"Prepare to be captivated by the journey you will take with Ah Veng! Readers will step into his story and never want to leave, thanks to author Herron's amazing ability to weave a tapestry of words into stunning prose you will want to read again and again."

—**Nancy Robinson Masters, award-winning author/explorer**

"Janna Herron brilliantly details a family's tribulation from Malaysia to the United States while capturing the reader's emotions through heart wrenching stories. Tuhan boleh . . . God is able."

—**Daniel Ford, EdD, Denton ISD executive director of Curriculum and Instruction**

"My tears were transformed into joy and hope for the future in this beautifully written book by Janna Herron, celebrating the life of her grandfather."

—**Steven Loewenstein, author of *A President, A King and You!***

"*Transforming Tears* draws you into the little moments that ripple like butterfly wings through one man's life—from the wonder of a little boy chasing butterflies to a grandfather looking back at all those moments of happiness and joy, hardship and persistence. Janna Herron tells her grandfather's story with compassion and love; we follow him from Malaysia to America, from the beginning to the end: 'Treasure awaits.'"

—**Margaret Williams, longtime journalist, writer, and editor**

Transforming Tears

by Janna Herron

ISBN 978-1-63393-990-5

Published by

 köehlerbooks™

210 60th Street
Virginia Beach, VA 23451
800–435–4811
www.koehlerbooks.com

TRANSFORMING TEARS

BASED ON A TRUE STORY

JANNA HERRON

VIRGINIA BEACH
CAPE CHARLES

"The plans of the Lord stand firm forever,
the purposes of his heart through all generations."

Psalms 33:11

Life is a book that is constantly being written,
woven intricately to make people who they are as a person.

Janna H.

TABLE OF CONTENTS

Kuala
Lumpur
★

Malaysia

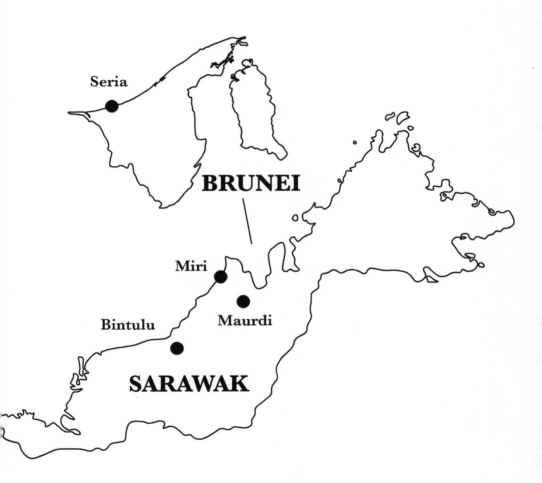

Seria

BRUNEI

Miri

Maurdi

Bintulu

SARAWAK

Life is short. Sometimes too short.
Some lives are shorter than others, but not a single person
is guaranteed tomorrow.
Not a single person can promise forever—only God is able.
He provides us with the words that allow the sharing of memories:
stories.
Stories of the old, stories of the young, stories that never end,
stories that live on.
These are the stories of life.
Truthful tales of time.

Three generations, the lives of a family—of five individuals.
Suffering. Unforgiveness. Miracles. Regret. Hope.
They all hold a key to a story that is eternal, carried into the future.

CHAPTER 1

ESCAPE

THE SECOND HAND OF A CLOCK ticked in the background, accompanied by a gentle tapping. The atmosphere of the room was thick with worry and uncertainty, the air eerily quiet except for the soft sounds of a machine and the agitated ticking of the tired, overworked clock. The gentle tapping could barely be heard, but suddenly, it stopped.

As the life of my grandfather hung in stasis, I remembered the stories he once told me, but there was something missing . . . significant gaps in that inspiring life. Gaps I regretted never asking about. I looked down at my hands, at the fingerprints I had left on that torn, ancient photograph, as I got sucked back into a time of unforeseen tragedy.

September 1936
Marudi, Sarawak, Malaya

"Son? Ah Veng? Ah Veng!" a man shouted, panicking for a moment when his child disappeared into the forest.

"Daddy!" the child giggled, running out from behind a tree. "Look, look!"

The man sighed with relief, ignoring the creature in his son's hands before grabbing the young boy and lifting him onto his shoulders.

"No!" Ah Veng squealed. "You made butterfly fly away!"

"You shouldn't scare me like that," the father scolded. "It's dangerous to step into the forest, especially for a butterfly that we see around the house every day."

"But elder sister said we're the only ones that can see them! So, they're special!"

His father groaned, continuing towards the river. "You spend too much time with your sisters."

"Well, I have nine and no brothers," he pouted, "and no one to play with 'cause everyone's old."

"So you play with butterflies instead?"

"Yes!" Ah Veng exclaimed in delight, reaching out to grab a handful of leaves from a tree. "It's true what elder sister said?" he asked.

The leaves drifted down upon the father's head, making his heart melt in adoration.

"Kind of. Everyone on the island can see our butterflies but not the people in the rest of the world. This is because they are an endemic species, which means they are native only to Malaya, and do you know what is even better?"

"What?"

"Our ancestors taught us that when we die, our souls reside within the butterflies, and when they come to visit, someone from our past is trying to connect with us."

"Ooh, they are special!"

"Yes," his father laughed. "Scientists call them *Graphium procles*, but what is it that we call them?

"*Kupu!*"[1] the boy shouted, giggling.

"That's right," his father said, lifting Ah Veng off his shoulders and setting him down on the riverbank.

---

1 Butterfly.

The small boy ran to edge of the water as soon as his father turned to uncover their hidden stash of fishing equipment. Peeking to make sure he was not looking, Ah Veng squatted and stuck his hands into the clear blue water. It sent a chill up his spine as he let the soft current flow across his fingers and wiggled them slightly to see if the water moved when he did. Giggling at the ticklish feeling, he pulled them out and turned towards the flowers blooming on the ground next to him. The milky white petals drifting and mixing with hints of yellow made him think of the eggs their chickens laid each morning. He inched closer and yanked some of them out by the roots, grinning in triumph when the comforting floral fragrance reached his nose.

"Ah Veng?"

He quickly dropped the flowers and swiveled around, bounding over to his father. He stared in fascination at the fishing rod in his father's hands, not hearing a word that he said.

"Ah Veng, are you listening?"

"Yes," he lied, nodding.

"No, you weren't. Now, as I said before, this is what I use to catch the fish that we eat so that we have food on the table, and one day when you are older, you will be the one to bring food home to the family," his father said, kneeling to look the small boy in the eyes before putting bait on the hook. "Now, watch me. *Menonton*."[2]

Ah Veng stepped closer, reaching out a hand to graze the rough bark of their fishing rod as he observed how his father handled a squirming worm, wincing when it flailed about once its body was impaled.

"Okay, now stand back," his father said, moving away.

The child obeyed and watched the string, as thin as thread, sail through the air, hitting its mark in the middle of the river and sinking below the surface, dragged down by frantic desperation.

"Wait, no, Daddy! The worm!" Ah Veng cried. "He's going to die!" Running, he tried to tug the fishing rod out of his father's hands.

---

2 Watch.

"No, son, stop. He's supposed to die."

"No, he's not!" the child shouted, grabbing the edge of his father's shirt. "Please don't let him die."

"Ah Veng, this is what fishing is. The worm helps us catch the fish, and the fish are our food and we need food to survive. You need to understand that," his father sighed, placing a hand on his son's shoulder. "I'm sorry; this is just the way things are."

The boy jerked away, upset.

"It's not fair," he mumbled, kicking at the rocks on the ground.

"Nothing is ever fair," his father replied. "You will understand more when you're older."

"Everyone says that."

Ah Veng turned away from the water and wandered back towards his uprooted flowers, settling down in the grass to pout as he looked further down the river. He closed his eyes for a moment and felt the wind blow, briefly breathing in the deep scent of nature before opening them to watch a mother duck tuck her little ducklings under her wing. Even at his young age, he admired all that surrounded him, recognizing that nature was the center of everything. Its vast beauty was captivating—everything about it: the way the wind shifted the trees, the way animals interacted, the way rain sprinkled its blessing down upon the earth, the way rivers flowed and flowers bloomed. Every inch of it a beautiful creation.

"Son, look. The line is moving, which means I've caught a fish."

The child shook his head, refusing to even look in his father's general direction.

"Oh, come on, you can't still be upset. Come over here and help me reel it in. It's fun, I promise."

"No," Ah Veng said. "I don't like fishing."

"How do you know that you don't like it if you don't try?" his father asked, slowly reeling in his catch to make sure that it wouldn't get away. "Come on, it doesn't hurt to try."

Ah Veng looked away.

"Okay, you don't have to today, but I expect you to learn when you're older. You'll be the man of the house, and that means working hard and providing food for the family."

"I know," the boy answered, picking at his mutilated flowers. He pulled off one of the petals and tossed it into the water, staring as it floated down the river, carefree and unaware of its surroundings.

"Look, you're missing it," the father said, tugging on the rod to reel in the last of the fishing line.

A sleek silver fish emerged from the water, twisting and turning in angry motions, clearly unhappy with the present situation. Ah Veng glanced over for a moment but quickly turned away because he knew that the fish was going to die.

"This one is perfect."

Ah Veng peeked over again, curious but afraid for the creature. He cautiously watched as his father grabbed ahold of the fish and squeezed to make it stop writhing. Holding his breath, he stared as his father reached inside the fish's mouth with his other hand to remove the hook.

"Ouch . . . it—Ah Veng . . ."

The boy leapt up but stayed frozen in his spot. His father's face contorted with pain as he frantically tried to pry the fish from his hand.

"Daddy?" Ah Veng asked.

"Help," his father whispered, stumbling to the ground. "Son . . . help."

Ah Veng started to cry. "Daddy, Daddy," he mumbled with fright, "what's wrong?"

"Help . . . go," his father hissed insistently, begging desperately with his eyes.

The child's crying persisted as his father's skin started to swell, beginning at the hand and spreading upward like a spider creeping towards its prey. A deep-purple color settled in as the poison sucked the oxygen dry. He choked and gagged, his eyes becoming red, bulging and straining as he desperately fought to breathe. All feeling had left his body, and he convulsed once before becoming as hard as stone, gazing deeply into an abyss of complete darkness.

"Daddy?" the boy coughed out through his tears.

He trembled and looked around in uncertainty. He had been left utterly alone. Panicking, Ah Veng started running, terror seizing his heart. He ran as fast as his little legs could carry him, ignoring the trail of tears he left behind in the wind. The trees seemed to close in on him, and he ran faster, pushing through bushes and tumbling out in front of their home. He pulled himself up and barged through the front door, running straight to his mother, saying, "Daddy, *bantu, bantu*"[3] repeatedly until she picked him up, shouted for his sisters, and ran back out the door towards the river.

But by the time they all got there, his father's body lay lifeless beside the bank, disfigured and discolored from the poison of one deadly fish. It was already too late.

* * *

Many tears were shed as the wailing commenced for someone deeply loved. Little Ah Veng somewhat remembered flashes of black cloth everywhere—symbolic of death. The loss of a loved one. A family being left behind.

Murmurs drifted through the crowd.

"What a shame."

"*Sangat sedih.*"[4]

"What will they do now?"

"*Tiada wang.*"[5]

"No support."

The crying of his mother was the worst. Beyond the grief, no one could bear the thought of being left with ten children to care for and no means of income. Ah Veng tugged on the bottom of his mom's shirt,

3 Help.

4 So sad.

5 No money.

begging to be picked up, but she merely pushed him away. The cold gesture instantly made him cry, but one of his sisters reached over and took him into her arms to comfort him.

"Shh, *tak mengapa, tak mengapa.*"[6]

Those words were his only assurance as the days flew past. His mother left the house every morning, not returning until night. Abandoned to fend for themselves, the older children had no choice but to care for their younger siblings. They had been robbed of their childhood, and even as the youngest, Ah Veng no longer felt like playing or having fun. Instead, he helped around the house whenever he was needed, and if he wasn't, then he spent his time beside the river, lost within his thoughts—lost in his own world.

He often zoned out, but a lot of his sisters did as well. They remembered their father even more than Ah Veng did, especially the eldest. No one really knew what to do except to keep going, oftentimes escaping from reality through their thoughts. Any diversion was an escape. The only thing pushing them along was their chores and housework as they waited for their mother to arrive home, rushing to greet her even though she dismissed their presence and shooed them away. They followed the same routine in everything they did until one very unexpected day.

"*Datang.*[7] See who I've brought home," his mother called from the door of their house one afternoon, much earlier than she normally arrived home. Some of the sisters looked at each other in confusion and worry as they slowly made their way to their mother. They gasped when the door squeaked open and she gestured to a tall man.

"This is my new husband, whom you are now to call father."

Ah Veng peeked out from behind the skirt of his oldest sister and instantly feared the stranger entering their home. He peered behind the man and drew back when he noticed that there were other children too.

---

6   It's okay.

7   Come.

"And these are your stepsiblings. I expect you to treat them well because their father has sacrificed a lot for us already."

The sisters and Ah Veng stood in silence, watching as their mother grabbed the stranger's hand and led him inside so that she could show him around the house. None of the kids moved, staring and boring holes into each other as if an intense wrestling match were about to start. Suddenly, the man's children grinned at one another and ran straight into the house, purposely pushing through their new stepsiblings and rapidly speaking about which room they wanted. Misery settled among Ah Veng and his sisters as they watched the spoiled strangers enter their home to take over their lives.

As the days went by, they were yelled at or slapped for doing anything that the other children did not like. Ah Veng and his nine sisters were treated as though they were unwanted, as if they were not worthy of love and were nothing but slaves. Only one sister would eventually have the courage to leave their abusive home. Wanting a better life for her younger brother, she chose to take him with her.

* * *

September 1940

Time ticked by. Just four years after his father passed away, Ah Veng stood in the place where he had died. Dark thoughts overtook his mind.

Earlier in the morning, his thirteen-year-old sister whispered in his ear that she was leaving, and he would be coming too. The news shocked him; he had never thought of abandoning the only place he had ever known. Perhaps he should be grateful for the chance to escape the control of their demanding stepfather, and yet something held him back.

Ah Veng stared at a frog hopping out from under a log and thought back to the incident that led his sister to make her decision to leave. That day never should have played out the way that it did, and Ah Veng blamed himself, even though he knew none of this was his fault.

It just wasn't fair.

* * *

"Hey, wake up," one of his stepbrothers yelled into Ah Veng's ear, shaking him violently to make him get out of bed.

"Stop," Ah Veng mumbled, pushing him away.

"Did you hear him? He just told me to stop," the stepbrother called to his older brother.

"What?! You little brat! Get up," the older brother said, kicking Ah Veng in the side.

"I just want to sleep," Ah Veng cried. "It's still dark outside."

"Too bad. You have chores to do."

"Not this early," Ah Veng whined. "Your dad would have told me yesterday."

"He didn't have to tell you anything. You're supposed to do everything we tell you to do, and right now, we're telling you to wake up."

Ah Veng rubbed his eyes and sat up, figuring that it would be better if he complied.

"Come one, move it," the younger brother said, nudging Ah Veng with his foot.

"I am," he mumbled, standing up to follow them outside. "What am I supposed to do?" he asked once they stopped in front of a tree.

"I want a coconut," the younger brother said, pointing up at the tree.

"What?" Ah Veng stammered. "I can't climb that."

"Sure you can. If your sisters can do it, then you can too."

"But they're bigger than me," Ah Veng argued.

"Stop whining," the older brother said, pushing him towards the trunk. Ah Veng looked back at the house. He wished that one of his sisters would wake up and save him from the torturous games of his stepbrothers. The boys seemed to feed off his fear and all the things that they made him do. Usually, the things were small, though—nothing like climbing a tree that was ten times larger than he was.

"Well, what are you waiting for?" they asked, glaring at him. Ah Veng didn't want to think about what they would do to him if he fled or didn't do it, so he put his hand on the trunk and wondered how he would climb it. He tried to remember how his sisters did, but he wasn't really sure.

"Hurry up. We don't have all day," the older brother said, tapping his foot on the ground and crossing his arms.

Finally, Ah Veng decided to hug the trunk and inch up slowly. He got a little ways and felt his arms and legs getting tired. It scared him, but he forced himself higher and higher until he was about halfway. He looked down and wished that he hadn't. The ground was quite a long way down. He gripped the tree tighter, scared to move any further.

"You scared up there?" the younger brother asked before bursting into laughter. His older brother laughed along with him.

"Gosh, you're so stupid," the older brother said, howling with laughter and rubbing his watering eyes. Suddenly, Ah Veng heard one of his sister's voices.

"What is going on out here?" she asked. He looked back towards the house to where she stood in the doorway. Dawn was just breaking, so he could see a little bit better. He saw her assess the situation and spot Ah Veng in the tree.

"Ah Veng!" she shrieked, running to the tree and pushing the laughing stepbrothers aside.

"You should have seen the look on his face!" they smirked.

"You all are sick. This is wrong and absolutely ridiculous! You should go pick on someone your own size instead of harassing those that are younger than you."

"Oh, look who's talking now. Someone finally has the nerve to say something," the older brother taunted.

Ah Veng's sister shoved him. For a moment, Ah Veng almost let go because he had never seen his sister so angry before. He quickly tightened his grip and watched the situation unfold.

"Going to do something about it?" the other brother provoked. "Well, too bad. You're just a girl."

"I dare you to say that again," she said, narrowing her eyes.

JANNA HERRON 11

"You're too girly, too weak, too defenseless. Aw, you poor—"

Ah Veng's eyes widened as his sister lashed out to slap their stepbrother. He was dazed for a moment as the other brother threw her to the ground.

"Stop," Ah Veng yelled down. "You're hurting her!"

"It's about time that you learned your lesson and your place," the older brother spat.

"What is happening here?!"

Their mother and stepfather now stood in the doorway. Ah Veng's mother was rubbing her eyes as though she had just woken up, and his stepfather looked furious.

"Boys?" he questioned.

"She slapped me!" the older brother cried. "Look!" He pointed at his face.

The stepfather marched over to them and took a careful look at his son's face before grabbing Ah Veng's sister and dragging her across the ground. She tried to fight back.

"What are you doing?" she whimpered.

"Teaching you a lesson."

"They made Ah Veng climb the tree," she yelled at her mother, who stood watching. "Do something!" she cried out, even though she knew that her mother would never do anything against their stepfather's wishes.

Ah Veng was frightened, but he also filled with a rage that he had never felt before. Glaring at his snickering stepbrothers, who stood whispering to themselves, he looked up and noticed that he wasn't afraid anymore. Instead of climbing down, he pushed himself to slowly inch higher until he reached the top where the coconuts were. Grabbing one of them, he looked down below and threw it, aiming for one of his stepbrother's heads. Surprisingly enough, the coconut hit its target.

"There's your coconut!" Ah Veng yelled. "I hope you're happy!"

"Ouch," the younger brother screeched. "That little brat! You're going to pay for that!"

For once, Ah Veng had his chance to laugh, and he didn't care about the consequences that would follow. Unfortunately, he was completely oblivious to how horrendous they would be.

He heard his sister scream somewhere towards the back of the house and watched as his stepbrothers sauntered off into the forest. It wasn't until they were out of sight that his mother walked to the tree and looked up.

"Can you get down?" she asked.

"I don't really know how," Ah Veng confessed.

"Just come down the way that you went up, but make sure you tighten your grip each time so that you don't slide."

He did just as his mother said, and eventually he was standing on solid ground again. His arms felt numb, and he had to lean against the tree to keep from toppling over on his unstable feet.

"Thank you," he said, glancing shyly at his mom. It was the first time that she had spoken to him directly since his father died.

"Please be careful," she pleaded, pausing for a second and then continuing, "I'm . . . sorry. You know I can't do anything. But please just don't make them mad, and do what they say even if you don't want to. It will make it less painful for all of us."

Ah Veng crumbled on the inside. He expected his mother to have pity, and yet the only thing he received was disappointment. She thought that the situation was his fault. Ah Veng hung his head.

"Ok," was all he said.

It wasn't until later that night that he saw his sister. She was curled in a ball in the corner of their bedroom.

"*Kakak*?"[8] Ah Veng whispered, tapping her softly on the shoulder. She flinched at his touch.

"Not now, Ah Veng," she replied, curling up even tighter.

"I just want to know that you're okay," he whimpered.

"I will be, I promise. I will be," she repeated.

"What about now, though? What's wrong?"

"I'll tell you when you're older."

---

8 Sister?

"That's what you always say," he whined.

"Ah Veng, you're too young and you won't understand."

"Stop saying that. I'm not, I'm not!" he said, stamping his foot. "I know he did something to you, I saw him drag you away and I just want to know that you're okay. I'm not too young to understand what I saw."

"Fine, look at my face. Look at it, Ah Veng."

He sucked in a breath when his sister lifted her head and winced at the sudden movement. There were bruises everywhere, and one of her eyes was swollen shut. He had to look away, tears in his eyes.

"I'm sorry," Ah Veng mumbled, starting to cry. "I'm sorry he hurt you and I'm sorry that I didn't do what they wanted me to do right when they told me, and I'm sorry that I didn't climb the tree fast enough and that—"

"Stop. Stop it, Ah Veng," his sister said, grabbing his hand and ignoring the pain that shot up her arm for doing so. "It wasn't your fault. You have to know that. None of this is ever your fault and it never will be. There was nothing that we could have done to prevent this. It is out of our hands."

"But . . . but I—" he sniffled, trying to make the words come out even though his sister wouldn't let him continue.

"No, you cannot blame this on yourself. Ever. Regret will eat you alive and you are still so young. I don't want you living in the past. Life is about moving forward. Do you understand?" she asked very seriously.

Ah Veng nodded.

"Are you sure?" she pressed.

"Yes," he whispered.

"Alright, now don't you worry because I will get us out of this mess one day. Now, that I can promise. It might take weeks, months or even years, but I promise you, Ah Veng, that one day, you'll have a better life. You deserve a chance and a life other than the one you were born into. I believe that everyone does. However, I can't help everyone. But what I will do is help the both of us and any of our other sisters that want to come along. Don't tell anyone, though," she added.

"I won't," Ah Veng reassured her.

"Good. Now run along. I need to rest, but remember, it will happen. Just wait; there will be a day."

* * *

Pulling himself from his thoughts, Ah Veng jumped at the sound of footsteps approaching, and he turned to see his older sister carrying a bundle in her arms. She motioned that it was time to leave their family and home behind. A tear hit the soil beneath him. The old life would be left behind. That beautiful river, left behind. Every trace of childhood—gone and left behind.

He took her hand, and they walked into the forest. Away from the only place they knew and towards the unknown.

CHAPTER 2

SURVIVAL

SOFT FOOTSTEPS WERE THE ONLY MAN-MADE sounds echoing through the backdrop of rainforest life. An unchanging landscape of trees entrapped them in every direction. Ah Veng did not know where they were going or if they were even on the right path. He was afraid to ask if they were lost, and he dared not cry out when he tripped over branches or scraped his arm on thorns. Everything went by in a blur. They had walked for what seemed like forever. Early on, he realized that they were not going to town at all, and it was not long before he lost count of the days that went by.

To pass time, he would sometimes quietly ask, "Can you tell me a story? *Sila?*"[9] And his sister would tell their parents' story. A tale of love—part of the distant past, and yet the story still lived on in the hearts of those that heard it. He loved to hear it retold and to remember the days when life was full of joy, happiness and light.

* * *

On one of those happy days, the sun had just started to set over the horizon as the family gathered beside the riverbank around their

---

9   Please.

burning firepit. Despite extreme poverty, they still found time to enjoy each other's company. Ah Veng's sisters laughed as they ran along the edge of the water. Crickets chirped in the tall grass, and owls called softly as night made its presence known. Ah Veng's father let out a roar as he chased after his children, who giggled and squealed as they raced to escape him. Ah Veng was a little over a year old at the time. He snuggled in his mother's arms, watching his squirming siblings with delight . The moment was so precious, so peaceful, so innocent, as if time had stopped to allow the family to bask in an untroubled time, oblivious to the pain that would befall them in the years to come.

Eventually, the brood's mother called her children over to sit around the fire, and they all came running with their father trailing behind. He sat beside his wife and tapped little Ah Veng on the nose, who giggled and grabbed his father's finger. The storytelling began, and his father's soothing voice lulled the young boy in and out of sleep. He hardly remembered the story. Only small words or phrases stood out to him, such as "love at first sight," "happiness," "I knew she was the one," "marriage," and "together forever."

The voice was the most prominent of his memories, along with the feelings of safety surrounding him like a soft cocoon. Ah Veng wished he could stay in those happy memories for eternity, but reality always pulled him back into a time where happiness and joy were mere illusions.

* * *

When the siblings first began walking, their strides were confident as they twisted this way and that, ducking under vines and pushing through bushes. Ah Veng chased one of their native butterflies at one point, the little bundle of bright blue flitting in all different directions. His sister leaned against a tree and giggled every time he jumped, reaching up as high as possible but not nearly high enough to even graze the butterfly's wing. The boy stared in fascination as the tiny creature flew higher and higher, towards the streak of sunlight peeking in from the treetops above.

"What if it's Daddy? His soul could be visiting us! Where is it going?" Ah Veng whined as he tugged at his sister's arm. A small smile lifted the corners of her mouth.

"Freedom," she simply said, her smile growing. "Now, why don't we eat something?"

They sat under a tree, and Ah Veng bounced up and down, excited to see what his sister had hidden in her little bundle. To his disappointment, there was not much.

"Sorry, little brother. We have to make sure that we have enough to last us a few days, so we can only eat a bit," she said as she handed him a small loaf of bread and a few nuts. He shrugged and nibbled slowly to savor every bite before taking a sip of water from their jug.

They were soon on their way again, winding through the maze of rainforest life and wandering into uncharted territory. The vines grew thicker as they went along, and it took more time to push through.

"Can we go around?" Ah Veng asked softly.

"No, I don't want us to get lost," his sister replied. Ah Veng furrowed his eyebrows at her reply. *Aren't we already lost?*

"But there's no trail," he whispered.

"I know," she said, grabbing another vine and pulling it out of the way. "There's not supposed to be. Don't worry about it too much. As long as we're going in this direction, then we'll be okay."

Ah Veng climbed over a rock while his sister held the vines up, allowing him to pass through.

"Here, hold this while I go through," she said, passing him the bundle. She let the vines swing back down before pushing her way under them and making it over the rock. Ah Veng stood waiting. Something ran over his hand, and he let out a yelp. The bundle fell to the ground as a spider crawled up Ah Veng's arm. He whimpered, shutting his eyes.

"Ah Veng! It's just a spider," his sister said, brushing it off of him.

"Is it gone?"

"Yes, now help me pick this up," she replied, bending down to open up the bundle. She froze when she saw a piece of pottery on the ground.

"Oh no, our jug is broken," she sighed. "But it's just the top part. We'll have to hold it carefully so that we don't lose more of our water."

"I'm sorry," Ah Veng said, bending down to help her arrange the rest of the things.

"It's okay. Just be more careful next time and don't freak out so easily. Do you think that you can carry the bundle? I'll carry the water to make sure that it lasts until we make it to the river."

"The river?" Ah Veng asked. "Like our river?"

"Yeah, we took the long way, but we are supposed to run back into the river eventually. It shouldn't be that much further, I don't think."

They started to walk again.

"Will we stop when it gets dark?"

"I don't know. It depends."

"Why does it depend?" Ah Veng questioned further. He realized that he shouldn't be asking so much, but he couldn't help interrupting the silence. It kind of scared him when the forest was too quiet.

"You know what's out here, don't you? We've told you stories, and I know that you've heard the sounds of animals some nights when we're still outside doing chores."

Ah Veng's eyes widened. "You mean like the scary monster stories?"

"Oh, those. No, not those. I'm sorry we even told you those stories. They aren't real and I hope that they didn't scare you too much."

"Then which stories?" Ah Veng asked, confused.

"You know, the ones that our aunties and uncles used to tell us when they came to visit. About the jungle life and animals in the wild."

"But those are scary too."

"They were?" his sister asked, raising her eyebrows. "Well, actually, they should be. It's real what can happen to people out here. Sometimes humanity is no match for nature because you can't fight fate and the natural occurrence of things," she continued.

"What? You're using big words again." Ah Veng pouted. "I don't like it when you do that."

She laughed.

"Sorry, I should have said it a little simpler. Basically, it is supposed to be scary because the jungle is alive and there are wild animals out here that are real."

"What happens if we see one?"

"I don't think that we will, but if we do, just stay really still and quiet. We don't want to startle them or look like we are a threat or a danger."

"I can do that," Ah Veng said.

"Of course you can. You learned how to do that back at the house, didn't you?" she replied with a sad smile.

"Yeah. I didn't want to make anybody angry."

"I don't think any of us did. But it's alright now. We're moving on from that past and we shouldn't dwell on it too much."

"Dwell?" Ah Veng asked, wondering what the word meant. It was a funny one.

"Think about. We shouldn't think about it too much."

Ah Veng's education had been limited since their stepfather never wanted to send him to school. Back when their father was alive, he made sure that each of his children went to school so they would have the opportunity for a career in the future, even though most people looked down on women who pursued an education or a job. Unfortunately for Ah Veng, their father passed before the youngest had the chance to attend the village's school. *He deserves so much better*, she thought, but her thinking was interrupted when she tripped on a root. Water sloshed out of the jar.

"Agh, there goes some of the water," she sighed, frustrated.

Ah Veng stared up at her. "It's okay. We shouldn't be too far from the river, right?"

"Yeah, you're right. We'll be okay. Yes, we will."

Night fell and the young boy was exhausted, but his sister kept walking and pulling him along.

"Please, *saya penat*,"[10] Ah Veng whispered, wincing as another sharp thorn dug into his arm.

His sister stopped and sighed. "Alright, we'll rest for just a while."

She walked over to the roots of a tree and sat down to lean her head against the trunk, motioning for Ah Veng to sit next to her. He curled up beside her, breathing in her familiar scent, and immediately drifted off to sleep.

* * *

He was flying somewhere above the treetops, gazing at the wonders below him. How is this possible? *he thought.* I'm flying! *The world was full of colors and creatures, full of vibrant life and adventure. He flew higher and then swooped down to enter the rainforest, looking in every direction and stopping to marvel at the things he found fascinating. A family of monkeys fighting over a banana. A mother owl nestling her owlings beneath her as they slept, awaiting nightfall. A wolf chasing his prey. A fox lapping water from a flowing river. A spider spinning his web.* Is this what freedom is? But . . . what all does nature entail? *He stopped to hover above a flower for a moment, until a bloodcurdling roar pierced the air.*

* * *

Ah Veng woke with a start and realized that the roar had been real. He started to say something, but his sister hushed him and held him close as they both watched in terror. A tiger emerged from the bushes, emitting a low growl. They had heard stories of Malay tigers deep within the jungle, but few saw the creatures and lived to tell the tale.

They watched the powerful muscles clench with each step, held captive by the beauty of the black stripes streaking the vivid orange fur. Everything was still for a moment. The tiger was narrowing in on his prey when, suddenly, a deer shot past, and the predator took off

---

10   I'm tired.

after it. Their fear dissipated as they sat there in silence, shocked by the sudden moment.

Ah Veng's sister stood up tentatively and stretched.

"Was that . . . a monster?" Ah Veng asked, eyes still round in shock.

His sister laughed.

"No, silly. That was a *harimau*."[11]

"Really? That's what they look like?"

"Yes," she replied. "They're beautiful creatures, aren't they? Dangerous but beautiful all at the same time. And to be so close to one." She shook her head in disbelief.

"Do people usually see them?"

"No, they stay away from people and villages. Only if you go deep into the jungle will you possibly run into one."

"Like we did!" Ah Veng exclaimed.

"Yes, like we did," she replied, smiling.

It was already daylight; they had rested for way too long. Ah Veng's sister opened up her bundle of food and handed Ah Veng another loaf of bread before taking one for herself.

"Are we going to run out?" Ah Veng asked, peering in to see how much was left.

"I don't know. I hope not," his sister answered. "I wish that I could assure you that we won't, but I honestly don't want to make a promise that I might not be able to keep."

"It's okay," Ah Veng said. "If we do, we can find something out here. Isn't there fruit in the trees or something?"

"Possibly, but remember, you can't simply eat anything. It could be poisonous."

"What's that word mean?"

"Poisonous? It means that . . . let's just say that it could make you really sick or possibly even kill you."

"Why would it do that?"

---

11 Tiger.

"Because some things are just not meant to be eaten."

"Even if they look like food?"

"Yes, even if it looks like it's edible—I mean, even if it looks like you can eat it," she explained, picking up the jar of water and handing it to Ah Veng so that he could have a drink. "We should start walking soon. The quicker we make it to the river, the better."

Ah Veng passed the jug back to his sister and wrapped the bundle before picking it up.

"Okay, let's go," he said.

"I suggested that we should start walking soon, not that we had to leave right now . . . you're in a hurry, aren't you?"

"I don't like being trapped in the jungle. I like looking at nature, but I don't like feeling stuck in it."

"That makes sense," she said, looking down at her younger brother in adoration. "Come on, I'm pretty sure that this is the way we were going."

Although she confidently started walking, Ah Veng's sister was actually not sure if they were headed in the correct direction or not. She couldn't remember which way they were going before they stopped to sleep. They weren't weaving through thick vines anymore, which meant that they were not going the direction that they came—a good sign; yet she frequently looked around, searching for anything out of place, though of course nothing looked different from one patch of jungle to the next.

"Isn't it supposed to be close by?" Ah Veng asked, starting to worry as darkness fell again. "Or did we just sleep too long last night?"

"No. I think it should be close . . ." His sister's voice cracked, and she wasn't able to wipe her tears away before little Ah Veng saw them.

"Don't cry!" he said. "I'm sure it's around here somewhere."

"I don't know, Ah Veng, I really don't know. Maybe I made a mistake."

"No! You didn't," he cried, trying to comfort his sister, who kept walking and wouldn't stop even though she was stumbling about.

Suddenly, she did stop.

"Do you hear that?"

"Hear what?"

"That," she said, putting a hand on his shoulder to make him stay still.

Ah Veng listened very carefully. "I don't hear anything," he said, frowning.

"Be very quiet, and listen in the distance. There's the soft sound of running water."

Ah Veng tried to do what his sister said.

"Do you hear it?" she asked.

He really couldn't but figured that it would make his sister happy if he said yes.

"I think so" was his reply.

She grabbed Ah Veng's arm, certain that the river was somewhere close by. Her pace quickened at the thought of fresh water.

"You're walking too fast," Ah Veng said, running to catch up. The water sloshed out of their jug in large amounts, but she didn't really seem to care anymore. It kind of scared him how crazy his sister looked at that moment—as if some creature had jumped inside of her and controlled her movements. Her desire for water and the river pushed all else aside. Ah Veng seemed forgotten as well.

And then, suddenly, it was there. Almost like a dream, glimmering in the sunlight, crystal clear and magical. His sister let out a squeal and rushed to the water's edge, dunking her hands in, submerging them completely.

"Come on," she called to Ah Veng, splashing him when he got close enough. The boy was still hesitant at his sister's rapid change of personality, but he finally let out a laugh and bent down beside her to have a drink of the cool water.

They laughed and splashed each other a bit more.

"See, I told you that it was close!" his sister exclaimed. She couldn't have felt more overjoyed at seeing clean water.

"It wasn't that close," Ah Veng pointed out.

"Well, okay. But it was close enough," she said.

"Sure," he replied, shrugging.

His sister splashed him again, and he laughed until a slight movement in the corner of his eye caught his attention.

"What's that?" he asked, backing away.

"What?" his sister said, looking around in confusion. "I don't see anything."

"*Di sana!*"[12] Ah Veng shrieked as his sister pulled her hands out of the water and scooted backwards just in time to miss the snapping jaws of a crocodile. She scrambled up, grabbed Ah Veng, and ran to the tree line. They watched the creature disappear below the surface of the water, disappointed in losing its prey. His sister let out a shaky breath and hugged Ah Veng tight.

"Oh, what would I do without you?" she said, staring at the place in which she could have lost her life if not for her younger brother. "*Terima kasih.*"[13]

Ah Veng simply shrugged and pointed across the river.

"How do we get over there?" he asked.

"Don't worry; we don't have to cross. Just follow alongside until it curves, and then we keep going through the forest until we get to a road," she said with a small smile and took his hand so that they could continue walking. The near-death experience made the happy moments of their short time at the river disappear into the background. "Not to worry. We shouldn't be that far from where we are supposed to go."

"That's what you said last time," Ah Veng whined.

"I know, Ah Veng, I know."

She climbed over a log and reached back to help her brother, but Ah Veng was already boosting himself up on a rock to try and climb over. She dropped her hand in defeat, hoping that her brother wasn't that angry with her.

---

12   There!

13   Thank you.

"Do you trust me?" she asked him after he jumped down.

"I . . . don't know."

"Please, Ah Veng. I'm trying. Can't you at least see that?"

"I do," he replied.

"You're not mad at me, right?"

"No, I just want to be out of here already."

"I know. I do too," she said softly, stepping around a puddle and quickly checking that Ah Veng was doing the same.

"I want you to know that you're a good sister," Ah Veng suddenly said.

"What do you mean?" she asked, confused, since she clearly had flaws in judgement.

"You helped me a lot. And you took a lot of my punishment for me while the other sisters were too worried about themselves. You cared. They didn't. It was always you that took me into your arms when I was crying or when I was upset. And now, you're actually trying to save me, to give me another chance. None of the others would have even cared enough to look at me or give me a glance."

"Well, that's not completely true. We all loved you. It's just that most of them were too worried that they would get in trouble if they . . ." She trailed off.

"If they what?" Ah Veng asked.

The sister stayed silent as her brother's words sank in; he sounded so much older and more mature than his actual age, and it honestly scared her.

"You didn't finish," Ah Veng said, tugging at her shirt.

"Oh, it's nothing."

"No, you were going to say something. I want to know."

"I just don't think our sisters realized that we needed to help each other instead of worry about ourselves. Their selfishness probably just made things worse."

"Well, why did stepfather and his kids treat us so bad? What did we do wrong?" Ah Veng asked, looking up at his sister with a plaintive look on his face.

Her heart tore because she didn't know how to answer.

"Ah Veng," she started, and then shook her head, starting again. "Some people are just cruel and they don't understand how their actions can hurt other people. They don't think before they take action, or they believe that what they're doing is harmless when it's actually not."

"I don't get it," Ah Veng confessed.

"I don't really know how else to explain it. Don't think about it too much. It worries me how you think so much and ask so many questions sometimes. But maybe you'll understand this better once you're older."

"I don't think that it's fair."

"I hate to have to tell you this, but life is never going to be fair, Ah Veng."

"Father said that too."

"Well, he was certainly right. It's up to us as individuals whether or not we live out our lives to the fullest. There are times where you have to learn to accept your life circumstances and make the best of it. Then there are other times where you have to stand up for yourself to make a change that will benefit your future self. Like now."

"Because we're leaving the old life behind and finding a new one?" he questioned.

"Yes, exactly," she said, smiling. "Now, what do you say we rest by that tree for a bit before continuing? It looks like you could use some sleep."

Ah Veng nodded and followed his sister to the tree to settle down for a nap, thankful that she had offered because his eyes could hardly stay open. Nighttime was taking over, and he had started to stumble since it was hard to see. Fortunately for him, he was so exhausted that sleep overtook him as soon as he sat against the tree, his head falling to rest on his sister's arm.

* * *

Birds chirped and called to one another as he made his way over the grassy plains. All was peaceful, and the air held the soothing ambience of nature's joy. Abundance characterized every aspect of the environment. A horse galloped by, free to run about as it pleased. Somewhere in the distance, a cow mooed. Nature lived in perfect harmony. Ah Veng landed in the grass, enjoying the breeze and the sun, feeling as though he were burrowed in a nest of some sort. It was nice—so soft and cuddly and safe.

* * *

Ah Veng woke to the soft rise and fall of his sister's chest. He didn't know how long he had slept, but he didn't think that he should wake his sister. She definitely needed the sleep. The sounds of her breathing comforted Ah Veng, made him feel safe, and for the first time, he didn't doubt her judgement in leaving their home in the first place. He snuggled closer to her, staring into the darkness and finally accepting that their old life was gone and that it should stay left behind. He also reassured himself that in the end, no matter what, they would survive.

He was sure of it even as the days dragged out. Time wavered as trees blurred together into a never-ending blob of green shifting in and out of focus. The sounds surrounding them became a howl, like the wolves they heard each time darkness fell. The smells of the forest gave Ah Veng a headache. He couldn't remember how long it had been, except that they had left the river, their only source of real comfort for survival, a long time ago.

Shortly after leaving the river, they ran out of food, but he didn't dare complain that he was hungry because when he looked up at his sister, he could see her determination to reach their destination. However, he didn't know where that was and was not sure if she did either.

At night they would briefly stop to rest, but it was never long enough because they feared the wild animals that might attack them while they slept. Energy drained from their bodies, making them more susceptible to predation. They came close to death several times. One night, they climbed up in a tree to sleep, thinking that they would be safe from harm. However, they woke to see several glowing eyes staring down at them, followed by the sounds of shrieking monkeys.

"Climb down and run!" she yelled, practically shoving Ah Veng out of the tree.

They were barely able to escape the wrath of those creatures, but not without several scrapes and bruises from running blindly through the night.

Another time, Ah Veng almost stepped on a snake. It hissed and threatened to bite, but they backed away slowly until it slithered into its burrow underneath the roots of a tree.

They ran out of water, and the Malayan humidity was overwhelming at times. They did not think to refill their water jug while they were at the river. Ah Veng was dehydrated, and his sister was too. Worry creased her face as she wondered whether she had made a mistake in leaving. She was unsure how much longer they would last.

"I'm so sorry," she suddenly said, breaking down and sobbing, stopping to support herself on a tree.

"It's not your fault," Ah Veng whispered, wishing that he had the strength to comfort her.

"But it is, Ah Veng, and you know that it is."

"No. It's nobody's fault. Remember what you told me?" Ah Veng asked, sitting on a rock to rest for a bit.

"I don't," she replied with tears still streaming down her cheeks.

"You told me to never blame myself for the things that happened to us in life because regret will eat us alive in the future."

"I said that?" she asked, wiping away some of the tears.

"Yes, after the incident happened."

"And you remembered?" she questioned in disbelief.

"Of course I did. Why wouldn't I?"

"I just wasn't sure if you always paid attention to what I had to say or not. But I totally forgot that I said that particular thing."

"Yeah, you did. Like I said before, you're a good sister," Ah Veng said, smiling up at her.

"You know what? We can do this. We're not dead yet, which means that we can keep fighting."

She removed her hand from the tree and forced herself to keep walking, and Ah Veng stood up to do the same, trailing closely behind. Only a little ways beyond where they had gained the confidence to keep trekking, they finally saw hope of the forest coming to an end.

It was about the middle of the day when they stepped out onto a dirt road. A rusty little gray car sat waiting. The older man in the vehicle immediately stepped out. Relief swept through them both, but the small boy moved behind a tree in confusion and fright as his sister let herself be hugged and kissed by the older gentleman. Questions filled his mind: *Who is this man? Is he helping us? Why is Sister forcing herself to let him do that?* There was so much that he would never understand until he was older.

"I was worried that you had changed your mind," the older man said.

"Well, it was much farther than you explained, and that would have been nice to know." She scowled and narrowed her eyes, feeling slightly light-headed.

"You're here now and that's what matters. But look at you, you're in desperate need of a bath."

"Yeah, I guess," she replied, frowning and wanting to say more but choosing against it since she did not want to anger him and was too tired to do so anyway.

"Come along, Ah Veng," she called, straining her voice. Her throat was raw and felt as though it were on fire. She wanted so badly to pass out but held herself together. Her younger brother peeked out from behind the tree again.

"Please, Ah Veng," she croaked, in desperate need of water.

Finally, Ah Veng emerged as his sister held out her hand in exhaustion to help him into the car before they drove away. The man had already gotten back in when she shut the door for Ah Veng. She moved to the front to sit in the passenger seat as the car engine started, and they set off down the road.

Just like that, they left all of their problems behind in search of a new life.

CHAPTER 3

NEW BEGINNINGS

AS THEY DROVE, AH VENG DRIFTED in and out of consciousness. He didn't recall when the car stopped or when he and his sister were taken into a medical facility. He remembered only the sight of bright-green forest leaves, the soft songs of chirping birds, the sweet scent of nectar from exotic flowers, the feeling of excruciating hunger, fear and uncertainty, the pain of every bruise and cut, and all the suffering from being on the verge of death.

* * *

He was flying again. Somewhere down below children were playing a game, running around in circles until they dropped to the ground laughing. Villagers spoke in cheery voices, their eyes lighting up every time they saw someone that they knew. Craftsmen diligently worked on their pieces of native art while women in the marketplace called out to get people to buy fresh produce. He swooped down to land on a lamppost, simply watching each person pass below him, wondering, What's their story? Where did they come from? How are they who they are today? *He stayed that way until night took all the people away, and then he, too, drifted off.*

* * *

When Ah Veng finally awoke, it took him a while to adjust to the brightly lit room and for his mind to settle on what had just occurred. He abruptly sat up and whimpered when his body protested at the sudden movement. His surroundings felt unfamiliar, and he instantly panicked when he realized that his sister was not present in the small, dusty room. The young boy eased out from under the covers to peek out the window. He saw stacks and stacks of wood piled high for what seemed like miles. *Why is there so much wood?* Harsh whispers came from the hallway, and he cautiously turned to make his way to the door.

"When is he going to get better? I need him to work!"

"You can't just throw him out there. He's just a child."

"Well, I need workers, and I'm not spending money on hiring workers. The deal was that I would take you away from your family if you married me and brought me someone that would be able to work for me. It's your fault that you decided to bring your younger brother."

"What else was I supposed to do?! Leave him behind too?"

Ah Veng's eyes started to water, but he forced himself to refrain from crying. He focused instead on the specks of dust littering the old doorframe. He leaned forward to take a closer look, lost his balance, and stumbled, pushing open the door and falling to the ground right between his sister and the strange tall man. He looked up from his sprawled position to see them staring in shock.

"How long have you been listening?!" the man demanded as he reached down and grabbed Ah Veng by the shirt.

"Don't hurt h—"

"I know what I'm doing! Listen here, little boy. If I ever catch you eavesdropping again, things will go very badly for you. You got that?" he asked, glaring as Ah Veng nodded in fright. "Good. Now get up and get dressed. There should be some work clothes in that closet there. I need you downstairs in an hour," he stated before giving Ah Veng's sister a stern look and turning to head down the stairs.

"*Saya minta maaf.*[14] I should not have done this, but we will make the best of it, ok?" his sister said softly as she helped her younger brother up from the floor and dusted him off.

He looked up at her with sad eyes and confusion before following her to the closet that the man had pointed to.

"Most of these are too big, but if we roll up the sleeves and the pant legs, then they should do for today until I can find time to sew them," she said as she handed him an oversized, worn shirt and a pair of black pants.

He looked down at the clothes in his hands and felt the tears fall when he saw the paint stains and holes, forcing him to realize that life was going to be much harder than before.

"I'm going to get you something to eat as you change. I'll be right back," his sister told him before leaving and shutting the door behind her.

He slid to the ground and clenched the clothes tightly in his hands, knowing that the door of his old life had shut behind him and he was going to have to pick himself up and just face it. It was time to grow up, to take life a step at a time, and to fight off the mocking call of horrific memories.

He pulled himself together and changed into the work clothes his sister had handed him. Not long after, he heard the footsteps of her return. She knocked softly prior to opening the door and stepped inside carrying a cup of water and a tray with an assortment of cut fruits and bread.

"Sorry it took so long. The cooks wouldn't let me leave until I told them a story," she said, rolling her eyes as she handed Ah Veng what she had brought for him.

"A story?" he asked.

"Yes, it's been about four days since we couldn't wake you, and I have gotten well acquainted with the cooks, maids and butlers of this house. They seem to adore me and always want me to tell them the stories of where we came from and how we got here."

---

14   I'm sorry.

"Why? We are not that far away."

His sister was silent for a moment.

"Well, Ah Veng, we actually are. You don't know where we are, do you?" she asked as he shook his head, even more confused than before. "We're in a village that is quite far from our hometown. It's called Miri. And Chong, the man that I am marrying, is the president of this village. However, he has taken on a project to expand, so that is why he needs workers like you . . . to help him build houses."

"Build houses?" Ah Veng gasped, wide-eyed.

"Oh, don't worry. There will be other workers too that will help you and tell you what to do. It will not be anything that you won't be able to handle, and you will also get to go to school every morning until noon so that you can be with other children. That'll be exciting, right?"

"School?" he questioned, growing more anxious with every word she said.

"Trust me, you're going to do great. Just do everything that you're told, and it will all be okay. *Saya janji,*"[15] she said, standing to walk around the bed to the window.

He nibbled on a piece of bread as he watched his once carefree and funny sister turn into someone totally different. She was so mature that her actual age probably did not matter anymore. It was as if her older self had been taken from some future time period and placed in this one.

She gazed out the window and said, "It's strange how life is able to change so quickly when least expected. Sometimes it is for the better, and for the times when it is not . . . well . . . life must go on."

Her stare lingered on the sky above the piles of woods as if she were searching for something more, but it only lasted for a second before she turned and walked back to her brother.

"You should probably eat a little more," she said, frowning at the plate, which still held quite a bit of food.

But Ah Veng shook his head and pushed the plate towards her,

---

15   I promise.

indicating that he was not very hungry.

"You'll need the energy, but okay. As long as you promise to eat a sufficient amount at dinner, then I'll let you pass on this."

Ah Veng nodded and stood to put the tray on the table beside the bed.

"You should probably get downstairs. I hope that you are not already late. I completely lost track of time. Don't worry about the tray. I'll take care of it once you leave," his sister said before pushing him out the door and to the stairs.

He tentatively took a step before looking back at her. She gave him a smile and a thumbs-up, so he continued down.

At the bottom of the stairs, Ah Veng noticed the cracks in the wooden floor, the dust on the railing, and the peeling paint on the walls. He shuddered as he realized how ancient the house was, and then turned the corner to find a very unhappy Chong staring down at him.

"You. Are late," he stated and grabbed the boy by the arm as he proceeded through the front door, dragging Ah Veng with him. "Come on. I don't have all day," he said, annoyed when the boy wasn't able to keep up.

"Where are we going?"

"To where the workers are, of course. Where else?" Chong responded, picking up the pace.

Ah Veng noticed the change in scenery and heard voices in the distance. He could make out the slight outlines of people where new houses were beginning to form. They bustled about and ran here and there in a flurry. Lost in his own thoughts and curiosities about what his new life would be like, he did not realize when Chong started to speak again.

"So, your job for today will be to simply observe and only help when you are needed. Some of the workers might ask for you to go get a tool for them, or maybe something else that they need. Don't ever argue. Just do what you're supposed to do and everyone will be happy. Got that?"

Ah Veng nodded before asking, "Why do you want to expand and build more houses?"

Chong halted immediately and bent down to look the boy in the eyes.

"One more thing. Do not ever ask me a question beginning with 'why.' It is none of your business and does not concern you. I hate when people question my credibility and reasoning behind the things that I do. So stay out of it. Questions like that could get you into a lot of trouble with me, and I don't think you will like that."

The child's eyes widened in fright, and he nodded hesitantly once more before stuttering, "I understand."

Chong frowned and then continued walking at his brisk pace. Silence accompanied them the rest of the way. Ah Veng did not even bother to look up and just stared at his feet, trying his best to keep up. He hoped that someone in the village would treat him nicely if his boss was to be this cold. The treatment reminded him of his mother once his father had passed away, and he had to suppress a shudder.

Soon enough, they arrived at the gathering of the other workers. Their voices immediately fell to hushed whispers as their boss approached them.

"*Bos! Selamat petang,*"[16] they exclaimed in unison, but Chong simply waved them off with a nonchalant reply.

"Why are you all just standing around? Get to work."

"Yes sir," they shouted and then quickly dispersed to their respective work areas.

Ah Veng found the courage to glance around at his surroundings and took a hesitant step towards a stack of wood in order to examine the way it was piled. He coughed when a worker dropped something beside him and a cloud of dust flew up, swirling around and sticking to his clothes. The work area stretched farther than the eye could see. Men called out to one another to pass tools down and marched around

---

16 Boss! Good afternoon.

in groups whenever they needed more wood.

"Hey, get over here," Chong shouted over the noise. Ah Veng's attention snapped back to his new boss, and he hurriedly ran to him.

"This is Ruwayfi, and he will be in charge of you every time you report to work. At the end of each day, he will give me a description of your efficiency. So don't expect to get away without doing anything just because I am not always around."

Chong then looked at Ruwayfi.

"I have a meeting that I must leave for, but you are well aware that all workers are not to leave their respective work areas until six o'clock, and I will be expecting a report from you at the downbeat of seven."

"Oh, and don't be late," he added once he turned to walk away.

Ruwayfi looked down at Ah Veng and scowled.

"Well, this is annoying. I'm not a babysitter," he said under his breath and pointed to a toolbox that sat on the ground not too far away. "Pick that up and follow me. I need to do rounds and check on all the other workers before we start on our assigned area."

Ah Veng reluctantly obliged and ran to catch up with Ruwayfi, who was already walking away. As they made their way through the construction sites, passing from one structure to another, the other workers stared at Ah Veng. Their eyes bore down on him as if they wanted him to know that he was not welcome among them and that he had no place there.

"Why are they looking at me like that?" he finally found the courage to ask.

"Who?" Ruwayfi mumbled, not really paying attention.

"The workers. Why are they staring at me?"

"Because you're a kid. Why else?"

"That doesn't make sense. Have they never seen a kid before?"

"How does it not make sense? Obviously kids aren't normally seen in the work area. They're usually in school, you know."

"Then why am I not in school?"

"Don't ask me. All I know is that our boss needed more people to work and somehow you showed up. Which doesn't seem like a good idea at all. You're too young."

"I'm seven," Ah Veng shot back.

"Exactly."

"I can help. Isn't that good enough?"

"No, because you still can't help with everything."

"Like what?"

"Like what?" Ruwayfi scoffed. "You have got to be kidding me. Kid, you better watch yourself. You haven't been alive long enough to even know what life is about."

Ah Veng was quiet for a moment before he decided to reply.

"You try watching your father die and then being screamed at and treated like you're nothing every single day by your stepbrothers and stepfather. Then try watching as your sister gets beaten almost till the point of death just because she stood up for me and then why don't you try going out into the jungle to try and survive without any food or water. Like I haven't been through enough," Ah Veng cried.

It was Ruwayfi's turn to be silent. He had stopped walking and turned to look at Ah Veng.

"I'm sorry, kid. I didn't know. Just thought that Chong got you from the school or something."

Ah Veng shook his head.

"Well, I'll tell the guys not to give you too hard of a time. I can't promise anything, but I'll try to look out for you."

"Thank you," Ah Veng said, smiling a little.

"For now, I guess I could teach you a bit about what we do or the different jobs that people have."

"They have different jobs?" Ah Veng asked.

"Yes. It might look confusing, but it actually isn't if the workers would just focus on their own jobs and stop worrying about what other people are doing."

"So, what is it that they're supposed to do?"

"Like, what are their jobs?"

"Yeah."

"Well, to start with, there's the boss and he's in charge of everything overall. That's Chong, and he's also the president of the village if you didn't already know. Then, below him, he has some administration people, but we never see them because they usually just stay in the offices. Next, there's people like me. I guess you could say that we're managers in a way. We're just supposed to monitor all that is happening and make sure that the workers are doing what they're supposed to be doing, and then we write reports or tell them to Chong at the end of the day. We also have to attend important meetings. Now, why? I don't know. They never make sense to me. Anyway, then there's the workers. That's you and everyone else around here."

"What do we do besides build the houses?" Ah Veng asked, trying to get a better understanding of how the system flowed.

"Technically, you don't do anything but build houses. However, you are usually assigned a specific job based on your work experience or your capabilities. The people who are more advanced, they work on the more difficult parts of the house, such as the roof or the foundation. We have plumbers and electricians that come in afterwards on our days off to work on the plumbing and electricity since we are not certified to touch those areas. So, the job that you are assigned just depends on your abilities."

"Is that why I'm just supposed to help with the easy stuff like handing out tools or anything else needed? Because I haven't had any work experience?"

"Yes! See, look at you. You're smart, and I am pretty sure that you will learn the art of construction in no time. You might even get to work on the more difficult parts by the time you are in your teen years. He's starting you young, which might be a good thing. I'm not really sure what he's going for, though."

"What do you mean?"

"It's just that he is usually not that desperate for new workers. But now he is, and he's still looking, which just confuses me because I'm not sure what he has planned. Also, he's going for people that are still really young. Like, you are a little too young, and I don't think that he meant to do that, but he's still wanting to hire kids that are in their teen years when some of them are still in school and haven't even reached adulthood yet."

"I don't know, maybe he wants more kids to learn."

Ruwayfi let out a laugh.

"You're funny. Chong would never do anything for the benefit of others. It's all for himself."

"But that's not nice."

"No, I agree. It's definitely not, but since we work for him, there's not much that we can do, and we're usually happy as long as we get paid."

"Will I get paid?" Ah Veng asked.

"I'm not really sure, kid. I would think so, but depending on the circumstances of why you're here, he just might take that aspect of the job away from you."

"I heard him arguing and yelling at my sister and then he got mad at me for listening in. He said something about a deal that he made with her."

"A deal?" Ruwayfi questioned with eyebrows raised. Now that caught his attention. "What deal?" he asked when Ah Veng didn't answer.

"I'm trying to remember. Something about marrying her to get her away from our family but that she had to bring someone to work for him. Yeah, that was it! And then he said something about it being her fault that she brought me . . ." Ah Veng trailed off, suddenly realizing something.

"He really does have something planned if he got angry at your sister for bringing you. Although he is typically strict and hardly ever smiles, he only gets really angry when things are not going according to his plan. And I'm really, really sorry, kid. You must have just gotten thrown out here, didn't you?"

"Yeah," Ah Veng said, nodding.

Ruwayfi looked closely at the young boy.

"Are you alright? You're not about to cry, are you? Please tell me you're not, because we're not good with emotions around here."

"My sister didn't actually care about me, did she? She lied, didn't she? About bringing me here for a better life and everything?"

"I'm not sure I understand."

"She was more concerned about saving herself than she was about saving me because the only reason she brought me along was to get herself away, isn't it?"

"Hey, hey . . . I'm sure she did care, but to me, it does seem as though she did it mostly for her own benefits. However, don't take my word for it. I'm certain that she thought of giving you another chance as well. Maybe she thought that you'd be able to learn more here than when you were back home and that you'd get to have more experiences. Come on, let's walk this way now so I can check on the other block. We can walk and talk," he said as they started to walk again.

"She could have told me the truth. She didn't tell me anything at all. Only that we would leave one day to find a better life."

"Ah Veng," Ruwayfi sighed, using the boy's name for the first time, "you have to realize that she was probably afraid that you wouldn't go with her or that you are possibly too young to—"

"Why does everyone keep saying that I'm too young?" Ah Veng interrupted, pouting.

"Because . . ." Ruwayfi then shook his head, choosing to ignore that question. "She was probably just worried, okay? Or she couldn't really think for herself. I don't really know. I'm just trying to come up with words to make you feel better, but I feel like I'm making it worse."

"Just a little," Ah Veng replied, looking away.

"Well, just know that sometimes things happen for a reason and we shouldn't question why they do." He stopped walking. "Before we check on that side, I want to show you where we store everything."

"What would you need to store?" Ah Veng asked, and Ruwayfi laughed again.

"Kid, you crack me up."

"How am I being funny? I just asked a question," Ah Veng replied, confused.

"Exactly," Ruwayfi said, snickering. "It's the type of questions that you ask. You're just so innocent."

Ah Veng was about to be offended again, but Ruwayfi continued talking.

"Ah, here we are. The storage shed, and it's where all the tools are kept. The workers meet here in the mornings, but since I'm not sure when you'll be coming to work each day, I can't really tell you where Chong will want you to meet. 'Cause you're going to school, right?" Ruwayfi asked.

"That's what my sister said."

"Okay, then yeah, I don't know. Do you know if you're going in the morning or in the afternoon? Because I doubt he'll have you go all day like the other children."

"I'm not sure," Ah Veng said.

"Alright, so I guess we'll wait on that."

"What's this?" Ah Veng asked, poking at one of the tools on the shelf.

"Which— Oh, I wouldn't touch that if I were you."

"Why not?"

"Because it's something that the more advanced workers use. I'm not really sure what it's used for or what it's actually called, but I do know that the older workers don't like it when people move or touch their stuff."

"Will they even know?"

"I mean, maybe, I don't know. Geez, kid, you ask a lot of questions."

"Sorry," Ah Veng said, giggling slightly. He was just curious.

"And you'd be surprised how much those workers find out. They can be scary sometimes. Alright, let's move on. We've got things to do," Ruwayfi announced, waiting for Ah Veng to walk out before shutting the door. "I think I am going to let you observe the guys working on that house over there," he thought aloud, tapping his pencil on the clipboard he was carrying around.

"Do I just watch?"

"For today, yes," Ruwayfi said, giving the boy a sad smile. "Well, unless they ask you to help with something. Then you should always do it. Don't argue or say anything and you'll probably earn their trust faster that way."

Ruwayfi walked up to one of the workers at the front of the house.

"Oh hey, Ruwayfi," the man said.

"Hi, Qawi. So I just wanted to let you know that little Ah Veng here will be observing all the workers in this area for the rest of today."

The older worker looked at the child with a disapproving glance and lowered his voice.

"Seriously?" he whispered to Ruwayfi. "I don't have the time to babysit some kid."

Ruwayfi shrugged. "Boss's orders," he said, "and, Qawi, I thought that at first, but cut the kid some slack. He's had a rough time already."

"Fine," the worker replied. "But it's not permanent, right?"

"Of course not. When is anything permanent around here?"

"You're right."

"Alright, Ah Veng, I'll see you around, okay? Be good," Ruwayfi called as he walked off.

Qawi turned and sneered at Ah Veng once Ruwayfi was out of hearing range.

"You've had a rough time, huh? Well, that's too bad. Sit over there," Qawi said, pointing to a little rock beside the house, and Ah Veng immediately did what he was told.

The rest of the day, little Ah Veng stayed seated on that rock and didn't dare say anything even though he was both hungry and thirsty. Qawi turned to look at him every so often and gave him mean looks, while the other workers that passed by would purposely kick his foot or mess with his hair. Ah Veng didn't understand why they were treating him like that, and with every passing minute, the boy's wounded self-confidence was further stripped away. He began to feel sorry for himself. It bothered him that he wasn't doing anything wrong and that it wasn't his fault that he was there in the first place, and yet he was treated just as badly as he was back home.

He curled up, pulling his legs in beneath him, trying to seem as close to invisible as possible. The harsh eyes of the workers and the conditions of the construction site bore down on the little boy, pushing him into a box until there was no air left to breathe. Only darkness remained.

CHAPTER 4

FREE LABOR

October 1940
Northern Outskirts of Miri, Sarawak, Malaya

THE WEDDING OF CHONG AND AH Veng's sister was bleak and dreary, held in the midst of newly constructed houses as the sun reached its peak. The humidity rained down upon the few people gathered. There was not a single genuine smile present among the small crowd, only a forced upturn of the bride's lips as she tried her best to hide her tears. She did not want this. She did not want to be a child bride and knew that her brother was too young to fully understand that she had dragged him into child labor. Her only hope was that he would forgive her once he was old enough to understand. She glanced over at him.

Ah Veng caught his sister's eye and frowned when he saw her tears. She turned away.

"Why's she crying?" he asked the housekeeper standing beside him.

"Shh, that's nothing for you to worry about. Just be a good boy for your sister, okay?"

Ah Veng nodded in confusion and decided to keep his mouth shut. His day had already been a bad one, and he certainly didn't want to make it worse.

Knowing that it was his sister's wedding day, Ah Veng leapt out of bed that morning, ready to get dressed, when he realized that he did not have anything nice to wear. He searched for his sister to ask her, but after walking around the house a few times, he still could not find her.

"If you're looking for your sister, she's not here," Chong said, leaning on the doorframe that led into the kitchen.

The young boy pulled his head out of the pantry and turned sharply when he heard his boss's voice.

"She's not?" Ah Veng asked.

"No, of course not. That's the thing with weddings. I can't see her get ready and she can't see me. You're completely clueless, aren't you? I still haven't decided what I'm going to do with you," Chong replied, shaking his head in disapproval.

"What you're going to do with me?" Ah Veng stammered, not sure what he meant.

"Yeah, I need young workers that are skilled, not clueless, and you're not learning fast enough. I might have to trade you in."

"My sister would never let you do that!" Ah Veng cried.

Chong's smile made him shudder. *The man can't get rid of me. I don't have anywhere to go.*

"She wouldn't? I don't think you know your sister as well as you think you do."

"Why wouldn't I? She's my sister!"

"And how often have you actually talked to her? How often have you seen her? Would you even notice if she's changed? What if she's had a change of heart? Or—"

"Stop!" Ah Veng yelled, almost breaking down in tears.

"Aw, is the little boy about to cry?" Chong taunted, clearly enjoying himself.

"I know for a fact that she wouldn't forget about me and she wouldn't ever want to get rid of me. All she wanted to do was save me and give me a better life."

"Oh, is that right?" Chong asked, his smile widening like a stretching rubber band that had almost reached its breaking point. Ah Veng turned away at its eeriness. Scared, he wasn't quite sure anymore. *Does my sister still care about me? She hardly talks to me anymore.*

"Ah Veng, unfortunately life works out for some people but for others . . . not so much," Chong said, smirking, "and people change. Oh, do people change, and it's such a beautiful thing when they do."

Chong stood upright from his position at the doorway and walked over to lean down and get eye level with Ah Veng.

"Guess who's the unfortunate one."

Ah Veng thought that the man's face was going to break from that creepy smile.

"I have all the money that I could want, a huge business, my own town, and in just a few hours, I'll have a beautiful wife. And what do you have? Well, you don't have to answer, cause the answer to that is simple. Nothing. You have absolutely nothing."

"Are you finished?" Ah Veng asked, matching Chong's gaze and holding it steady.

He would not cry. He would not give this man the satisfaction of making him cry.

"No, because I want you to understand that your sister would do absolutely anything for me because she's scared that she'll lose this house and my money. I can guarantee that if I tell her I'm trading you, she'll let me. I mean, why wouldn't she if I told her that I was giving you to an even better company," he said, laughing.

"You're mean. Did you know that?" Ah Veng asked.

"Of course, but I'm not stupid like you. You know, I might actually keep you around. Just for the fun of it and free labor. Yeah, that's what I'll do."

Chong straightened up again and walked back towards the doorway.

"Do I have something to wear?" Ah Veng asked before he even thought about why he'd ever ask this cruel man.

Chong laughed. "You're kidding me, right? Of course you do. Your work clothes. You have work to do after the wedding."

And then he finally walked out of the room and left Ah Veng all alone.

The priest was saying something now, but Ah Veng didn't really care. He was still disturbed by everything that Chong had said that morning. *And what is free labor? If that means working for free, it's hardly fair.* He wasn't really sure. He feared both getting kicked out to work for some other company and dealing with the torture that his boss and many of the workers threw him.

People were clapping, and it snapped him out of his thoughts. His sister and Chong were now holding hands and facing them. Chills ran down Ah Veng's spine at his sister's forced smile compared to the glowing face of Chong. It felt wrong. He turned to walk away, not wanting to watch anymore. Strolling along the parade of newly built houses, he made it to the construction zone, sighing as he looked back towards the celebration in the distance.

* * *

Ah Veng had no place in Chong's house, but he continued to obey commands and lost count of the days, simply moving through the routine of his new life. He would get up at the crack of dawn, get dressed in worn work clothes and then head downstairs for a quick breakfast before grabbing his backpack and walking to the small school just around the corner. At around noon, he would swallow his lunch as quickly as possible before running off to the construction site.

He hardly spoke a word and usually kept to himself at school. The other kids merely stared at him in disgust because of the clothes that he wore. Work was not much better since the adults always bossed him around, and when he did not do a task fast enough, they would shove him to the ground, saying that he was useless. Back at the house, his sister was pregnant and never in the mood to talk to him anymore; she was always crying or busying herself with chores. Sometimes, the young boy wondered if his solitude was some sort of punishment for

not being able to save his father. His mother had often blamed him
for his father's death.

* * *

"Anda! Anda! Itu kerana anda!"[17] Ah Veng's mother screamed as a
few of his sisters held her back. Her eyes were blood red from crying as
she screamed. It was only a few weeks after his father's passing, and his
mother had returned home from her daily outings a little after dinner.
Ah Veng was helping to clean up after the meal when he accidently
dropped a plate. The sound of it breaking echoed throughout the room
as it splintered into tiny fragments across the floor.

His mother walked through the front door with anger in her eyes
and hit him before he even had time to look up. She yelled until Ah
Veng's sisters held her back and tried to drag her out of the room,
which simply turned her cries into hysterical screams.

The innocent boy merely cradled his face with one hand as he bent
down to pick up the broken pieces with the other. Tears crowded his
vision, and eventually one of his sisters helped him clean up the mess
before gently prying his hand away from his face to tend to his slightly
swollen eye. Although the yelling had turned to muffled sobs, the screams
of his mother still resonated in the back of his mind, never to be forgotten.

* * *

"Hey, are you daydreaming again? We don't have all day! How
many times do I have to tell you that?" Qawi snapped before shoving
a hammer into Ah Veng's hands and pushing him towards the wall
they were working on. "Now, get to it. The boss says that we have to
stay on track since buyers are impatient, and we have to finish this set
of houses soon or the company will not be happy. What is it that we
always say? Hmm?"

---

17   You! You! It is because of you!

"Efficient wor—"

"*Bersuara!*"[18] Qawi barked.

"Efficient workers mean happy bosses, and happy bosses mean higher wages," Ah Veng stated, giving his superior the hardest glare he could muster.

Qawi merely laughed and patted him on the head like a dog.

"That's a good boy. Now get to work."

Ah Veng hated Ruwayfi for putting him under Qawi's supervision. He wanted to follow Ruwayfi around instead, but Ruwayfi said that Ah Veng had to work on the houses and that there wasn't anyone else willing to supervise besides Qawi. Now, that was hard to believe.

He hammered another nail into the wooden structure harder than he normally did. It just wasn't fair, and he knew that he said that a lot, but he just couldn't fit in anywhere at home, school, or work. It seemed as though everyone around him hated him, and he couldn't figure out why. He wasn't doing anything wrong. In fact, he was trying his best to do everything right.

"Kid! We need some water," one of the workers yelled from the back. Ah Veng threw his hammer down and stood, grumbling to himself.

"I don't think so," Qawi said, putting a hand on Ah Veng's chest and stopping him from walking past.

"I need to get them water," Ah Veng replied, trying to move around him.

"Not with that attitude. Pick up that hammer and put it down gently. Tools cost money, you know?"

Ah Veng sighed and bent down to do as he was told.

"You better fix your face. I know you don't want a bad report to go to Ruwayfi or Chong."

"I'm sorry," Ah Veng said, looking down at his feet.

"It's fine. Don't let it happen again. Now, go get them some water like they asked."

---

18 Speak up!

Ah Veng ran off towards the well, thankful to be away from everyone for a while, but when he reached the well, there was a little girl standing there, giggling at something down in the water below.

"What are you doing?" Ah Veng asked.

The girl turned, frightened and unsure of who was speaking to her. She chewed on her bottom lip. "Ummm . . ."

"Kids aren't usually out here. They're usually at school."

"Well, you're out here," the girl retorted, apparently offended.

"'Cause I work out here," Ah Veng shot back.

"Well, my uncle works here."

"So? That doesn't give you a reason to be here," Ah Veng said, narrowing his eyes.

"I don't go to school here. We're visiting my uncle and his family. They said I could do whatever I wanted, and I wanted to go to work with him. So I don't see why you have to get so upset. I was just staring down into the water and watching it ripple."

"Oh," Ah Veng said, feeling kind of stupid.

"You should come look," she said, pointing down into the well.

Ah Veng approached and peered over the top. He watched as she blew gently down onto the surface of the water. Little ripples interrupted the calm surface. It was mesmerizing—such a small but beautiful effect.

"It's pretty," Ah Veng said, looking up to smile at the girl.

"I know, right? I like watching it because it reminds me how even little things matter and one thing can cause another thing to happen that causes another one, just like the ripples."

Ah Veng stared at her, impressed.

"You're smart," he said. "Like, really smart."

"Thanks," she said, giggling. "A lot of people tell me that, but I never believe them. I just like books and school. A lot."

"That's—" Ah Veng started to say when a shout interrupted him.

"Ah Veng! Hurry up, will you? Stop talking to that girl and do what you're supposed to do!"

Qawi stood beside the house with his arms crossed.

"Sorry," Ah Veng said to the girl, wincing as he quickly drew up a bucket of water.

As he walked away with it, the girl called out to him.

"Thank you for talking to me. It was nice!"

Ah Veng looked back and gave her a small smile as he prepared himself for a scolding.

"Who told you that you could stop and socialize?"

"What's socia—"

"Never mind that," Qawi cut him off. "When have you ever been able to take a break and just talk to someone?"

Ah Veng hung his head.

"That's what I thought. Now get in there and give them their water. I'm sorry, but today is just not your day. I'm going to have to tell Ruwayfi. I thought that I could be nice for once, but sorry, kid. You've got to learn your place and what it means to be a worker."

Qawi looked at the boy in pity as Ah Veng walked off to serve the other workers water. *Perhaps I was too harsh,* he thought. *But the kid has to learn somehow, and someone has to teach him. There's no other way to do that than to isolate him and make him feel like no one cares about him. It will make him tougher. Those are the people that end up receiving the most blessings in the end anyway.*

"Poor kid," Qawi mumbled before getting back to work.

* * *

November 1941

A little over a year after the siblings first arrived in Chong's village, Ah Veng's sister had her child, a little girl that the couple named Damia. The little attention he received before the birth was now fully taken away by the new addition to the family. Ah Veng simply sighed and went about his life like normal. He was used to being ignored and found that his work in both school and construction eased his pain and desire to live a normal childhood.

"Come on, you're eight now," he whispered to himself every time he felt like crying. "*Anda seorang lelaki besar.*"[19]

He would also talk to nature itself, thinking that maybe there was a god for each of the wonderful plants or creatures that covered the planet. He had heard the construction workers talk about gods of nature, and since he had nowhere to turn, he decided to trust these nature gods.

The animal he prayed to the most was the owl in hopes that its association with the spirits would allow him to feel his father's spirit watching over him. Guilt often overwhelmed him, and he desperately begged to be forgiven for letting his father die. Even if that fate had been inevitable, he still wished that he had run to get help sooner. He also prayed to the owls for wisdom and patience. On difficult days, he looked to the birds for hope and to the butterflies for the will to live and move forward. However, the tiger was what kept him going; each day, he prayed for the power and energy to fulfill his duties.

His time in the rainforest and his fight for survival had given him a connection with nature itself. Although he had stood on the verge of death during his journey, there was still a peace within him which seemed to acknowledge that he was protected—a child of mother nature. Believing that higher beings watched over him gave him the strength to push forward, hoping that one day he could finally carve out a life of his own.

Every day was harder than the one before, but he persevered. There was never a time in which he was not ridiculed at school and scolded at work. The other children laughed and chased one another while Ah Veng ran to get to the construction site on time. They read and studied hard each afternoon and evening to further their education while Ah Veng was doing manual labor, hammering away on a house. The other kids went home to loving families and nice dinners while Ah Veng

---

19 You're a big boy.

arrived at his house late at night to choke down a cold meal before bathing and falling into bed. This was what life was like for him, and yet not once did he complain to a single soul.

* * *

December 1947

Damia, Ah Veng's six-year-old niece, bounded up to him and threw her arms around his leg.

"Don't goooo," she whined and looked up at him with a pouty face and sad eyes.

"You know I have to," Ah Veng sighed and picked her up to swing her around. "Your daddy says that there's work to be done."

Damia frowned when he put her down and stamped her foot.

"Well, that's not fair."

"I know," he said. "I used to say that all the time too, but there is nowhere else to build houses unless we travel farther into the countryside."

"Blah, blah, blah. I want you to stay and play with me. Mommy's always too busy with the baby," she pouted.

"Aw, I'm sorry, but I will be back tonight, and maybe I'll tell you a story if I hear that you were good, alright?"

She hesitated before nodding and turning to run into the house. *That child is too wild,* Ah Veng thought, feeling sorry that his sister had to put up with her. He followed the other workers as they lined up to grab their tools and head onto the waiting bus for another day of work. He sent a brief mental thank-you to the nature gods for the school holiday. It meant more time for him to concentrate on his work and stay lost in his thoughts, and less time being humiliated by the other kids in his class.

Over the past few years, Ah Veng had gained respect from the other workers once he realized that a good work ethic could work wonders.

It meant less scolding, and no one was constantly looking over his shoulder or watching him while he worked. However, school was still difficult for him since he was never accepted among those his age. They thought that he was too mature, too quiet, too different from the rest of them. He was contemplating dropping out before high school started next month. His brother-in-law was sure to agree to that since he wanted Ah Veng at the job site more often.

Ah Veng stared out the window, watching the scenery pass by. *Yes, that's what I'm going to do.* He observed the rows and rows of houses that they had spent years working on and admired all the hard work that had gone into building each one. They were now helping another village expand, but it was miles away, so they had to travel by bus each morning.

The bus slowly halted, and the workers stood up to file out one by one. Ah Veng stayed seated, usually the last one to leave since he liked to thank the driver and was in no rush to enter the heat. He sighed and picked up his toolbox before making his way to the front of the bus.

"*Terima kas*—" he started to say, but the bus driver cut him off.

"I don't know why you do it."

"Do what?" Ah Veng asked.

"This," he replied, waving his hand in the air.

"Construction?"

"All of it," the driver said.

"I don't think I understand."

"You're basically a slave. The other workers get paid. You don't. You're doing free labor. All you get is a small room to sleep in, a sandwich for lunch, and a cold dinner at night. And yet you're the nicest person I've met. The only one to thank me for simply doing my job. So I don't understand why you, a nice young man, are working for that brother-in-law of yours when you could be out finding your own life."

"Why would I need to do that?" Ah Veng asked.

"What? Finding your own life?" the bus driver laughed. "Because you can't go about doing free labor your whole entire life. Don't you want to find a wife one day, maybe settle down in a house and have kids?"

"Never really thought about," Ah Veng honestly replied.

"Well, you certainly shouldn't work for free. You might want to talk to your brother-in-law about that."

"I'd rather not."

"Why? It can't hurt to ask."

"Trust me, I've tried."

"And? He just said no?" the driver asked skeptically.

"No, he laughed," Ah Veng said. "I know what you're thinking," Ah Veng continued. "He is pretty much nice to everyone except me."

"Do you know why he treats you like that?" the driver asked.

"Not really. I guess it had something to do with the fact that my sister brought me along when I was young, and he wanted someone older that would be more efficient in working."

"That's weird for someone to hold a grudge about."

"Yeah, you're telling me. Especially after he had kids. I thought that I would become more a part of the family, but instead, I just became even more invisible."

"That sounds awful. I'm sorry about the way you're treated. I hate when people don't get the respect that they deserve. You really ought to get out of there as soon as possible."

"I don't know," Ah Veng replied.

"Just think about it," the driver said with a soft, genuine smile.

And Ah Veng did. He thought about it every morning when he got on the bus, he thought about it while he worked, he thought about it before he went to sleep each night, and the more he thought about it, the more he liked the idea of leaving. The question was how. There was no way that his boss would simply let him go, and it might break his niece's heart if he did leave. He was also not sure if he was strong enough to leave behind the only family he had, even with the mistreatment he received.

The thoughts festered in his mind for over three years. He wasn't sure if he was just scared or if a small part of him wanted to stay with the only family he really knew. But each day the bus driver gave him a sad smile of pity and shook his head.

"Still not going to, are you?" he asked one day.

"I don't know," Ah Veng replied. "I just don't think I can."

"You can't or you won't?" the driver questioned with raised eyebrows, and Ah Veng shook his head, stepped out of the bus, and kicked at a few stones littering the ground.

"Tomorrow," Ah Veng finally said with determination, looking back up at the driver. "I'll leave tomorrow."

CHAPTER 5

HOMELESS

HE KEPT HIS WORD. WHEN HE got home that night, he packed up all his stuff and placed it beside his bed. Then in the morning he hugged his sister for the first time in many years before throwing his arms around his niece and nephew, planting a kiss on their heads.

"What are you doing?" his sister asked with wide eyes pleading him to say anything other than what she knew she was going to hear.

But he still said it.

"I'm leaving," he replied and then walked out the door, grabbed his tools, and got on the bus just like he had done every day for the past few years.

But this time was different. It would be his last.

As he sat staring out the window, he wondered what his new life would be like. He thought about all of the things he could do but was unsure if he would be able to find a job or even a place to stay. Doubts stirred in his mind, but he forced himself to think of the positive. He needed to; he was being taken advantage of and could no longer stay there if he was to find a life of his own.

The drive dragged on forever. He sighed when the construction site rolled into view. Stacks of wood, piles of trash, half-built houses—it was nothing new, except he would not be going to work that day. He watched as each worker stepped off the bus and set off towards their assigned area. His would be left empty that day, and they would have to find someone to fill his position.

He turned to see the bus driver's eyes on him, so he stood and headed to the front.

"Today is the day, huh?" the driver asked, his face filled with both concern and relief.

"Yes, I was wondering if you—"

"Of course, of course," the driver stated, cutting Ah Veng off. "You know that I'll take you wherever you want to go."

"Well, that's the thing—" Ah Veng started to say.

"You don't know, do you?" he asked, and Ah Veng shook his head.

"Good thing I know just the place. You might even be able to find a job there and everything."

"Really?" Ah Veng questioned, reassurance flowing through his body. Everything might actually work out.

"Yes, but it's not too far from where you use to live, though, and it's going to be quite a drive. I hope that's alright."

"Yes, of course."

"Well, alright then. Take a seat anywhere you like. We have somewhere to be!" he exclaimed, throwing the young man a delighted smile over his shoulder as he placed the bus into drive.

Ah Veng grimaced at the man's enthusiasm but was grateful to be getting a ride instead of having to walk. He watched the only world he had really known slowly dissipate into the background. For the second time, he was leaving a part of his life behind. The first time, he had left his childhood. *And now what? My young adulthood?*

* * *

Ah Veng soared above the clouds. Flying was an escape. But where there was beauty, there was also ugliness, and where there was good, there was evil. The world was composed of all. He flew below the clouds only to be swept away in the storm—into a current of lightning and rain. Down below, people screamed. A hurricane was brewing, growing, becoming stronger with every flap of his wings. Why do storms happen? Do they have a purpose? *he wondered as he fought to stay aloft, but the rain pelted down harder, overpowering all else, and down he went, spiraling out of control.*

* * *

"Hey, kid, we're here," the driver said, shaking Ah Veng awake.

"Wha—" he started to say and then jolted fully awake, taking in his surroundings. He looked out the window and saw rain drops showering streets and buildings that looked so much nicer than what he was used to.

"Where are we?" Ah Veng asked in amazement.

The driver's smile grew before he said, "*Selamat datang ke pusat Miri.*"[20]

Ah Veng thanked the bus driver multiple times before watching him drive away. The words "Good luck kid, I believe in you" rang loud in his ears.

He wandered the street, wondering where he should go first. Already drenched, he tried to decide quickly. A sign caught his eye that read *Restoran*,[21] so he walked in. Immediately he was greeted by a friendly face,

"*Hai*,[22] how can I help you?"

"I'm looking for work," Ah Veng replied. "Do you—"

"*Maaf, tidak*,"[23] the man said quickly, and Ah Veng was out on the streets again.

He looked up and down the street once more before braving the rain and dashing to a bookstore across from the restaurant. A bell dinged as he pushed open the door and stepped inside.

---

20 Welcome to the center of Miri.

21 Diner.

22 Hi.

23 Sorry, no.

"Hai, welcome. Can I help you find something? We have many new selections of books that are on sale at the moment."

"Actually, I wanted to ask if you were hiring."

"Oh. I'm sorry, but all positions are filled. You might want to check at the hardware store on the corner."

"Okay, thank you," Ah Veng said, giving a small wave and stepping back outside.

Clutching his bag to his chest, he jogged towards the corner that the bookstore owner had pointed to, shaking the water from his hair and clothes once he reached the door. It opened, and he slipped in after a couple stepped out. There was no one at the counter, so he wandered towards the back.

"Are you looking for something?" a voice called from behind.

He turned, slightly startled.

"Yes, I was looking for the owner because I am searching for work."

"I would be the person you are looking for, then. Do you have identification?"

"I'm sorry, what?" Ah Veng asked.

"You know, an ID that shows who you are. It's a card with your picture and information on it."

"No. I worked for my brother-in-law and he never mentioned anything like that."

"Well, then I'm sorry. No ID means I cannot hire you, and it is likely that nowhere else will want to hire you as well."

"May I ask why?"

"Sure. I mean no offense, but I don't know you, and how can I know that what you tell me is true if I do not have proof of your background? Plus, it's just policy to hire workers with ID since most people without one have no work experience or are labeled an ex-convict, and I am not saying that you are. I just don't know you."

"Oh, okay, I guess that makes sense. Thank you," Ah Veng said, quickly sliding past and making it to the door.

"I'm sorry," the owner called, but Ah Veng was already outside.

He tried asking a few other places just to be certain, but the same thing happened time and time again. It did not take long for him to learn that there was no use; no one would hire him if he did not have identification.

"Excuse me, where can I get an ID?" he asked a couple walking by, but they merely shook their heads and walked on.

"Sir, do you know where I can get an ID?" he asked another man that strolled by, but he, too, continued to walk on, muttering, "They don't just give those out, you know."

Ah Veng sat down, defeated. Perhaps the bus driver thought he had an ID, but Ah Veng hadn't even known he was supposed to have one. *Did they tell us at school?* he wondered. He had dropped out his first year in high school. *Why didn't the workers ever talk about needing one?* It just didn't make sense.

He finally got up and wandered a few streets down, wondering where he was going to sleep that night, when a voice called out to him, "Wait!"

He froze and spun around to find a small boy running towards him. Confused, he stepped to the side and let the kid catch up.

"You don't have anywhere to stay, do you?" the little boy asked.

"No," Ah Veng answered cautiously, wondering why the child knew and what he could possibly offer.

"Well, there's a place you could stay a few blocks down. It's where all the people like us stay."

"People like . . . us?" Ah Veng questioned.

"Well, yeah," the boy said. "You know, we're homeless, so we usually stick together since we don't have anyone else. And you looked new so I followed you around and noticed that you couldn't find work and were asking people about getting an ID."

"Oh, did you now?" Ah Veng replied slowly, unsure if he could trust the child, especially if he was being stalked by the young boy.

"Come on!" the kid said, taking Ah Veng's arm and attempting to drag him down the street, but Ah Veng shook him free and followed behind instead.

They walked for a few blocks before they reached a wide alleyway filled with people. Clothes littered the ground, and other useful pieces of trash were piled up against the wall, but what caught Ah Veng's attention was a very old man sitting in a chair. He had all sorts of treasures piled high around him, including toys, dishes, furniture, and various musical instruments. Ah Veng wondered why he had all of that stuff and started to ask, except the little boy was gone. He looked around in confusion but stopped when he realized that everyone had stopped what they were doing in order to stare at him. The old man motioned to him, and Ah Veng tentatively took a few steps forward.

"If you're looking for the boy that brought you, don't bother. Also, the things that you're missing, don't go looking for that either."

"The things that I'm missing?" Ah Veng asked with his brows furrowed. It was then that he realized his bag was gone and there was nothing left in his pockets. "Hey, did that kid take all my stuff?" he demanded in anger.

"Sleight of hand. Tip number one," the man stated simply. "Tip number two: better learn to hide the things you don't want stolen. And tip number three: do what you can to survive."

"What is this?" Ah Veng questioned in frustration. "Some sort of game or something?"

"Well, yes, actually. It's what we like to call the theft game," the man replied with a huge smile, showing a mouth full of rotten teeth. A gap in between the front two was wide enough for the man to stick his tongue through, and Ah Veng shuddered at the ghastliness of not only his surroundings but of the people who were there. *This is sick*, he thought and turned to leave.

"Oh, and one more thing before you go," the man said. "Watch your back."

He howled with laughter, and everyone else laughed with him. Ah Veng ran out of there as fast as he could.

He slept on the opposite side of town that first night.

* * *

June 1954
Central Miri, Sarawak, Malaya

The deserted streets stood silent and still as clouds covered the moon, shielding the main source of light. No cars passed by, and no animals were in sight as they slept in their respective homes. The street corner was barely lit as the lamppost flickered on and off. A hunched figure curled up beside it, trying to read a newspaper he had found earlier that day.

A boy ran towards him and grabbed the paper from his hands before turning and sprinting down the street.

"Hey, that's mine!" Ah Veng yelled after the child before grumbling and standing up to glare after the boy, not in the mood to chase him.

He bent down to pick up his small sack of belongings and sauntered off to find a place to sleep for the night. Another homeless child ran past him on swift but quiet feet, probably looking for something to steal. That was all that ever happened here.

A smile played along Ah Veng's lips as he settled in a small alleyway to get some sleep. He made sure to tuck his little sack beneath him so that nothing would get stolen. It had happened all too often when he first became homeless, but eventually he learned all the rules of the theft game.

He swatted at a mosquito flying around his face. Bugs were a constant problem, and he always had trouble sleeping. He longed for a bed to lie on and a proper meal to eat. *Is that too much to ask for?* he thought before finally drifting off.

* * *

A sharp wail pierced the air, reverberating off every object in the vicinity. Ah Veng swiveled in that direction and arrived at a patch of dry, shriveled grass. The ground was cracked, splintering and crumbling to pieces. Drought had ruined the land. He flew a little higher to see the source of the wail. Villagers gathered around a water well. There wasn't a single drop left. How were they supposed to survive? Water was a necessity.

The sound of a roar cut off the wail. A river had completely dried. Animals were fighting over the last drops. Water flowed no longer. Both people and animals were fighting to survive. That, too, left its mark.

Who, then, would prevail?

The strongest, toughest, most powerful of them all.

Survival of the fittest.

* * *

A ray of sunlight woke Ah Veng early the next morning. He stood and stretched before picking up his sack and walking out onto the street. People were already bustling about as shops opened. The newspaper boy rode his bike up and down the street yelling, "*Ahkbar, ahkbar.*"[24]

Ah Veng's stride quickened with excitement when he remembered that today he would be able to choose something from the old man's pile, a reward for diligently pickpocketing for the man. It wasn't something that he wanted to do, but he had to survive someway, and it seemed like the only option at the time.

* * *

"So you decided to come back," the old man had said, cackling with amusement when Ah Veng returned after his first night alone in the town.

"I didn't have a choice," Ah Veng muttered. The man simply laughed harder. The creepy sound made Ah Veng uncomfortable.

"Smart choice," the man said, wheezing from all his laughing.

---

24 Newspapers, newspapers.

"Hanina, get him a sack, will you?" he demanded, and a woman bent down behind the chair and handed Ah Veng a little brown sack.

"What do I have to do?" Ah Veng asked with a sigh.

"Just fill the sack up each day and deposit the things in that corner there. When you do, you'll get food in return. It's that simple. Also, if you bring me extra or something really valuable, you might just get a reward in return," he said and winked.

* * *

Ah Veng pick up his pace. He weaved in and out of the crowds, his mind set on one particular thing. *The guitar.* When he wasn't pickpocketing, he spent a lot of his time in the music store. Eventually, the owner of the store agreed to give him free lessons with the one condition that he had to get a guitar. That meant stealing it, getting it as a reward, or somehow earning enough money to afford one. Well, now was his chance. He broke into a run and rounded the last corner, skidding to a halt in front of the alleyway. It was deserted.

"What?" Ah Veng stated in bewilderment.

Someone moved behind the piles of things the old man had collected over the years.

"He died," the voice called. "Everyone went to bury him."

"Oh," Ah Veng said with disappointment. "From what?"

"What do you think? Old age," the voice replied.

"Right," Ah Veng said cautiously, wondering why the person did not want to reveal himself.

"You can take what you want, you know."

"But—"

"He's not here anymore, and besides, none of it belonged to him in the first place," the voice said.

Ah Veng shrugged. That much was true. He reached down to grab the guitar and then took off running. Hugging it tightly to his chest, he did not stop until he reached the music store. A bright smile lit up his face the whole way, and it glowed even brighter when he barged into the front door.

"I got it!" Ah Veng exclaimed.

The store owner spun around in shock.

"Now, how did you manage to do that?" he asked.

"I got it from—" Ah Veng stopped abruptly; he'd almost let the reward system and his secret pickpocketing slip. "One of the older homeless men passed away, and he knew that I really wanted a guitar, so he gave me his just before he died," Ah Veng redeemed himself, looking down and trying to make his excuse convincing.

"Aw, well, I'm sorry that he passed, but happy for you at the same time. So, when do you want to start lessons?"

"Um, right now?" Ah Veng laughed nervously.

"Well, come on over here! I just finished polishing up my own guitar."

"It's alright with you, though, right?"

"What? That we start right now? Of course it is. I know that you've been waiting a long time for this. It's the least I could do."

"Thank you so much!" Ah Veng exclaimed.

The owner of the store let out a laugh. "Besides, I love teaching music, and students that are enthusiastic about learning are more fun to teach. Sometimes I have trouble with those kids that don't want to play but their parents are making them."

"What! There are kids that don't want to learn music?" Ah Veng asked in shock, not understanding why anyone wouldn't want to learn.

"Well, it's not everyone's forte, you know?" the owner replied, cracking up.

Ah Veng looked at him, confused.

"Sorry about that," the owner said. "It's a joke, a pun, whatever you call it. 'Cause forte means 'loud' in music, but I used it in the sentence to indicate that music is not everyone's area of interest."

"Forte," Ah Veng said slowly, "means loud. Like, play loud?"

"Yes, it means to play loud. It's a dynamic. Dynamics are the indicators that tell us how loud or soft we need to play. There's a symbol for each dynamic level. Here, let me find a piece that's relatively easy. Wait, before we do that, I need to see if I should teach you to read music or if you play by ear."

"What do you mean, play by ear?"

"Whether you can play what I can play just by watching me and hearing it. So, do everything that I do."

Ah Veng paid close attention and mimicked all of his teacher's motions.

"Good, so that's how you strum. And when you pick . . . yes, exactly. So now, try playing this."

The owner played a few notes, and Ah Veng played the little melody back.

"Alright, now this one," he said, playing one that was a little longer.

Ah Veng played it exactly the way it sounded.

"Hey, you're really good! So this means that you do play by ear, which makes it a lot easier. You figured that out a lot quicker than any other student I have had."

"Really?" Ah Veng asked.

"Yeah. I knew that I had a good feeling about you. I see great things in store for you in the future."

"Thank you. You have no idea what it means to have you say that."

"It's no big deal, and I mean it, too. Now, let's learn some of those dynamics I was talking about earlier."

Ah Veng couldn't believe his luck. Destiny must have led him to this little music store where someone actually had faith in him. It seemed like a dream. He tuned back in to what his teacher was saying, excited to learn something new and to get the opportunity to embark on a new adventure.

The lessons flew by like a breeze, and just two weeks later, Ah Veng was already performing on the streets.

He quickly picked up not only the guitar but the harmonica as well. People started going out of their way to hear him play, occasionally throwing coins into his sack. He loved the attention, and although he still didn't have a place to call his own, he was able to buy himself a meal each day. That was enough to satisfy him, and he made sure to thank the gods for his good luck since others were not so lucky. He wondered what happened to the other homeless people when their leader died. Were they still stealing? Or were they trying to find other ways to make money like he was?

At one point, he ran into the boy that had stolen all his belongings that first day he ended up in the town. Surprisingly, the boy was with a nice-looking couple. Ah Veng called out to the kid before he could run off again.

"Hey, I want to talk to you," Ah Veng shouted, and the boy immediately slumped his shoulders. He slowly walked over to where Ah Veng stood waiting.

"I just wanted to let you know that I don't blame you for stealing my stuff," Ah Veng said, and the boy's head snapped up.

"You don't?" he asked in shock.

"Of course not," Ah Veng responded. "After all, it's survival of the fittest, am I right?"

"Yeah, I guess you're right," the boy said with a small smile.

They shook hands and then parted ways. The child headed back to his adopted family while Ah Veng walked off in the opposite direction, guitar in hand, searching for an audience to play for.

CHAPTER 6

RECOLLECTIONS OF WAR

July 1954

THE SUN HAD JUST STARTED TO rise when the young man sat down at his street corner to begin strumming a tune. It was still early, but he enjoyed watching the sun wake up their side of the world. He also loved the gradual start to the morning, usually staying lost within his own thoughts, wondering what he would like to think about that day. A stray newspaper flew by and landed beside him. It was a day old, but he still picked it up to read it. The headline on the front page read, *GENEVA AGREEMENTS SIGNED—July 21, 1954.*

"I'd forgotten that the French Indochina war is still going on," a voice said behind him.

Ah Veng was startled and turned to see who had spoken.

"Well, actually, as of yesterday, it should be coming to a close," a tall man dressed in business attire said with a thoughtful expression.

His hair was combed back neatly, jawline steadily shaven, skin gleamingly smooth and many shades lighter than Ah Veng's, and although his demeanor was overall intimidating, the man's eyes flickered with a soft kindness that immediately gained Ah Veng's trust.

"Yeah, I had honestly forgotten as well," he finally replied.

"People seem to forget things too often, especially war. They would rather not remember the ghastly horrors and unpleasant feelings, but the stories are important. That's what people don't realize," the man stated, sitting down beside Ah Veng.

"You don't have to sit," Ah Veng blurted, the words tumbling out before he had a chance to think.

"Oh, I don't mind," the man replied and then paused before saying, "You shouldn't let what I wear intimidate you because it is what's in the heart that really counts."

Ah Veng was dumbfounded by this man's words. No normal businessman would ever have a conversation with a homeless man, let alone sit right next to him on the side of the street. He noticed that the man was steadily watching him.

"I'm Jian-min, by the way," he said, sticking his hand out.

Ah Veng hesitated before reaching out his own to shake the man's hand.

"I'm Ah Veng."

"Well, nice to meet you, Ah Veng. So, what do you think about the conference and signing of the agreements and everything?" he asked.

"What do you mean?" Ah Veng started to ask and then realized that Jian-min meant the newspaper he was holding. "Oh, this. I'm not sure. I didn't have a chance to read it yet."

"That's quite alright. I could sum it up for you if you'd like," Jian-min offered.

Ah Veng simply shrugged, realizing that the man probably thought he couldn't read.

"Let me see where to begin . . . hmm . . ." Jian-min glanced over at the paper before starting, "Basically, the French were obsessed with fortune in Indochina and specifically Vietnam. They completely took over the country, tyrannizing everything and implementing this and that simply because they wanted to. 'The French protectorate' is what people call it, and it must have made the people go insane at not having the freedom to govern their own country. I mean, it's just like the British rule our country right now, and before them, the Dutch. We might not openly talk about it, but I'm sure that we all want our independence, am I right?" Jian-min said and winked.

He didn't wait for Ah Veng to respond before continuing.

"So then this whole uprising occurred where a revolutionary organization called the Viet Minh was created. Shortly after, the war started—it was 1946, I believe—and nothing was accomplished. When I say nothing, I literally mean nothing. The war was a stalemate. Hardly anything was resolved. If you think about it, the war is still going on now and it's 1954! Well, actually, it should be dwindling down since the signing of the Geneva Agreements yesterday. Hopefully . . . although I have my doubts. Vietnam will be temporarily divided at the 17th parallel for two years until a president is elected and the country is reunited. But dividing a country doesn't sound like a good idea to me, even if it's temporary. All sorts of things can happen in two years before the election of a president, and reuniting the country? How do you know people won't . . ."

Ah Veng zoned out. Jian-min kept going on and on. Ah Veng wondered why this man wanted to talk to him in the first place. *Political reasons? Economic?* Malaya was trying to gain independence at the moment, but then again, they always were, from what he had overheard. He shook his head, trying to sort everything out. The information was definitely interesting, but it bored him, and he didn't like the topic of war anyway. There was a reason for that; it was one of the many things he'd like to forget from his childhood.

* * *

It was pitch dark as Ah Veng tried to trace his way back to Chong's house. He had worked overtime at the construction site since a deadline was closing in, and he was exhausted, just wanting to crawl into bed. Bugs swarmed, and the sudden hoot of an owl made him jump. *How late is it?* he wondered as he stumbled yet again and let himself fall to the ground. He just lay there, looking up at the stars. *So, so tired.* He so desperately wanted to let himself drift off to sleep.

The night sky twinkled up above. Suddenly, a streak of metal and blinding white lights disrupted the scene. Ah Veng bolted to his feet. Planes never flew above their little town and especially not at night. He broke into a run and didn't care that he wasn't really sure where he was going. Somehow, he made it back to the house. He threw open the door and ran into the kitchen where he found Chong and his sister talking with two other men. They were dressed in nice clothes and held themselves as if they were of importance. The only difference between them was that one man was shorter than the other.

"Do you know when . . ." Their voices trailed off as they turned to look at Ah Veng.

"Oh, there you are," his sister sighed with relief and walked over.

"There was a plane," Ah Veng said, trying to catch his breath. "It just flew by, and I don't know why, but that doesn't usually happen, right? Planes are not supposed to fly around here. It . . . I think it was going that way," he stammered, pointing.

His sister froze, and the other adults in the room stared at him, wide-eyed.

"They were planning something; I knew it," one of the men said.

"The British are too oblivious to think that our country could potentially be threatened as well," the shorter man added, shaking his head.

"So, what happens now?" Chong asked. "There has to be something that can be done."

"Sorry, but I'm afraid there isn't. The British would never listen to a word we have to say, and besides, you never know what is actually going to happen. A plane flying by could practically mean anything," the short man replied. He picked up his hat from the table and placed it on his head before saying, "We should get going before anything else happens tonight."

"I hope that you get back safely. It's dark out there," Ah Veng's sister said softly, holding the door open. However, they weren't able to step through before the sound of planes drowned out all else. A loud explosion shook the ground, and their whole world trembled. Time froze and then moved in slow motion. The sky lit up and rained down shooting stars of fiery light. As people awoke from their slumber, some screamed, paralyzed in terror, while others ran and scrambled to take cover, shielding their children, not allowing them to look out the windows at the horror.

Ah Veng was on the ground, covering his ringing ears and staring into the distance where planes dropped bombs from the sky, watching explosion after explosion. The fire danced in a taunting manner as if it were winning some game; as if the sky held all the power in the world. Chong crawled over and pushed the door shut, snapping Ah Veng from the grasp of hypnosis. The flickering flames disappeared from view, but chaos commenced.

"*Saya takut,*"[25] Ah Veng whispered.

"We need to find safety somewhere," one of the men yelled.

"Like where? There isn't any place. I haven't had time to build a shelter underground," Chong shouted back. The planes and explosions were so loud now that all Ah Veng wanted to do was curl up somewhere and forget about all that was happening, but next thing he knew his sister was dragging him out the back door.

"If we can make it to my place, I have a storage shelter below my house sort of like a basement. It hasn't been opened in years, though, and it's small, but we can probably all fit," the short man said, but Ah Veng could hardly hear him.

Another plane flew past, and they all broke into a run.

"This way," someone shouted as they ran through the neighborhood.

---

25 I'm scared.

People stood outside, mesmerized by the terrors unfolding behind them, while some peeked out from windows or stayed hidden within the shadows. Ah Veng didn't dare look back. The dancing pattern of explosions was already engraved in his mind—a nightmare never to be forgotten.

Suddenly, they veered to the right and stopped at the door of a house. The short man pushed the door open and fumbled around on the ground of his living room. Chong and the other man ran to help as Ah Veng's sister shoved him inside and shut the door behind them. A chair and table were pushed away, a rug thrown to the side, and a latch opened to reveal a hidden ladder leading down into darkness. The short man lit an oil lamp and clambered down the rungs.

"Come on down," he yelled, and one by one they went down into the opening.

Chong shut the door, enclosing them as if they were being buried alive in a box with nothing but their only source of light—a tiny glow of hope.

The area was small, and there was not much room to move around. Ah Veng felt claustrophobic but was glad that the terrible sounds were not overpowering anymore. He could hear himself think again. He rubbed his ears to soothe the throbbing and slid down to sit on the ground. Dust flew up and he coughed, finally noticing that everyone was silent. The solemn stares were empty as they strained to listen to the faint sounds in the distance, waiting for the moment when the bombing would stop.

Eventually, after what felt like hours, the sounds stopped completely, and the short man climbed out to take a look.

"I'm quite certain the bombing is over now," he called from the top of the ladder. "You all can come on up now."

Ah Veng stirred and followed his sister up the ladder and then outside. The smell of smoke hit them in the face, and they coughed at the stench, unprepared for the sight. People slowly emerged from their houses, talking in hushed tones and staring into the distance in bewilderment. Most of their forest was gone, meaning that their wood for construction would have to be found elsewhere. Smoke rose from the horizon in two directions, blackening the sky that was just about to break for dawn.

They were lucky; their houses were not destroyed like most of the villages close by. The closest bombs around their homes were the few that hit their forest. Ah Veng knew that they would likely be hired to rebuild houses for the villages that were affected. They would need all the help they could get. He walked over to where Chong and his sister were talking to some of their neighbors.

"We just need to stay calm," Chong said with assurance. "I know we don't like the British very much, but I'm sure they will fight since they don't want their territory taken from them."

"Fight?" one woman scoffed. "They don't even have a naval base here. Instead, they put it on Singapore because they always said that nothing would happen to Malaya. They probably didn't even consider that we might need protection too."

"Well, I'm sure they'll send troops," a man stated. "They are probably already fighting right now."

"Yeah right," the woman said, rolling her eyes.

"Let's just hope they don't come back," someone else called from the crowd.

"Maybe someone should be on the lookout for any more planes or signs of danger."

"I'll do it," the short man volunteered.

"As for everyone else, just keep your families safe and make sure you have enough food and water. Maybe a few men can group together to go and check on the other villages as well. They'll probably need supplies, and the wounded will need medical attention," Chong said before people started talking again.

A few men started organizing a group to check on the surrounding areas.

"Do we know if there is anyone missing, before we head off to the other villages?" someone asked from the group.

People looked around as mothers counted their children and fathers looked for relatives and close family friends. Many were shaking their heads.

"Whoever isn't here is most likely still holed up inside their houses or shelters," another person suggested from the side.

"That's true, but just checking to be sure. Does anyone need anything?" Chong asked. "If not, some of us can part ways now, and those that stay behind should knock on doors and check on the people still in their homes. You might have to knock loudly and announce that the bombing has stopped so that those still in their shelters know that it is safe to come out. Any questions?"

The people looked at one another and shook their heads in response.

"Wait," a man yelled. Everyone turned to look at the man running towards them. "My son," he yelled. "He was in the forest!"

"Okay, okay, calm down," Chong said, catching the man when he reached them and holding him by the shoulders to steady him. "What happened?"

"I shouldn't have done it," the man cried. "I sent him into the forest last night to get more firewood and he didn't come home and then the bombing and we still haven't found him. Someone help . . . please."

Chong looked around at the men in the group.

"What are you all waiting for? Let's go. We have a child to find."

With Chong and the hysterical man in the lead, others following quickly behind, the group left with the angry shouts of woman in the background.

"I swear, this better not happen again! We can't afford to lose our loved ones."

"The British better fight. If not on our behalf, then for their own pride!"

* * *

As it turned out, the British did have troops to fight. There was no way they would let Japan step all over their territory, and even though they were thrown off guard, they fought hard. It was the first major battle of the war in the Pacific, but the efforts of the British were thwarted. Malaya was conquered within two months, and there wasn't much that they could do.

Ah Veng sat deep in thought about his country's past as Jian-mind chattered on. It was crazy how much could change in so little time and how war affected people in so many different ways. He couldn't possibly imagine what the fighting soldiers had to endure.

"So what do you think about that?" Jian-min asked.

"Huh?" Ah Veng said, glancing over at the man.

"About everything going on right now?"

"Oh, um . . . it's alright, I guess. A little messy though," Ah Veng murmured.

"Well, that's war for you," Jian-min said with a hearty laugh. "At least Vietnam kind of accomplished something, even if it might lead them to another war. Meanwhile, Malaya has got to do something besides sit here and let other countries run us over."

"But at least those other countries protect us," Ah Veng argued.

"Yeah, but to what extent? If you really think about it, how well did they actually protect us? Remember what happened with World War II? Oh wait, you were probably too young to remem—"

"I wasn't," Ah Veng said quickly, cutting Jian-min off. The businessman stared in shock at Ah Veng's reaction since he hadn't really spoken until now.

"You . . . weren't?" Jian-min said slowly, and Ah Veng shook his head.

"I saw the first plane, then more of them, the explosions, the bombings, the chaos of terror, of fire, of smoke, of people screaming, of dead bodies, all of it. I was there."

Jian-min sucked in a breath and turned to face Ah Veng with bright, curious eyes before asking, "What was it like? I've always wanted to know but I've never met anyone that was in the midst of the bombings."

"A nightmare," Ah Veng simply stated.

"Come on, I know there's more than that. Please. I would really like to know," Jian-min begged with pleading eyes.

Ah Veng sighed, shifting slightly before running a hand through his hair.

"I was only eight at the time, but once you experience and see something like that, it never leaves your mind. It was all unexpected. Nobody in our village thought that anything could ever happen to us, and then when it did, people were confused and angry. They mostly blamed the British for not protecting us, and yet they did. The British really did try because there was no way they would want to lose our territory. I mean, look at our country now. The British still rule it. If they wanted to save themselves, they would have abandoned us, practically handing us over to the Japanese forces. But they didn't and they tried fighting. That's what should count. It's that they tried, even if they lost.

"As for the bombings, it was terrible for us all, but for some, it was way worse. I worked at my brother-in-law's construction site and I remember when we had to help the surrounding villages. It was such a horrible sight to see. Houses burned to ashes, corpses lying around, bones piled up, everything covered in black. I was still a child and yet I had to help the other men carry bodies. They always made me carry the dead babies or children . . ."

Ah Veng trailed off. Tears were streaming down his face, and Jian-min looked stricken.

"You were a kid," he said, "and they made you do that?"

"Yeah, and then I had to help rebuild houses or run here and there to make sure that people had enough food to eat or enough water to drink. The work never seemed to stop. I don't think anyone even had a good night's sleep."

"I can't even imagine," Jian-min said softly, "but you're alive and you can live to tell your tale."

"I guess," Ah Veng replied with a shrug, wiping the tears from his eyes.

"And what about the troops? Did they not fight around the villages in that area?"

"Probably not. We had a messenger come a few times a week to tell us what was going on with the war and all. It was devastating to hear about the other countries or areas that were bombed," Ah Veng answered.

"Oh yeah, I remember how the other countries were affected as well. It's so sad. I never thought that it was that horrible, but hearing you tell your experience just made it a hundred times more real. I only have knowledge from textbooks or articles, not personal experience."

Ah Veng fidgeted with his guitar. The conversation made him uncomfortable.

"What happened after Japan defeated the British Indian troops? Or what do you know about it? I am only familiar with the power they held in running our country government-wise."

"I honestly don't know. All I heard was that the Japanese made empty promises."

Jian-min let out a laugh. "Yeah, they definitely did," he said.

"Can I ask you something?" Ah Veng said suddenly.

"Umm, sure."

"Why would you want to talk to a homeless guy like me?" he asked.

Jian-min stared steadily into Ah Veng's face, not at all bothered by the question.

"Well, why not?" he replied calmly.

Ah Veng had to break eye contact. The deep brown of the man's eyes bore down on Ah Veng, searching deep into his soul, and he didn't like the vulnerability.

"It's just that you're a businessman and I'm quite the opposite. A person without a job, a person without a home. No one wants to talk to people like me because they think that we are either thieves or that we deserve to live on the streets."

"I hate that people think like that," Jian-min said, his eyebrows furrowed. "It's not fair, and honestly, I just needed someone to talk to about everything going on in that newspaper there, so I decided to leave for work early and see if I ran into anyone. And what do you know, you were sitting right out here."

"Oh, so you're the one that threw the newspaper down beside me," Ah Veng said.

"Yeah, I was," Jian-min said with a sheepish grin. He glanced down at his watch. "And I think that it's about time I head off to work."

It was then that Ah Veng noticed the streets were already crowded with people and that the sun had made its appearance a long while ago.

"You didn't care that people were already out and about," Ah Veng stated as Jian-min stood up to leave. He continued, "You didn't care that people saw you were sitting here, talking to me?"

"Of course not," Jian-min answered. "Remember, the heart is what counts. A lot of people still need to learn that. Appearance shouldn't matter because what makes up a person is their character and what lies beneath. And I really have to go now, but it was nice talking to you. I'm sure that I will see you around. Remember, don't beat yourself up about your status and where you came from because it's where you're heading in the future that should make all the difference in the world." He winked and then disappeared into the crowd.

A smile crept onto Ah Veng's face. He rarely met anyone nice, and he was extremely grateful.

"*Terima kasih, dewa alam,*"[26] he whispered before placing his guitar in his lap to play a joyous and light-hearted tune.

* * *

After Jian-min left, Ah Veng thought that he would never see the businessman again. It seemed highly unlikely that anyone would want to

---

26 Thank you, nature gods.

take the steps to help rescue someone from the streets. Sitting down and talking to someone was totally different from actually helping someone.

But he was wrong. That evening, when the streets were crowded with people rushing back to their homes after work, Jian-min came back down the street, pushing a bicycle along with him.

"This is for you," he said once he reached Ah Veng, who looked up in shock.

"I can't take that," Ah Veng exclaimed. "It's yours."

"No, it's not. I bought it for you since I got paid today at work."

"Why would—" Ah Veng started to ask, but Jian-min kept talking.

"I thought that maybe you would want to travel farther and see if you can find work, and if not, then at least this gives you a different type of transportation. Walking can get awfully boring at times. Well, for me personally. But I want you to have this; otherwise I wouldn't have bought it. I realized after talking to you this morning that I should do something for you or a least get you something since I made you tell your story when you didn't really want to. Sorry about that."

"It's alright," Ah Veng responded. "But this . . . this is too much. How much did it cost? Once I find a job one day, I can pay you back—"

"No need," Jian-min interrupted. "It's all yours. I would recommend learning to ride it first before simply hopping on. You might want to do it at night since the streets are so crowded during the daytime."

Ah Veng wanted to argue, but he knew that it was no use. He reluctantly put his guitar aside and stood to take the bike.

"Thank you," he said, admiring the gift he had been given.

He tried to take it all in. The bike itself was a soft gray, shiny enough to sparkle in the sunlight, the handlebars a milky white much like the color of the flowers beside the riverbank of his childhood. He had never been filled with so much gratitude before, and for once, he was happy.

"No problem," Jian-min replied. "Take care of yourself now."

"I will," Ah Veng whispered, still grinning from ear to ear, once the kind man had already walked off.

* * *

A few scrapes and bruises were acquired the first time he tried to ride the bike. He fell multiple times, but once he got it down, it felt like he had missed out on so much. He let out a shout of excitement as he flew down the streets, beaming and glowing at his tiny accomplishment. It was one step forward—one step towards the possibility of a new life. A little over a year after he had been given the bike, Jian-min helped him take the next steps.

* * *

"Hey, watch it," someone yelled.

Ah Veng was running. He glanced over his shoulder at the teens chasing him.

"Ugh, why don't they pick on other people?" he grumbled and turned another corner, veering away from the place he hid all his things. He knew that it would be bad news if they found it.

"We're going to get you eventually," one of the boys yelled, and the rest of them hooted and hollered with laughter.

It was a game to them. There was almost always some kind of game involved, and this one was what they called "the hobo chase." He hated giving them the satisfaction of the chase, but he didn't want to know what they would do once they caught him, either. Suddenly, he ran into someone and tripped and fell.

"He's down, he's down," the boys yelled.

Ah Veng curled up and covered his face.

"Get him!" they shouted.

"Not so fast," a familiar voice said.

Ah Veng looked up. Jian-min stood in front of him. The boys slowed to a stop.

"Move aside, old man. We're just having a little fun."

"No. I will not move aside. You can have your fun elsewhere."

"Did you just say no?" one of the boys said, lunging for Jian-min. One of his friends held him back.

"Hey, man, just leave it alone. We can find someone else to mess around with."

"But he told us no, and no one ever tells us no."

"It's whatever, I'm serious. Let's just leave," his friend begged.

"Fine, but we're not letting it go a second time if we run into something like this again. Got it?" he turned to ask his buddies, eyes narrowed at them.

They simply nodded and ran off in the opposite direction. One of them tugged on the angry boy's arm. "Come on," he said.

"Wait, I want this old man to know that people don't like when rich people like him stand up for the poor," the kid sneered.

"I know perfectly well what society entails," Jian-min said calmly. "Remember, I've been alive a lot longer than you have, young man."

"You might know, but you're stupid enough to defy it," he shot back.

"Why don't you get on out of here like all of your other friends," Jian-min answered, annoyed by the conversation.

"Dude, come on," his friend said, pulling him back a bit more.

"You'll regret everything eventually," the boy called out as he let his friend drag him off down the street.

"Blessings conquer regrets in the long run," Jian-min said softly, shaking his head in disappointment at the younger generations the world was raising.

He spun around and leaned down to help Ah Veng up.

"Sorry about them," he said. "They're a lost cause. Rich kids that don't have anything better to do than terrorize the streets. The sad thing is that their parents don't teach them morals or manners or anything, and most kids are sent off to boarding schools."

"It's alright," Ah Veng said, dusting himself off. "I'm just glad that you were the one I ran into instead of someone else."

"The funny thing is, I was actually looking for you," Jian-min said.

"You were?" Ah Veng asked. "Why?"

"I have thought about it for a long time now. Everyone deserves a second chance no matter what walk of life you come from. And sometimes it takes a person to help give someone a second chance. I want to be that person."

"I don't think I understand," Ah Veng said slowly.

"Sure you do," Jian-min replied. "I think it's just that you don't want to accept it, just like you didn't want to accept the bike I gave you at first."

"But how could you possibly help me? I can't get a job anywhere."

"Well, I have an extra bedroom. It used to be a storage room, but I spent the last few weeks cleaning it out."

"So, a place to live?" Ah Veng piped up. "Like, an actual bed?"

Jian-min laughed. "Yes, an actual bed, and you'll have meals every day as well. You could have as many as you want. As for a job, you don't have to get one now. We can worry about that later on. Just take things one step at a time, you know?"

"Yeah, but I feel bad. You're being too kind. I can't just stay at your house all the time."

"Why not?" Jian-min said. "No one else lives there and I have an extra room."

"I don't know. It's just that there are so many homeless people out on the streets, so why—"

"Why you?" Jian-min finished Ah Veng's sentence.

"Yeah," Ah Veng said, and Jian-min sighed before saying, "I have been looking for someone to bless for a long time now, but there was never the right person. Many were too bitter or too greedy. And then I met you. The first time I looked deeply into your eyes, I saw a deep suffering lying within them, a suffering of a pain-inflicted life, a desire to fight for a better future, but an uncertainty of what to do or if a better life was even possible to reach. I knew that you were the one that I would help. I watched as people walked past you sleeping on the side of the streets. I watched as no one ever stopped to care. You deserve better. That's why I'm doing this."

Ah Veng was silent for a moment before he laughed nervously, saying, "I don't know what to say. Thank you, I guess."

"Oh, it's nothing," Jian-min said, throwing his arm around Ah Veng. "Now, how about we get your stuff and head to your new home."

"Home," Ah Veng whispered, testing the word out, slightly amused at the emotions that erupted at that one simple word.

CHAPTER 7

THE GOOD SAMARITAN

March 1959

"YOU KNOW, I THINK THAT IT is about time you got an ID card and a real job," Jian-min said one day as Ah Veng sat down at the table for breakfast.

"And how am I supposed to do that?" Ah Veng asked, eyebrows raised.

"I'll vouch for you, of course, and if they make us pay, then I'll pay."

"You don't have to do that." Ah Veng frowned. "You've already done enough."

"I want to, though. You deserve it," Jian-min insisted.

"Alright," Ah Veng sighed in defeat. "What do we have to do?" Over the past few years of living with the man, Jian-min always won these types of conversations; it was no use trying to argue.

"I'm pretty sure we just have to go into the office."

"And where's the office?" Ah Veng asked.

"It shouldn't be too far."

"Right," Ah Veng said, rolling his eyes. "Next thing you know, we'll be lost again."

"Again? When was the last time we got lost?"

"Yesterday. You wanted to go to that marketplace. Remember?"

"Oh, right." Jian-min laughed nervously. "I mean, we found it, right?"

"Yeah, after a few hours of walking in circles. How long have you lived here again?"

"Just a few years."

"And yet you still haven't figured out where everything is. I only know the street corners and my specific hideouts because I never paid very much attention to the shops or buildings unless I needed to go to one of them, but you work in an actual office," Ah Veng accused.

"I guess I don't really check my surroundings very often. But I'm sure we'll find it, and I'm confident that you'll get a card. I know some people who work there."

"Okay, okay," Ah Veng said and bent to finish his breakfast as Jian-min stood to get ready.

Around noon, they finally stepped out of the house. People rushed up and down the street as storm clouds rolled in.

"We should probably grab an umbrella," Jian-min said and turned to go back into the house. "I'll get yours too."

Ah Veng sat on a step to wait, knowing that Jian-min would probably have to shift everything around to find even one umbrella. He was always losing things.

A small boy caught his attention when the kid bumped into someone on the street. The person glared at the child and mumbled something before walking on. No one else noticed, but Ah Veng saw the treasures that the boy held in his hand and stuffed into a sack, making them disappear from sight.

He smiled nostalgically at the street corner where the pickpocketing had occurred and where he had met Jian-min. It was the corner that changed his life.

The door opened behind him, and there stood a very perplexed Jian-min without an umbrella in his hands. He scratched his head and said, "Umm, I can't—"

"You can't find them, can you?" Ah Veng said, trying to hide his smile.

"It's not funny," Jian-min insisted. "I just forget where I put things."

"How do you survive at work?" Ah Veng said, shaking his head and standing to follow Jian-min back into the house.

"Well, I only have a desk to worry about at the office. This is a whole house," Jian-min stated, waving his hands in the air.

Ah Veng refrained from laughing yet again and opened up a closet in the hall. He pulled out the two umbrellas that were sitting in a box.

"What? I looked there; I swear I did," Jian-min stammered, mouth hanging open.

"Obviously, you didn't look hard enough," Ah Veng pointed out before handing him one of the umbrellas and walking to the door.

Jian-min followed after him, cursing softly.

"Come on. We have somewhere to be, right?"

"Yeah, yeah," Jian-min said, briefly cracking a smile before grumbling about how his memory needed to be checked.

They stepped out onto the street and into a slow drizzle—like the last drops of water leaking out from a jar. An angry cluster of clouds rolled in like waves.

"I know we usually get a lot of rain, but this storm looks different," Jian-min stated, pausing to look up at the sky.

"I'm sure it's fine. Are we actually going to use these umbrellas? Don't tell me we brought them for nothing."

"Oh, right," Jian-min said, laughing before opening his just as Ah Veng did the same.

They ran down the street, huddled under their shields from the rain now pelting them in larger drops.

"Let's go this way," Jian-min said, pointing to the right.

"Are you sure it's this way?"

"No. We'll find out, though."

"That's not helpful at all," Ah Veng yelled over the sound of pouring water.

"Well, we can always ask if we get lost."

"Why don't we ask right now?"

"Because I'm pretty sure that I know where it is."

"That's definitely not what you said this morning. You didn't sound confident at all."

"Trust me on this one. If we get lost, it will only be for a bit."

"Only for a bit," Ah Veng snorted. "Yeah no, I'm asking someone."

"Aw, come on," Jian-min whined. "You can't be serious. I know it's on this street."

"Nope, I'm asking. There's a guy over there outside that building. I'll ask him."

"Hey, that is the building!" Jian-min exclaimed. "The one with the man outside. I told you I knew where it was."

"Are you sure?" Ah Veng asked, skeptical.

"Yeah, just read the sign. It clearly says, *JABATAN IMIGRESEN MALAYA.*"[27]

"Oh," Ah Veng said, stopping in front of it.

Jian-min stopped beside him with a huge grin on his face.

"Told you I knew. So, I'm not going crazy yet. That's nice to know."

He opened the door, and the two of them walked in. A few people sat in the chairs, filling out forms, and a man at the counter was typing at a computer. At first, Ah Veng was shocked to see that the office had a computer, but then again, it was a government office, so it made sense that they would be able to afford them.

"*Selamat petang, apa yang boleh saya lakukan untuk awak?*"[28] the man at the counter asked before lifting his gaze and lighting up a bit. "Jian-min? Hey, my friend, what are you doing here?" he asked in English.

---

27 Immigration Department of Malaya

28 Good afternoon, what can I do for you?

"Lokman, long time no see," Jian-min replied and shook his friend's hand over the counter.

Ah Veng was surprised. It suddenly occurred to him that he never did ask Jian-min what his job was and what type of office work he did.

"I'm just here to get this young man an ID card," Jian-min said, motioning to Ah Veng and lowering his voice. "Do you think you could do that for me?"

"Of course," Lokman replied, nodding, "I could put him under late registration, but you would have to sign off as his advocate. Is that alright?"

"Yes," Jian-min said with a sigh of relief. "I was worried that it would be more difficult than this. Everyone always makes it seem as though it is."

"Yeah, it's really not that bad of a process," Lokman agreed. "They just don't want to go out of their way to help others. There wouldn't be so many homeless people on the streets if they did because literally the only thing that most of those people need is someone to sign as an advocate, and that's it. Well, unless they have some sort of criminal record or other reasons for keeping them out of work."

He pulled up something on his computer and then looked at Ah Veng.

"I'm just going to ask a few questions so that I can find your birth certificate. What's your full name?"

"Ah Veng."

"No, your full name," he said, raising his eyebrows and looking at Jian-min.

"Yeah, it's just Ah Veng."

"You don't have a last name?"

Both Jian-min and the government official were staring at him now.

"Umm, I don't think so," he answered.

"Everyone has a last name; it comes from your parents."

"I'm not sure—"

"Ah Veng, you don't remember, do you?" Jian-min asked softly, a look of concern on his face, and Ah Veng shook his head.

"Just use mine," Jian-min said.

"What?" Lokman questioned. "What do you mean use yours?"

"Yeah, that's what I said. Let him have my last name. Put in his name as Chia Ah Veng."

"You're sure you're okay with that?" his friend said, inquisitively.

"Yes, as long as he's okay with it as well."

"Are you?" Lokman asked.

"Jian-min, you've provided so much for me already. I couldn't possibly take your name as well," Ah Veng said.

"I want you to have it. All those other things I gave to you are only materials. They eventually break down, but a name . . . a name lasts for your whole lifetime. This way, when you finally go out to find your own life, you'll still have something to remember me by."

"I really appreciate it, I really do, but—"

"I'm not taking no for an answer. Please, don't say you don't want it just because you feel bad. You've done this several times and I know you're thankful. You don't have to keep refusing."

Lokman watched the exchange silently, not expecting the bond between the two to be so strong. He knew that Jian-min had a soft spot for the homeless on the street and those that were less fortunate. It was one of the reasons why he was kicked out of working in the government office a few years back and was now stuck in normal business deals.

He felt bad for his friend. Jian-min never learned how Malayan society worked. Social classes stayed separate; they were taught to live in their own worlds. Lokman might have been tempted to help the less fortunate, but he knew better than to jeopardize his job. However, watching the two interact made him think that maybe, just maybe, people should stop living in fear.

He shook his head slightly, suddenly noticing that they were both staring at him in silence.

"Oh, umm, did you decide to accept it?" he asked, clearing his throat.

"Yeah," Ah Veng replied, "I did."

"Alright, so on to the next question. Let me see. Do you remember where you were born?"

"No, sorry," Ah Veng said.

"It's okay. Umm, how about, when's your birthday?"

"Birthday?" Ah Veng asked.

Lokman glanced at Jian-min in bewilderment, thinking, *Where did this boy come from? The jungle?* His friend merely shrugged.

"Yeah, you know, the day you were born," Lokman said.

"No, I was never told."

"Well, we can probably figure that out by how old you are. So, how old are you right now?"

"Now," Ah Veng said, clenching his teeth together and sucking in a breath. "I can't remember. The years kind of all ran together. I lost count."

"Oh my," Lokman said. "So, I'm guessing that there's probably not a birth certificate on file anywhere. You know what, I'll make you one and it will just say late registration on it. Yes, that's what I'll do."

"What do we do about him not having a birthday, though?" Jian-min asked, slightly worried.

"Make it up," Lokman said. "Just choose one and pick a year based on how old you think he is."

"Make it up?" Ah Veng asked. "Are we allowed to do that?"

"Shh," Lokman hushed. "It doesn't really matter, but don't go letting people know that it was all made up. I'll just type all this up, and I'm making up names for your parents as well; is that alright?" he asked Ah Veng, who nodded in agreement.

"Ah Veng, look at me for a second," Jian-min said, and the young man turned towards him. "Hmm. I would say that you look about 25 years old, which would mean 1933. That's the year we are going to say you were born. As for the day . . . this is like a new life for you, a new independence. That's it! Malaya's independence day, August 31st. That's going to be your birthday!" Jian-min exclaimed with excitement.

Some of the people in the room looked up from what they were doing to stare at them.

"Too loud, my bad," he mumbled before asking Lokman, "Did you get that?"

"Yes. So we're going to say August 31, 1933; is that correct?"

"Yeah," Jian-min said, and looked to Ah Veng, saying, "You're okay with that, right?"

"Of course."

"Now, I filled in the little information that we did know and then the things we made up, but we might actually be able to find out where you were born," Lokman said and opened a drawer to pull out a Malayan map. "Were you born in Miri, or did you travel here somehow?"

"My sister and I, we walked, a really long way. It took us days, maybe weeks, but it was through a jungle, and then we followed a river—"

Jian-min interrupted Ah Veng, pointing to a spot on the map. "That, there's a river right there that flows into the outskirts of Miri."

"Yeah, that's Baram River, but the question is where they started out at. That river flows for miles and miles."

"If I remember correctly, my sister said something about reaching a bend in the river and then going through the jungle again until we reached a road where a car would pick us up."

"Well, there's several bends right here," Lokman said, "and if you trace backwards, using the river, that would mean that you came from somewhere around this area."

"Marudi, maybe?" Jian-min offered.

"Yeah, let's say that. It's a pretty small village, though. Do you remember anything about the place of your childhood?"

"Not much, but it was definitely a small village," Ah Veng said.

"Okay, so we'll say that you're from Marudi, Sarawak. And we're almost finished. I just need to fill out that I was the administrator and today's date, which is March 12th, 1959."

"Is a birth certificate the same thing as an ID card?" Ah Veng whispered to Jian-min.

"No," he said, shaking his head. "Information is pulled from a birth certificate in order to create an ID card, but every person needs to have both."

"Oh, I guess that makes sense."

"Now that the birth certificate is all set, I'll print you an official copy and then I'll generate your ID card, which I will need a picture for," Lokman said, sifting through his lower drawer and pulling out a camera. "Stand to the right a bit. Shift over a bit more. There, now smile," he said to Ah Veng. "If the two of you want, you can sit and wait, or you could go somewhere and come back before we close since the processing might take some time."

"How about we go somewhere?" Jian-min asked Ah Veng.

Ah Veng shrugged. "Sure."

"Alright, we will be back in a bit," Jian-min said to Lokman.

"I'll be right here," he called as Jian-min and Ah Veng stepped out the door.

They wandered down the street a bit. The rain was still coming down, but it was very light, a soft, feathery touch to the skin. They didn't bother opening their umbrellas.

"Let's go this way," Jian-min said. "I have somewhere that I want to show you and a few people that I'd like you to meet."

"Where?" Ah Veng asked.

"I'm not telling. You'll see."

"As long as we don't get lost."

"We won't, we won't. I go to this place several times a week. It's where I always disappear to, as you like to say."

"I thought that I wasn't allowed to know," Ah Veng said hesitantly.

"Well, technically no, but I like bending the rules a bit, and the men that I want you to meet do too. Just don't ask questions. Whatever we tell you is the information you're going to get," Jian-min cautioned before stopping to look around. When he saw that no one was paying attention, he grabbed Ah Veng and ducked under a ruined fence into an alleyway.

"What?" Ah Veng hissed, startled.

"Come on," Jian-min said quietly, opening a door that was hidden in the shadows and could only be seen if you knew it was there.

The two of them stepped inside, and Jian-min shut the door firmly behind them. It was pitch dark. Ah Veng couldn't see Jian-min anymore.

"Jian-min."

No reply.

"Jian-min," Ah Veng whispered a little more urgently.

Still no reply.

"Hello?"

"Hang on," Jian-min's voice said somewhere in close proximity. "I'm getting a lamp so we can see."

Relieved, Ah Veng soon heard a match being lit. The man he trusted came back carrying a source of light.

"Sorry about that. Here, hold the lamp. You might feel better knowing that you have light, and I can pretty much walk these halls without it."

"Is this some sort of conspiracy hideout or something?" Ah Veng asked as he took the lamp from Jian-min.

"Now, those types of questions are going to get you in trouble," he replied very seriously. "Remember what I said about asking. However, I will answer that by simply saying . . . maybe."

Ah Veng held the light up and noticed that Jian-min had a huge grin on his face. It sent chills up his spine. How well did he actually know the man?

"Whatever it is, you all must really not want to be found," Ah Veng said, observing each turn they made and how the halls were intricately woven together into a maze.

"It is preferable that we are not even known to exist. And, ah, here we are," Jian-min said, knocking three times before pushing open a door.

Light flooded out, and Ah Veng blinked a few times before following Jian-min inside. He shut the door behind him and noticed men sitting around a table, staring at him. Jian-min was already talking.

"This here is Ah Veng. The one that I've been wanting you all to meet."

"Oh, that's right," one man said, immediately standing to cross the room and shake Ah Veng's hand. "How do you do, young man? We have heard many great things about you."

"I'm fine, thank you," Ah Veng said nervously.

He averted his eyes and looked around the room until he noticed that there were maps and notes and all kinds of things plastered to the wall. He didn't want them to think he was snooping. Instead, he focused on the man who brought him here.

"Well, what are you up to, Jian-min?" one of the other men asked.

"Oh, the usual, except today we went to register him for an ID card."

"Wow, you looking for work?" the man asked Ah Veng.

"Yes sir."

"I happen to find people jobs. I could get you offers if you would like."

"I would really appreciate that, sir."

"Alright, I will make sure to stay in touch with Jian-min about it then," he said with a kind smile.

"Do you know what we do here?" a man with glasses that sat on the tip of his nose questioned skeptically, scrutinizing every movement Ah Veng made. It was unsettling, as if something bad were about to happen.

"Um, no," Ah Veng said, furrowing his eyebrows with concern about where the question would lead.

"Smart answer," he replied. "Would you like to know?"

"I would, but I will only listen to what you would like me to know."

The room was silent for a moment, and Ah Veng went over the words in his head, wondering if he had said the right thing. Finally, the man smiled.

"I like this kid," he said. "He's clever, and honest. What do you say, guys?"

"Accept him? Isn't he still too young?"

"I don't think so. How old are you?" another man asked.

Ah Veng had a hard time remembering which man was which, and he didn't know names to associate them with.

"Twenty-five," Ah Veng answered, completely confused about what was going on.

He looked again at Jian-min, who seemed to avoid looking at him.

"Yeah, he actually is a bit young, but how about honorary member, at least. That way he can come to the parties and socials, but not the meetings."

"He wouldn't be able to know everything going on, either."

"But it's better than nothing, and we'd still get to see him around. I'm sure Jian-min wants him around."

Ah Veng shifted slightly, feeling awkward at the atmosphere and how the men were talking about him as though he weren't there.

"That's it!" someone exclaimed.

Some of the men stood to clap Ah Veng on the back or hug him.

"Um, what?" he asked.

"You're now an honorary member of *Perjalanan Persaudaraan*.[29] Congrats!"

"What exactly does that mean?"

"It means exactly that. We're a brotherhood that loves our country, and we dedicate our entire lives to helping Malaya reach its full potential."

"Oh." It suddenly dawned on Ah Veng: the reason why Jian-min always loved going on historical rants, the reason why he was always up to date on the events that happened each day, the reason why he disappeared sometimes for hours on end, the reason why he was so kindhearted towards people on the streets and the reason why he had helped Ah Veng to begin with. It all made sense now. The brotherhood basically comprised who Jian-min was as a person.

The men were still talking to him.

29　The Journey of Brotherhood.

". . . so we deal with the fight for independence, the injustices within the government system, the people on the streets, the job searches, practically anything you can think of that deals with making our country better as a whole."

"There are also a lot more of us. We have branches in so many different areas," another man chimed in.

"That's true too. And as for you, we can only tell you so much until you choose to actually join when you're older. Which you don't have to if you don't want to. It would totally be your choice. But as for now, knowing that you're always with Jian-min, we figured it would be easier for you to be able to tag along sometimes," the guy with the glasses said with a wink. "And Alan here said that he would help you find a job. He always keeps his word, so you should be hearing from him soon."

Jian-min spoke up for the first time since he had started avoiding Ah Veng's gaze. "Thank you all so much. I was worried there for a bit."

"Aw, no problem, brother, and there was nothing to be worried about. We always trust the people that you point out or choose."

"Yeah, well, we should head back to the government office now, but it was nice to see you all. I'll see you again in a few days."

"Alright, be safe. And, Ah Veng, glad to have you as a part of our cause."

"Thanks," he said with a small smile. He followed Jian-min out of the room, back into the dark hallway. He was handed the lamp again, and they returned through the maze of halls, completely silent until they got back out onto the streets. The silence eventually became unbearable, and so Ah Veng decided to break it, realizing that Jian-min probably didn't know what to say.

"I can't believe this is happening," Ah Veng finally said, and Jian-min's head snapped up to look at him.

His response was delayed, but he seemed to be back to himself again.

"Well, it is," Jian-min laughed. "I'm really happy for you. I really am."

"It doesn't seem real that I have the possibility of having a life. It couldn't have happened without your help. Only a Good Samaritan would have done what you did over these past few years."

"I appreciate your words, but I'm pretty sure that anyone can be a Good Samaritan if they actually take the time to search deep inside their hearts," Jian-min said.

"I don't think so," Ah Veng replied.

"Why do you say that?" Jian-min asked.

"Because tens of hundreds of people walked by me every day and yet only one person took the time to stop and have a conversation. It takes someone special to be considered a Good Samaritan. Not just anybody can be one; it's the people that have a heart or a burning passion to do good in the world. It's the people that have a desire to put the needs of others before themselves."

Jian-min was silent for a moment, and then he finally said, "You're starting to sound a lot like me."

He let out a laugh. Ah Veng grinned, thinking about what Jian-min meant as they continued on their walk.

CHAPTER 8

INDEPENDENCE

May 1959
Southern Outskirts of Miri, Sarawak, Malaya

IT WAS AN ORDINARY MORNING WHEN Ah Veng walked out of his room to find his coworkers shouting about something, again.

"I'm pretty sure that's mine," his friend Zhen shrieked.

"No, I've always had that in my room," one of the other guys yelled back.

"You took—"

"Goodness, you all sound like a bunch of screaming girls," Ah Veng interrupted, walking into the kitchen. "You'd think that you would be more mature, but it seems you never did grow up."

The men stopped their fighting and turned to listen. Ah Veng wasn't the oldest person in the corporation, but he was the oldest in their workhouse, so the men seemed to respect him. He didn't even know how he got stuck with all the younger workers; most of them were fresh out of high school.

"Seriously, you all are adults, in the working world. I'm not saying don't have a little fun once in a while, but all this fighting and arguing, every single morning. It's getting just a bit annoying. If you all put your things where they belong, you wouldn't have this issue anyway."

Ah Veng picked up an apple and bit into it.

"Sorry, we'll try to be better about that," Zhen said, hanging his head and handing a shirt he had grabbed back over to the guy he was fighting with. "Here, you can have it."

"Hey, it's almost eight. We're going to be late," Cheng suddenly observed, looking at the clock on the wall. He actually had some sense and was the closest to Ah Veng's age, just two years younger.

"I'm just waiting for you all," Ah Veng simply said, shaking his head to hide his laughter as he watched the men scramble from the room to get ready.

He walked out the front door to wait on them outside. He had been working there a little over a month, and it had been about a week since he'd seen Jian-min. He usually found time to ride his bike into Central to visit on his days off.

He looked back towards the front door to see if the men were coming. He liked the community, even if he didn't really enjoy the work he was doing for the electrical company; workers were allowed to stay in a workhouse assigned to them and were paid eighty dollars a month to buy food, clothes or anything else they might want.

It had been difficult to leave Jian-min's home.

"You're sure that this is what you want to do?" Jian-min had asked as Ah Veng packed up his stuff.

"It might not be the job that I want, but I know for sure that it is a step that I have to take."

"That makes sense," Jian-min answered, nodding.

"Don't worry. I will visit whenever I can," Ah Veng said.

"I know that you will. I'm not concerned about that. I was just worried that you were doing something that you might not want to do."

"Well, it might help me find a job that I will eventually enjoy. And it is the only job offer I got that seemed decent enough. The others would not provide me with enough to live on my own, and I have to do something. It's been almost a month since I got my ID."

"True. Just look after yourself."

"I will," Ah Veng said with a smile and then walked out of his room and to the door to set his things down.

He checked the other areas of the house to make sure that he got everything.

"I guess that's it then," Ah Veng said, turning to face Jian-min, who helped him attach his things to his bike.

"Alright, your bike should be all good to go," Jian-min stated, standing.

They were silent for a moment, and then Jian-min spoke up.

"I'm sad to see you go, but I want you to know that I'm really proud to see you move on to make a life for yourself. Look at you. You're becoming a real man," he laughed, clamping Ah Veng on the shoulder.

"Thanks for everything," Ah Veng said and then stepped forward to hug the man that saved him from the streets, the man he considered to be a second father.

"Of course, kid, and I'll still always be here. Don't forget your old man, and make sure you come visit."

"For sure, for sure," Ah Veng laughed and then took his bike out the door and onto the streets.

He rode across town to reach the countryside, following the directions that he had been given. Although the ride was long, it was not difficult to find his destination. The workhouses were much bigger than normal residential houses.

He had just hopped off his bike when he was greeted by one of his bosses.

"You made it. Ah Veng, am I right?"

"Yes sir," Ah Veng replied with a smile and reached out to shake the man's hand.

"Great, I'm Wei. So, basically, you'll be learning how to deal with electrical wires and home systems. Our company specializes in all the electrical wiring within homes and then occasionally throughout the town as well. We send a majority of our workers out to the new homes they're building around Miri, and then a small portion gets sent into the central areas to do repairs."

Ah Veng froze at the possibility of seeing his brother-in-law or the men that he used to work with when he was a child.

"We had to stick you in the younger workhouse because we are kind of tight on space. However, you will get your own room. Most people have to share, but we thought that since we are making you live with workers much younger than you, we would allow you to have your own room."

"Oh, thank you," Ah Veng said, still queasy. *Will my brother-in-law recognize me? It has been years since I've seen him.*

"So, you know about your living accommodations, the pay and the rules and everything. Why don't I show you where you'll be staying, and then we can head out to where most of the workers are for today."

"Sounds good," Ah Veng said, unfocused. Somehow, he managed to pay attention to his surroundings and where they were headed.

They passed a few houses before they reached the one where Ah Veng would be staying. They all looked the same except for a small colored flag pushed into the ground at the edge of the yard to indicate what group stayed where. Wei was explaining them.

"Your house's color is white 'cause, well . . . because most of the men in here are innocent. I really do hope you don't lose your mind living with them."

"It's fine," Ah Veng said, leaning his bike against the side of the house before following Wei through the front door.

"Here's the kitchen, the living room," Wei said, pointing before going up the stairs. "There are some bedrooms down there as well, but most of them are upstairs. And here's your room."

Ah Veng stopped at the doorway and looked in. Although it wasn't that big, he was thankful to be getting his own space.

"What about the bathrooms?" he asked.

"There are two upstairs: that last door there and then the last one on this side. There's only one downstairs, and it's at the end of the hall by the bedrooms."

"Okay, do you mind if I bring my bike up here to leave my stuff in my room before we head out to where the other workers are?"

"Sure." Wei shrugged and they walked back down the stairs.

He went into the kitchen as Ah Veng went back outside to get his bike, taking his time to really look at the street lined with at least a dozen other houses. There were so many different flags; he realized that he should have asked specifics about the colors because the only one he heard was his own. He was not certain he liked being stuck in the "innocent" house, and he shook his head as he walked his bike into the house and carried it up the stairs.

When he came back down, Wei was waiting for him at the door.

"The bus should be a little ways down the street at the spot you and the other workers report to at eight every morning. That's where your house gets your assignment for the day, and then you all get sent out on a bus. Do you have any questions so far?"

Ah Veng shook his head as they approached a wooden bus.

"After you," Wei said, and so Ah Veng went up first, taking a seat right behind the driver.

"You know where we're going, right?" Wei asked the driver before sitting.

"Yes, the southeast region."

The bus started, and Ah Veng moved closer to the window to watch the passing scenery, wondering what it was going to be like, finally working again.

"So, you're born in Marudi, is that correct?" Wei asked, writing something down on the clipboard he was carrying.

"Yes sir," Ah Veng answered.

"I have a friend that lives out there, come to think of it," he said, looking up. "It's a pretty small village."

"Yes, it is."

"So, when did you come to Miri?" he questioned.

Ah Veng refrained from squirming in his seat at the unsettling inquiries.

"I was about seven, I believe, when my sister and I left." Ah Veng realized his mistake after he said it and knew that he should have kept his mouth shut.

"Your sister?" Wei asked. "Where is she now?"

"Married," Ah Veng quickly stated, hoping the conversation would switch to something else before he gave away too much information.

Wei eyed him curiously but went back to jotting something else down. Ah Veng let out a sigh of relief and almost jumped up when the bus came to a stop. He froze when he noticed the familiarity of the construction sites. Once they stepped off the bus, the sights, the sounds and the smells of the area made Ah Veng flinch at the remembrance of his childhood. Some of the workers stopped what they were doing when they saw the bus roll to a standstill, and even more of them paused their work in order to stare at Ah Veng. Their eyes seemed to rake over him, judging whether or not he was worthy to be working with them.

"Where is Cheng?" Wei asked the men closest to them.

"Inside," they replied, pointing to one of the houses. Ah Veng noticed that the workers of the company were mixed with the construction workers, as if they were working together. Under Chong, the electrical company always worked after the house was already built, which never did make any sense. *Maybe this is more efficient*, he thought.

"Someone tell him to come out here," Wei said, and one of the men immediately ran into the house.

"Who's Cheng?" Ah Veng asked.

"He's one of the guys that lives in your house and is closest to your age, about two years younger, I think. He has his own room as well, and I think it would be best for you to work with him so that he can teach you everything you will need to know."

The worker returned with a shorter man, who was so dark that his hair almost matched the color of his skin.

"You called?" Cheng asked, raising his eyebrows at Wei.

"Yeah, remember the new guy I was telling you about?" Wei answered, and Cheng nodded. "Well, this is Ah Veng, and, Ah Veng, this is Cheng. I'll leave you two to get acquainted in a bit, but before that, Cheng, it is your responsibility to look out for him now until he figures everything out. I trust that you'll do all that you're supposed to and make sure that the other guys leave him alone. They always seem to pick on the new guys for some reason," he said, looking around, trying to spot some of the troublemakers before continuing. "Anyway, I'll stop bothering you all and check up on the other areas."

Once Wei walked off, Cheng turned towards Ah Veng and smiled. "Well, I wish that I could say that this job is exciting or something, but it's really not. Welcome to the working world, my friend."

* * *

Ah Veng snapped back to the present when he heard the sound of a bus engine and realized that the first bus was leaving.

"Where are they?" he grumbled and turned to throw open the front door. "Hey, we're late," Ah Veng yelled just as the men bolted out of their rooms and towards the doors. "What was taking you all so long?"

The men stared at one another.

"Please tell me that you all weren't fighting over clothes again," he sighed.

"It's just that Kai was missing his—"

"I don't even want to hear it," Ah Veng said, putting his hand up. "It would be wise if you all just go ahead and get on the bus before it leaves us behind, because if it does, then we'll really be in trouble."

"Alright," they said softly, complying.

Meanwhile, some of the other men were still trying to get their shoes on.

"You know what, just carry them and put them on in the bus," Ah Veng said, "or I'm telling them to leave you all behind."

That did the trick. All of them rushed out the door in a hurry and ran all the way to the bus. Ah Veng followed behind, laughing at their reaction to his empty threat because the buses would never leave them behind. There wouldn't be any reason to. The worst that could happen was a scolding from the bosses and possibly having to work overtime.

On days like this he actually enjoyed living with the younger guys. They were gullible and susceptible to believing everything he said just because he was older. He laughed again, shaking his head. He was the last one to get onto their transport to another day's worth of work.

* * *

August 1959

"Ah, you came!" Jian-min said excitedly, throwing open the front door.

"Why, of course," Ah Veng replied, grinning.

"Well, come in, come in." Jian-min motioned and held the door open a bit wider.

Ah Veng stepped inside and took a deep breath, not realizing how much he had missed the house.

"Would you like something to drink? Water, tea, anything?"

"Water would be fine, thank you," Ah Veng said before wandering upstairs to set his bag down in his room.

He glanced around and noticed that nothing had been touched, as if it had waited for him to come back. He was only there for three days, but it was surprising that his bosses let him take the days off at all. They were not very willing until they learned that Jian-min wanted him to visit because tomorrow was Ah Veng's birthday and Hari Merdeka.[30]

He walked to the window and pushed open the curtains to let in some light, looking out briefly before heading back downstairs.

"So, I've been working on a new project," Jian-min said.

"Really? What is it?"

30 Independence Day.

"You'll have to wait and see," he replied, laughing.

"You can't just tell someone that you're working on something and then not tell them." Ah Veng frowned. "Is this about my birthday or something?"

"Maybe," Jian-min said, his smile widening as he handed Ah Veng his cup of water before sitting down at the kitchen table.

"Well, if it is, then you're terrible at keeping it secret 'cause now I know that you're planning something."

"I didn't say I was planning something."

"Well, it seems like you are."

"All I said was that I'm working on a new project, so how do you know it's for you?"

"Because tomorrow's my birthday and I'm here for a few days and you just seem way too delighted at my responses."

"Hmm . . . interesting," Jian-min said, stroking his chin before bursting out in laughter.

"Seriously, I deal with enough childish people at work and then I come back to this. What happened to the old Jian-min?"

"Oh, he's in there alright."

"In there? You make it sound as though you're possessed or something. Are you? Are you?!"

Jian-min just laughed even harder, covering his face with his hands.

"Alright, I'm about to walk out because clearly something's not right in your mind."

"Okay, okay. Goodness, you need to lighten up a bit. You must be too serious at work. There needs to be some fun in life too, you know."

"Yeah, yeah, just tell me what was funny."

"Look at your cup," Jian-min said, as he let out another snicker.

Ah Veng quickly held the cup away from him and realized that it had a tiny hole on the bottom. It was dripping water on him the whole time and he didn't even realize.

"Seriously? Seriously!" Ah Veng demanded, but he felt himself cracking a bit, and soon he was laughing just as hard as Jian-min was.

"This is like the worst joke ever."

"It took you so long—"

"Hey, you were distracting me!"

"I couldn't help myself," Jian-min said defensively.

"So this is your new project, huh? Making cups that don't function properly?"

"Nooo," he answered. "I'm making cups in general. I've taken up ceramics for a local art shop."

"Um, okay, and why? Apparently you're not very good at it considering there's a hole in my cup," Ah Veng mused.

He hadn't realized how much he missed the old man.

"Because I was getting bored around here and needed something else to do. And hey! I did that on purpose; it's a joke!"

"Well, I guess. But of everything you could have chosen, cups, really?"

"Why not? They're fun to make! You ought to try it sometime."

"No thanks. I think I'm good," Ah Veng replied, carrying the dysfunctional cup to the sink to pour the rest of the water out.

"Oh, by the way, the Hari Merdeka parade is at nine tomorrow, so make sure you wake up before then."

"Where is it at?" Ah Veng asked.

"Just outside."

"Oh, okay, so by early that technically means rolling out of bed right before then."

"Absolutely not," Jian-min said. "You better be down here in time for breakfast and dressed decently, too, because once we step out to watch the parade, we are not going back into the house until late at night."

"What, why?" Ah Veng whined. "I thought this was supposed to be my break from going places and working."

"Because we have to participate in the festivities, and there's also a few surprises in store for you."

"Greeeat, I love surprises," Ah Veng groaned, rolling his eyes.

"It is your birthday after all."

"I've never celebrated my birthday before now."

"And that's why this one is special," Jian-min replied. "Now, come on. I want to show you where I make the cups and set up shop."

"Alright," Ah Veng sighed, knowing that it would make Jian-min happy to hear him comply for once.

* * *

Later that night, Ah Veng stared up at the ceiling, thinking deeply about his life and about life in general, along with all that it entailed. *What's the meaning of it all?* he wondered. *Does everyone have a specific purpose? A specific role?* He glanced towards the window. Moonlight streamed in, and the stars were twinkling. It was a clear night, for once, where the night sky seemed close enough to reach out and touch. Slowly but surely, Ah Veng drifted off to sleep and slipped back into the long-awaited dream world for the first time in years.

* * *

The colors were a blinding array, twisting and contorting, commanding attention. Ah Veng flew through the northern sky, admiring the light, amazed at such a beautiful sight. He swooped down to see the snow-covered mountaintops, where tiny flakes floated down to land among piles of white fluff. A flake fell in slow motion right next him, allowing him to take in every curve, every outline, and every pattern that went into creating that tiny, perfect design. He followed it down as it fell, and then landed softly beside it on the snow, shivering at the freezing temperatures. An arctic fox bounded across his view and buried itself deep under the snow, popping its head up to look straight at Ah Veng. Suddenly, he felt the snow give way underneath him, and down he went.

* * *

Ah Veng woke with a start and realized that he had fallen off the bed—or rather, he had been pushed off the bed. Jian-min stood above him with one hand on his hips and the other holding Ah Veng's blankets.

"Up, up, rise and shine. Happy birthday, my friend! You're 26 now!" Jian-min said, grinning down.

"You can't be serious. It's not morning yet," Ah Veng groaned.

"Last time I checked, the sun was out."

Sure enough, light was streaming in the window. Ah Veng groaned again.

"Can't I sleep in a bit longer? I never get to sleep in."

"No, come on," he said, holding his hand out to help Ah Veng up.

"Ugh, fine," Ah Veng sighed, taking Jian-min's hand.

"It's a big day. Oh, I'm so excited!" Jian-min exclaimed, unable to stop smiling as he walked out to let Ah Veng get dressed.

"He's more excited than I am," Ah Veng mumbled, shaking his head. He didn't understand the point of celebrating a birthday.

He threw on random clothes and went downstairs. Jian-min turned around when he entered the kitchen.

"No sir, that will not do," he said, pointing at Ah Veng's attire.

"What do you mean no? It's just a shirt. I don't see what the big deal is."

"You'll see later. Now go change into something more decent. There should be something in your closet if you don't have anything."

Ah Veng wanted to argue but decided that there must be a purpose to it, so he walked back upstairs to change. By the time he came down again, breakfast was on the table.

"See, that wasn't so hard now, was it?" Jian-min said. "You're making your birthday seem as though it is the most dreaded day on the planet when it should be one of the best."

"I just don't see the point in doing anything for it. You're just getting a year older. Everybody ages."

"Well, that's true, but at the same time, it also means that you're getting a year wiser, more knowledgeable and a tad bit more mature."

"I guess, but still—"

"Nope, we're not talking about this anymore. Let's eat before we run out of time. I don't want to miss the beginning of the parade."

"It's just a parade, and it happens every year," Ah Veng said, rolling his eyes and sitting down at the table.

"Where is your Malayan pride? How many times do I have to tell you that it is important to be proud of your country," Jian-min scolded before taking a bite of his roti canai.[31]

"I know, I know," Ah Veng defended. "I am proud to be Malayan. All I'm saying is that it's just a parade."

"A very good one, though," Jian-min pointed out.

They quickly finished up the rest of the meal, making small talk before they dumped the dishes in the sink and stepped out onto the streets to find it crowded with people.

"Goodness, if I knew that it was going to be this crowded, I would have woken you up earlier," Jian-min stated.

"Well, I'm glad you didn't because I would have been even grumpier."

"You know, I thought that you actually having a job and working would have changed your ways, but apparently not," Jian-min said, looking around to see if they could find a closer spot.

Ah Veng shrugged. "Let's stay here. I don't see any other places," he told Jian-min.

"Alright," Jian-min said for once. It was probably one of the only times he complied with Ah Veng's wishes. "Do you remember that time when we first found out Malaya was independent?" Jian-min suddenly asked.

"Um, yeah," Ah Veng responded, crossing his fingers that Jian-min was not about to go on another historical rant.

"Ah, the good times. I still can't believe the British were in control of our country since 1786. Do you know how long ago that was?" Jian-min asked.

---

31   A Malaysian flatbread that is Indian-influenced.

Ah Veng inwardly groaned, knowing that the rant was about to happen; Jian-min didn't let Ah Veng say anything before continuing,

"They planted some trading post on Penang Island, and some of our dumb sultans of smaller states thought that it would be okay to accept British advisors just because they seemed good at ruling. What? Ha, no. That was a bad move. And then a bunch of immigration happened from China and India just because more workers were needed. There was so much going on over the years as territories and states were split this way and that, which I just don't get why they never could leave us alone . . ."

Ah Veng felt bad for not really listening, but he was much more interested in when the parade was going to start since he wanted to get it over with. He wished that he had glanced at the clock when they walked out because he wasn't sure how early they had left. Against his will, his mind drifted back to that auspicious day—the Malayan declaration of independence.

* * *

"Ah Veng! Ah Veng! Did you hear? Did you hear?" Jian-min shouted, barging in through the front door of the house.

"Hear what?" Ah Veng called from the kitchen.

"We're independent!" Jian-min exclaimed. "Like, it's official and everything."

"Independent?" Ah Veng asked. "From Britain?"

"Yes, from Britain. Who else?"

"Well, I just wasn't quite sure what you were talking about."

"Yeah, yeah, of course from Britain. It's finally happened! I've been waiting so many years for this day and it's actually here. The corporation has worked so hard for this."

"How did it happen? I'm sure the British didn't just hand it over," Ah Veng speculated.

"Well, the British actually kind of did."

Although he knew that Jian-min wasn't supposed to tell him details, he couldn't help but ask, "What's that supposed to mean?"

"Aw, Ah Veng, you know I'm not allowed to tell you everything. I'm sworn to secrecy. But I will tell you that it had something to do with communism and that our new prime minister was our former chief minister."

"So, Tunku Abdul Rahman, right?"

"Yup, that's exactly who it is! And he's going down in history as our first prime minister as an independent country. Isn't that exciting?"

Suddenly, cheers erupted outside. Jian-min grabbed Ah Veng's arm and dragged him out the front door. People were holding flags and walking up and down the street, chattering uncontrollably. Occasionally, shouts and cheers went up. Most of the people were shouting, "*Merdeka! Merdeka!*"[32]

* * *

Ah Veng stepped back into reality when he realized that the crowds around him were shouting, meaning that the parade was starting. He joined in, unsure of how many times they had already said it.

"Merdeka! Merdeka! Merdeka!"

It was a tradition to shout "Merdeka" seven times during independence day; otherwise the day was deemed incomplete. This was first conducted the day Tunku Abdul Rahman became prime minister in 1957.

"Look, look," Jian-min said excitedly, nudging Ah Veng with his elbow.

"What?" Ah Veng asked, confused, and then he saw it. A huge sign was being held by the second group in the parade, decorated with a Malaya flag that had streaks of red and white, their native butterflies painted to make up the blue portion of the flag around the moon and

---

32   Independent! Independent!

fourteen-pointed star. Above the flag, it read, *HAPPY BIRTHDAY, AH VENG. IT'S YOUR INDEPENDENCE DAY TOO!*

A lot of the men were his coworkers from the electrical company, but some of them he didn't recognize. They started singing *Selamat Hari Jadi*,[33] and everyone in the crowd joined in. Ah Veng held back his tears and looked at Jian-min. His mentor, his friend, his father figure had done so much, and the emotions were overwhelming.

It was then that he realized how lucky he was. It was then that he saw a future for himself. It was then that he finally recognized the possibility of his having a fulfilling life. A fiery independence burned within him.

---

33 Happy Birthday.

CHAPTER 9

THE GIRL

January 1960

"HURRY UP," JIAN-MIN SAID, TAPPING HIS foot impatiently as he held the door open.

Ah Veng threw on his jacket and pulled on his shoes.

"I'm coming, I'm coming," he said, annoyed that they were running late yet again. It was his fault this time, but usually it was Jian-min's.

"I don't want them to start eating without us."

"It's not that big of a deal," Ah Veng said, rolling his eyes.

"Umm, yeah," Jian-min retorted. "It's food."

"And the food will still be there even if we're just a few minutes late."

"Oh please, you know that it runs out sometimes."

"I doubt that it will tonight, though. Isn't this party an important one because the ladies were all invited as well?" Ah Veng asked.

"Yeah, it's the first time they're trying this. They want to get to know the women around Miri that are involved in pursuing the same beliefs we are," Jian-min said, shutting the door as they finally left the house.

"There are other groups, then?"

"Of course there are. They just stay hidden as good as we do."

Ah Veng thought about the different possible ways of creating a hideout and eventually got annoyed again. There were too many parties happening during this time of year, and they all made him uncomfortable. It wasn't that he didn't like socializing. The people were just too nosy and liked to ask very personal questions. He had to find ways around some of them so that they wouldn't know his background.

"Where is it again?" Ah Veng asked.

"Alan's place, since he has the biggest house amongst all of us."

"It's big enough to fit everyone?"

"Well, probably not, but some people will be outside, and some will be inside so I'm sure it will balance out. He likes to plan for things like this and we usually leave it to him."

"I don't get the point of all these parties," Ah Veng groaned, knowing that he was about to get another lecture for doing so, but not caring at that moment.

"Ah Veng, seriously. We've been over this. It's called networking, and you have to get used to it in life because it's what's going to help you survive out there."

"But they ask too many questions."

"To get to know you better, yeah. How else are people supposed to know who you are as a person and recognize the qualities that make up your personality? You never know when you might get lucky and find yourself a super good job just because an important person likes you. Or at parties like tonight, you might even find yourself a girl," Jian-min said mischievously.

"Ew, no," Ah Veng said, scrunching up his face in disgust.

"What's bad about that? You're bound to get a wife sometime."

"You didn't," Ah Veng pointed out.

Jian-min fell silent and looked away before finally saying, "I actually did."

"What?!" Ah Veng responded, mouth hanging open. It amazed him how much he still didn't know about the man after so many years with him.

"Yeah, a year after we married, we found out that she was pregnant, but there were complications during the birth and both her and the baby didn't make it. I couldn't ever bring myself to remarry after that happened, even though it's been years and years."

"I'm . . . sorry, I didn't know," Ah Veng said softly, noticing the pained look on Jian-min's face and how he rubbed his eyes to keep the tears from falling.

"It's alright. Let's not talk about it anymore because tonight we're going to have a great night," he said with a grin for Ah Veng.

"Yes, we are." He smiled back as they walked up to a decent-sized house.

It was painted white, a picture-perfect home with flowers lining the edges and a nice little fence to encompass the yard. The house was way nicer than any Ah Veng had seen in the other parts of Central Miri.

Jian-min pushed open the gate to the yard, and they walked up the pathway to the door. He knocked. They heard indistinct chatter, as well as light music in the background. The door flew open.

"Jian-min! And Ah Veng! What a pleasure to see you," Alan exclaimed. "Come in, come in. We're just about to start eating."

They stepped inside, and Ah Veng automatically regretted being a part of the brotherhood and having to attend these events. There were too many people and it was way too crowded.

"Hey, guys, look who's here," someone called.

Men came over and shook their hands or patted them on the back.

"Ah Veng, so glad to see you again," one of the older guys from work said.

"You too," he laughed.

"Dude, you should check out the women that are here," his friend Zhen said, suddenly showing up beside Ah Veng, who flinched a bit.

"Umm, no thanks. I think I'm good."

"Come on, man, you always do this. Live a bit, will you?"

"I'm just not interested."

"How do you know you're not if you don't even look?" Zhen frowned, shaking his head. "I'm taking you over there anyway," he said, dragging Ah Veng away from Jian-min, who was still conversing with Alan.

"Why does everyone keep forcing me? It's like you all want me to get married or something."

"Of course we do," Zhen snickered.

"Shouldn't you be focused on finding your own girl or something? Stop worrying about the love life of other people," Ah Veng said, pulling his hand away from Zhen and stopping to cross his arms.

"You're so stubborn," Zhen replied, narrowing his eyes. "Unfortunately, you're not a very good actor. I know you're curious."

"Nope, I'm not," Ah Veng said, frowning.

"Fine, bet you can't make it the whole night without seeing a girl you like or at least talking to one."

"Is that a dare?" Ah Veng asked. "Because you know I hate those types of games."

"You're making excuses. Come on, it shouldn't be that hard if you're serious about not caring about girls and getting married in the future and all that fluff. Plus, whoever wins has to buy dinner for a blind date."

"No way. I don't have that kind of money to waste on going out to dinner. And I am most certainly not going on a blind date."

"It's just one evening, and it wouldn't be too bad if the girl's good looking," Zhen said, waggling a finger in front of Ah Veng's nose.

"Alright, fine," Ah Veng stated. He shook hands with Zhen and sealed the deal.

"Great," his friend said and smiled as he walked away.

"Oh, there you are," Jian-min said, walking up to Ah Veng, carrying a plate piled with food. "You haven't got food yet," he observed.

"I haven't got the chance to get anything yet."

"Well, I'll go with you."

"So that you can get more?" Ah Veng snickered.

"Nooo." Jian-min laughed nervously. "I like food; don't judge," he whined.

"Hey, maybe you're the reason why they run out of food," Ah Veng teased as they approached the line.

He saw a girl staring at him and tensed. The clothes she wore had wealth written all over them. Her dark hair flowed past her waist, and her skin was the perfect shade of brown. They made eye contact. Her eyes were just as dark as her hair.

"Hey, man, what are you doing?" Zhen said, stepping in front of him with a big grin on his face.

"Nothing," Ah Veng said perhaps a little too quickly.

"Oh really," Zhen said, raising his eyebrows.

"Just getting in line for food, right, Jian-min?"

"Hmm?" Jian-min looked up from his food. "Oh, yeah."

"Right," Zhen said. "I'm watching you."

Ah Veng nodded. "Of course you are."

Zhen walked off again to talk to girls.

"Why's he watching you?" Jian-min questioned, a look of confusion on his face.

"It's nothing," Ah Veng replied, shaking his head.

He stole one more glance at the girl, who was still looking in his direction. *Maybe everyone is right. It actually wouldn't hurt to try and pursue a girl*, he thought. There wasn't even a reason why he wasn't interested in thinking about girls or marriage. He was simply used to being around guys and never saw many girls.

However, he really didn't want to lose the bet.

"It's your turn," Jian-min said, snapping Ah Veng out of his thoughts.

"Oh, thanks," he replied and started piling food onto his plate.

He thought about how he might outsmart Zhen as he followed Jian-min into the living room. They sat at a table in the corner where his companion immediately started talking with some of the other men. Suddenly, Ah Veng had an idea. It was dumb and childish, but he couldn't think of anything else.

He spotted scraps of paper and a few pens on the shelf of a cupboard. He excused himself, saying that he wanted to wash his hands before eating. Looking around to see if anyone was paying attention to him, Ah Veng shoved a few pieces of paper and a pen in his pocket.

"Excuse me, sir, do you know where the restroom is?" Ah Veng asked a man who was eyeing him curiously.

"Yeah, it's upstairs. First door on your right."

"Thanks," he said.

When he found it, he quickly locked the door behind him, took the pieces of paper and pen out of his pocket, and thought about what he should write. Finally, he decided on something simple and wrote, *Can't talk now, but you're pretty and I'd love to get to know you. Where can I meet you one day?*

His heart beat loudly in his chest. The feeling was exhilarating, and, oddly enough, he was nervous not because of possibly losing the bet, but because he wasn't sure what the girl would think and if she would even find a way to reply. He tried to calm down as he shoved the pen and extra pieces of paper into his pocket before folding the little note. Then, when he was ready, he clenched the note in his fist and stepped out.

"Hey, so that's where you've been this whole time," Zhen said, leaning against the wall on the other side of the hall.

"I needed a break. There's too many people down there," Ah Veng said lamely.

"Uh-huh, okay. You sure you weren't hiding out so that you wouldn't accidently run into a girl that would start talking to you?" Zhen replied, moving away from the wall.

"Maybe just a little," Ah Veng said with a sheepish grin.

"Well, get back downstairs. It's not fair if you're doing that."

"Alright, alright, I'm going," Ah Veng complied, looking back to see if Zhen would follow.

To his relief, his friend walked into the restroom and closed the door. Ah Veng hurried down the stairs, knowing that he needed to find the girl quickly. As he turned the corner to go back into the living room, he bumped into someone and started to say sorry but realized it was the girl. His eyes widened, and he didn't even think before shoving the little note into her hands and rushing away from her, afraid that someone might have seen the exchange. He wasn't sure if Zhen would have other people watching him, too, but knowing his friend, he probably did.

The whole situation seemed ridiculous; he was playing another one of his friend's silly games. Zhen played way too much, and it often got him in trouble at work.

He didn't remember sitting back down at the table, but someone was trying to get his attention.

"Ah Veng," Jian-min said a little more insistently, snapping his fingers in front of Ah Veng's face.

"Huh, what?" Ah Veng said, startled.

"You were zoning out again," Jian-min replied with a concerned look. "Are you okay?"

"Yeah, I'm fine," Ah Veng answered and started to pick at his food, which had already turned cold. He wasn't very hungry anymore.

"You missed the toast."

"I did?" Ah Veng questioned, wondering how long he had been gone.

"Yeah, but they haven't done speeches yet."

"Oh."

"You know, you don't look that good. Why don't we leave a bit early tonight? I don't want you to come down with something."

"But you like staying," Ah Veng pointed out.

"I usually do, but I'm not really feeling it tonight. So, what do you say? Do you want to leave?"

Ah Veng looked around the room, trying to spot the girl, but she was nowhere to be found. He didn't want to leave until he got an answer from her, but then again, this was his escape from possibly losing the bet. Finally, he said, "Yeah, let's go."

Jian-min thanked the men they were sitting with as Ah Veng looked around again. He wondered where she went off to. *Possibly to get more food? Or to talk to someone?* Jian-min motioned to Ah Veng and he followed. He got more anxious the closer they got to the front door. Suddenly, someone bumped into him, and he felt something get pressed into his palm. He didn't dare look back because he knew who it was, and his heart raced.

Zhen stepped in front of them.

"Woah, where are you all going?"

"We're leaving for tonight," Jian-min replied.

"Leaving? But it's still early," Zhen whined, looking at Ah Veng.

"Sorry, but we have to go," Jian-min said.

"Well, alright then. Have a good night."

When Jian-min moved to tell Alan they were going, Zhen pouted at Ah Veng.

"You got lucky. If it weren't for your caretaker there, I would have thought that you were bailing out on me."

"Of course not," Ah Veng said, and then decided to play along. "Why do you think I took the bet? I knew that we had to leave early."

"Clever," Zhen said, narrowing his eyes as if he knew something was up. But then he bounded away, calling behind him, "See you at work next week."

* * *

Ah Veng was back at the workhouse after his time off, and he still hadn't opened the note. What it might entail terrified him, and he was unsure if he really wanted a relationship. But at the same time, he was curious. *Life is about adventures, right? About taking risks and trying new things or changing every once in a while.* The note could crush his curiosity or raise his enthusiasm to try something new. It went both ways. The good and the bad. *So, which one will choose me?* he wondered.

The note was under his pillow. It would be so easy to get it over with. He had to read it eventually. His hand twitched. *Come on, Ah Veng.* Finally, he caved in and snatched his pillow away to pick up the note. He stared at it, unsure once again. Ah Veng had finished his job early that day, but the other workers were still out working. No one would know.

Slowly and tentatively, he unfolded it. The words read, *I sell tickets at TEATER FILEM BINTANG*[34] *on Monday through Friday. Come see me.*

His heart beat faster in his chest and he felt lightheaded. He laughed out loud at the thought of being in love with a girl. It seemed unreal, considering where he came from; he'd never known what the term *love* actually meant. He wasn't sure that he did now. He fell back onto his bed, holding the note and wondering if he was crazy enough to ride his bike to her work.

Minutes later, he found himself on his bike, pedaling towards the movie theater; it was the one he always rode past to get to Jian-min's. He wondered why he'd never paid attention to it.

Suddenly, he got really nervous. *What if the girl doesn't want to see me anymore?* he thought. *Or maybe she will be too busy to talk.* He wondered if he should just turn around and forget about it, but it was too late: the theater was right in front of him. He slowed and got off his bike to walk it closer to the entrance. He froze when he saw her. Someone behind him yelped a bit at his sudden stop and mumbled, "Watch it, man," before moving around him.

She was handing out tickets from a little box office right next to the front door. However, she looked different. Her hair was a lot shorter, falling around her shoulders, and her skin was a little lighter than it was in the house that night at the party. But her face was the same. He was sure of it. The eyes held that same glow of a darkening night. They were the same color as her hair. He approached and she looked up from a piece of paper she was writing on.

"Would you like to buy a ticket?" she called out, smiling at him.

Ah Veng felt like he was drowning. He shook his head, unable to make his mouth open to let words come out. Frustrated, he crossed the street so she wouldn't think that he was creepy for standing and

---

34   Star Movie Theater.

staring at her. *How stupid I must have looked*, he thought. He should have said something when he had the chance. *Maybe I could wait for her to leave work.* He walked into an alleyway right across the street so that he could keep an eye on her.

"Got an eye for that girl, don't ya?" someone said behind him. Ah Veng jumped and spun around to find a homeless man sitting on the ground.

Remembering his own experience living on the streets, Ah Veng's heart automatically went out to the man.

"Maybe," Ah Veng said with a grin.

"Well, let me tell you. Women are not always as they seem. Now, you might get lucky with one that is sweet, but sometimes they're deceiving, cunning, and can be misleading as they twist and squeeze your heart this way and that. They turn into these little creatures with bloodthirsty powers that suck all the will from you and all of your freedom. Take it from someone that has personal experience. That's the whole reason why I'm out on the streets."

Ah Veng backed away. The man spoke as though he had lost his mind years ago. To Ah Veng's relief, when he looked out towards the street, the girl was leaving the theater.

"I have to go," Ah Veng said and then turned to flee.

The man yelled after him. "I'm warning you, kid!"

Ah Veng walked faster to catch up with the girl, but he made sure to stay quite a distance away from her. *Is it weird that I am following her?* he wondered. He was too scared to actually say something to her or start a conversation.

He stopped walking and pretended to look inside a shop when she glanced over her shoulder. *She doesn't suspect something, does she?*

He stayed even further back and looked more closely at their surroundings, realizing that they were nearing the eastern part of town, which was the really poor area. He could have sworn that the girl was rich because of the clothes she had been wearing that night. But then again, she could have just borrowed the clothes from a friend, or they could have been hers; most poor families were able to afford at least one decent outfit.

He was slightly disappointed. A girl that actually had money could help him out a lot. However, he knew he'd be lucky if a girl married him at all.

They walked for such a long time that Ah Veng lost track of how long it had been. The town and the shops were left behind as they entered the kampong[35] areas. It would be dark by the time he arrived back at the workhouse, but for once he didn't really care. They passed a cemetery, and the girl walked even faster, as if she was afraid of it. She constantly looked around, walking on the far side of the trail to avoid the tombstones protruding from the ground. Ah Veng hung back, not wanting to terrify her. *Does she always have to walk this far?*

He left his bike in the bushes because it was easier to follow on foot. He stuck to the tree line in case he had to duck into the jungle to hide.

It couldn't possibly be safe for her to walk this far every day, he thought. However, poor villagers had to find work someway, and if it involved walking, that was the least of their problems. Ah Veng visualized the girl's features. He loved her face, and her voice. *Is that weird?* His emotions confused him.

Suddenly, the girl veered off on a smaller path that led to a house. He crept closer, pushing himself a little further into the trees. The house was small and broken down. He couldn't tell what the original color was, but it was now a mucky brown with spots of gray paint peeling off. One of the windows was shattered, and the door hung open as if it couldn't close all the way. His heart hurt for her. The lower classes suffered in unspeakable conditions while the rich fed off and benefitted from everyone else. Life just wasn't fair. He turned and made his way back down to where he had left his bike, content that he had seen her safely home.

Ah Veng spent the whole way back to the workhouse deep in thought, wondering what he was going to do and whether he could ever force himself to approach the girl. He prepared himself for the

35   village.

probing questions his coworkers were bound to ask. They knew that he never went out in the evening, or at night after work. He stopped. Lights were still on in the house, and he heard the men laughing. He tried to open the door quietly, but they knew, and when he stepped through the door, wheeling in his bike, they all came running.

"Ah Veng! Where have you been?!" Zhen demanded.

"Yeah, we've been worried sick," Cheng chimed in, and the other men agreed.

"Calm down," Ah Veng said. "I just went to see Jian-min, and he wasn't feeling good, so I stayed for a bit longer."

"Oh, well, you could have told us," Zhen replied, rolling his eyes. "You know, so we wouldn't freak out about you not being here when you usually are."

"We thought you got fired or something!" one of the other men yelled out from the back.

"I'm sorry. I didn't think that it would be that big of a deal. But I appreciate the concern. I'll be sure to let you know next time," Ah Veng said, running a hand through his hair.

"Alright, alright, everyone leave him alone now. He's probably tired and wants to go up to his room," Cheng said, making a shooing motion with his hands.

"Thanks," Ah Veng told him with a small smile before leaning his bike against the wall and heading up the stairs. When he reached the top, Cheng called out to him once more.

"Ah Veng?"

"Yeah," he answered, turning to look back down.

"We really were worried. I know that it may seem like the guys don't really care at times and that they're too immature. But they do care. It's just a different way of showing it. Seriously, let us know next time."

"I will," Ah Veng said. "I'll go ahead and give you a heads-up that I'll be going out a lot more now."

"Alright, thanks for letting me know. I don't want to keep you. I know you're tired. So, goodnight."

"Goodnight," Ah Veng replied, heading into his room and shutting the door.

He collapsed onto the bed, feeling more confused and lost than he was before he had opened the note. *Should I have just left it alone?*

* * *

Music was playing. A sweet melody drifted on a light, feathery breeze. It carried over the blossoms blooming alongside the field on trees of various colors. Blossoms of pink, purple, blue, yellow. Colors of the rainbow. The breeze shifted, lifting him up and pushing him closer to the source of that beautiful tune. He was so close. It was louder now, pulling and calling for him. He tried to fly closer. Tried to move around the hill blocking his view. But his efforts were useless. The wind pulled him back, and he fell softly to the ground.

Then suddenly, he was there. It was a marriage ceremony. A beautiful picture of love and happiness, of life and meaning. The music stopped. Everything fell silent with anticipation for that one special moment. The scene became fuzzy and blurred around the edges.

* * *

Ah Veng woke when it was still dark. He looked at the window even though he knew the curtains were closed. The dream replayed in his mind. *What do all these dreams mean? And why am I always flying? Is there something special about being in the air?* he thought.

This one bothered him. Perhaps he was supposed to get married one day. Or maybe he was just supposed to be tortured with knowing that other people were when he couldn't even bring up the courage to talk to a girl. *The girl* . . . He needed to talk to her. If he didn't, he risked losing her. *Next week,* he told himself, staring up at the ceiling. *I'll talk to her next week.*

* * *

It was already the next week and Ah Veng still hadn't talked to the girl. Instead, he followed her home every day to make sure that she got there safely. His coworkers were suspicious, knowing that he was not running off to visit Jian-min every single night, and Ah Veng started to worry that they might follow him one day, but instead, Zhen found the courage to blatantly confront him.

"Hey, where are you heading off to?" he said, stepping in front of Ah Veng one day when he was leaving.

"To Jian-min's, where else?" Ah Veng said, rolling his eyes and trying to shove past his friend.

"You can stop that act right now," Zhen demanded. "I ran into Jian-min at the market. He says that he hasn't heard from you at all in the last week."

Ah Veng's face fell. There was no lopsided grin on his friend's face. Zhen seemed so genuinely serious that Ah Veng shifted uncomfortably at the change.

"Something's wrong with you and everyone is worried. I don't think you realize that. It's not like you to just disappear for hours on end, and you hardly spend time with us anymore. All you do is work and then disappear. Not to mention, you hardly talk at all and you stayed locked up in your room on the weekend."

Ah Veng stayed silent, unsure of what he should say or do. The truth would be embarrassing after causing such a fuss, but if he lied again, it could cause an even bigger problem.

"Just think about it. You can tell any of us what's going on. It doesn't matter. Just think about it for the sake of us and so that we can stop worrying."

Zhen moved away from Ah Veng and started walking upstairs.

"There's a girl," Ah Veng blurted out, unable to control himself.

"What?" Zhen said, spinning around on the steps.

"I saw her at the party, and I promise that I didn't talk to her and I didn't even know if I really, really liked her or not, but I wrote her a note and passed it to her, and she passed a response to me and told me where she worked and—"

"Woah, woah, slow down," Zhen said, walking back down the stairs. "You've been leaving every day after work to go see a girl?" he asked incredulously.

"Yeah," Ah Veng said, turning away sheepishly.

"You've got to be kidding me!" Zhen said laughing. "Is she the one, then?"

"What do you mean?" Ah Veng asked.

"Like, you know, the one that you want to marry?"

"Umm, I don't really know. I kind of still haven't talked to her," Ah Veng said, wincing and rubbing the back of his neck.

"You what?"

"I haven't talked to her."

"Then what in the world have you been doing when you go see her?"

"Umm . . . follow her."

"Ah Veng! Do you know how creepy that is? Does she even know that you're following her every day?" Zhen asked, shaking his head.

"I don't know. She might, or she might not."

"Dude, you need to talk to her. That's so weird. You can't just watch a girl work and then follow her around afterwards. It doesn't work that way. You're getting nowhere."

"I know, I keep telling myself that I'm going to, but then I get freaked out—"

"Today. You need to talk to her today because you seriously can't keep that up. One day she might notice and tell the police or something. And then, man will you be in trouble."

"I don't know," he told Zhen.

"Come on. It's not that hard. You just go up and start having a normal conversation with her and then possibly offer to walk her home after she gets off work or something. Who is this girl, anyway?" Zhen asked.

"I'm not really sure. I don't know much about her."

"Ah Veng, Ah Veng, Ah Veng," Zhen tsked, shaking his head again, "you're head over heels and it reminds me of some lovesick puppy. You have got yourself a major problem. But don't worry; you can fix that tonight if you'll actually talk to her."

"Alright, I'll try to," Ah Veng sighed.

"Nope, not try. You're going to," Zhen said, narrowing his eyes. "I do not want to be visiting you in jail one of these days, so you better do it."

"I will, I will," Ah Veng said, waving him off as he pushed his bike out the front door.

"I can't wait to hear all about it tonight," Zhen called with a grin, closing the door for him.

Ah Veng's heart beat wildly in his chest. He had to stop every once in a while to wipe his sweaty hands off. *It's not that big of a deal,* he kept telling himself, and yet he was still nervous. The theater came into view, and Ah Veng almost considered turning around, but he kept riding until he got to the front. After leaning his bike against the wall, he walked closer. The box office that the girl usually worked at was empty. His heart fell, disappointed that she was not there. Suddenly, someone poked him in the chest.

"Hey, I've been meaning to talk to you," the girl said.

Ah Veng jumped back in surprise, speechless.

"Why have you been following me every day?" the girl demanded, putting her hands on her hips and narrowing her eyes.

"Umm . . . I . . ." he stammered.

"Well?" she said, tapping her foot, annoyed.

"I just wanted to talk to you," Ah Veng finally blurted out.

"Talk to me?" she asked, raising her eyebrows. "That's hard to believe."

"Why?" Ah Veng questioned.

"Because no one follows someone to their house every day just because they want to talk to them. Only a crazy person would do that."

Ah Veng felt offended. "I didn't mean to. I told myself to say something, but I couldn't . . ." He trailed off, rubbing the back of his neck nervously.

"What do you mean, you couldn't?" she asked, clearly not recognizing that Ah Veng liked her.

"I don't know."

"If you want to buy a movie ticket, you know that you could just go up to the counter and ask instead of following people home. Just a tip, you know, so people don't think that you are a creep or something," she said, turning to walk away.

Great, now she thinks I'm stupid and that I'm a creep, Ah Veng thought.

"Wait," he called out.

The girl turned back around.

"What?" she snapped.

"Can I walk you home after you get off of work?" he asked quickly so that he wouldn't lose his nerve.

"I don't see why not since you've already been following me for over a week," she said, rolling her eyes. "My shift ends in about an hour, so either wait inside or go somewhere and come back, because it's also creepy when you stare at people while they work. Oh, and it's rude," she added.

"Okay, thank you. I'll be back!" he exclaimed.

"Don't thank me," the girl grumbled.

"Right," Ah Veng nodded and scurried back to his bike.

He was slightly dizzy and excited about everything that had just happened. He had actually talked to the girl and he was going to walk her home. Glancing around, he wondered where to wait. A bookstore on the other side of the street seemed like a promising place, so he crossed the street and went inside. His mind and emotions were all over the place. He picked up a book, but quickly put it back when he noticed that it was a love story. He couldn't handle one of those at that moment. *Does she like me back? Or is she just being nice?* he wondered, terrified that she might not even notice that he liked her.

Nothing like this had ever happened before. It scared and confused him, and yet it also excited him.

He finally decided to curl up by the window where he could still keep an eye on her. It may have been creepy, but he didn't really care. He took in every feature. The way her eyebrows furrowed when someone gave her the wrong amount of money, the way her smile lit up her eyes, the way her hair blew whenever someone rushed past or the wind fluttered. He couldn't take his eyes off of her. *The girl.* So mysterious and yet so concrete. He didn't know her name or even who she was, but he knew for a fact that he was in love.

* * *

"I hope you know, I saw you," the girl said, glaring at Ah Veng when she met him at the bookstore after finishing her shift.

"What do you mean?" Ah Veng asked.

"Oh, don't act so innocent. You were watching me from the window in there," she said pointedly.

"Right," Ah Veng replied, trailing off and tapping his finger on his lips. "Sorry about that."

"Sure you're sorry. I bet you'll still continue your creepy stalking ways even after I tell you not to. At least you're walking me home instead of trailing behind me, acting like some kind of ghost."

"I just didn't want to startle or scare you," Ah Veng said, frowning.

"Well, let me tell you, it's a lot scarier when someone is following you everywhere you go rather than simply walking up to talk to you."

"Oh. I didn't think about it like that."

The girl rolled her eyes. "Boys. You all are so dumb. Now, come on. I don't want you to have to walk home in the dark."

"I don't mind."

"Of course you don't," she said.

"No, really. I'm used to it. Well, I was actually more accustomed to it in the past."

"And why is that?"

"Because—" Ah Veng stopped himself from saying what he was about to say. He didn't want the girl to know that he had been homeless before, so instead he simply said, "My old job made us work overtime quite often."

"Ah, that's understandable. I always worry that I will be asked to stay later, but they know that I live far and have to walk or ride my bike, so they haven't ever kept me longer than my actual shift."

"Well, that's considerate of them."

"Ha, yeah right," she scoffed.

"What? Is it not?"

"No, it's just that . . . never mind," she said, shaking her head.

"Do they not treat you very well?" Ah Veng asked.

"Nope," she replied, looking away.

"I know how that feels," he said. "I'm Ah Veng, by the way. What's your name?"

The girls smiled up at him. "Guess," she said.

"I doubt that I could get it right even if I tried. Aren't there millions of girl names out there?"

"Yeah, but mine's special."

"I feel like every girl would say something like that. Can you give me a hint?"

"Hmm . . . not until we get close to my house."

"Aw, come on. How can I guess right now if I don't have a hint?" Ah Veng begged.

"Alright, I'll help you out. It's something that's red."

"What?" Ah Veng asked. "But there's so many things that are red."

"Exactly," she replied, smiling.

"Umm, I don't know. Apple, Strawberry, Tomato—"

"Oh gosh, you're terrible at this. Stop it. What kind of person would name their kid after fruits?" she said in disgust.

"Hey, you never know. And how I supposed to guess your name with such a vague hint?"

"Okay, what if I told you that it's a flower?"

"Oh, how about Hibiscus?"

"Ew, no," she said, scrunching up her face. "Why would someone be named that? Do you have any common sense at all?"

"I mean, it is Malaysia's national flower, so I don't see why someone wouldn't be named after it. That's pretty special, right?"

"Okay, true. But no."

"I don't think I'm going to get anywhere with guessing wrong. Can you just tell me?" he pleaded.

"Hold on; we're almost there," she said.

"Where?"

"To my house—where else?"

"Okay, but what does that have to do with you telling me your name?"

"I'm going to show you."

"You're going to show me your name." Ah Veng laughed. "Now that's funny. Do you have it written somewhere?"

"No, I'm serious," she said, stopping at the road that split off and led to her house.

A little bush of red roses stood hidden around the bend in the pathway. She carefully reached down and looked for one without too many thorns to pluck off.

"You're kidding me, right? There's no way your name is Red Roses."

"No, silly," she said, standing up and handing Ah Veng the rose. "I'm one person, so it's just Rose."

"Oh, I guess that makes sense. It's pretty," he said, staring down at the small but vibrant flower.

Rose simply laughed. "I should probably get inside."

Ah Veng glanced up.

"See you tomorrow," he called after her.

"I guess I don't have a choice, do I?"

Ah Veng couldn't stop smiling, even after he turned away to head back. It was crazy to think that had he not gone to the party, he would have never met the girl. He twirled the flower in his hands, finding it hard to believe that he had fallen in love with a Rose.

CHAPTER 10

RED ROSES

June 1960

Ah Veng kept glancing down at his watch. Time moved too slowly, and it aggravated him. He sighed before checking the meter on the house.

"What's wrong with you?" Zhen asked, walking up beside him.

"Nothing," Ah Veng said, writing down some numbers on the clipboard that he was holding.

"I don't believe you. You're always anxious these days. Something's up."

"I promise you, it's nothing."

"Nothing, huh? I bet it has something to do with the girl. She didn't dump you, did she?"

"No," Ah Veng said, offended that his friend would think that a possibility.

"Hey, I was just wondering. Nothing to get upset about."

"I just want to be finished with work so that I can go see her. That's it."

"Nah, man. I know it's more than that."

"Like what?" Ah Veng asked, crossing his arms and leaning against the house to stare at Zhen.

"How am I supposed to know? I'm asking you."

"Well, that's too bad," Ah Veng replied and straightened up to walk over to the next house.

"Really? You're just going to leave me hanging like this?" Zhen called.

"You'll figure it out eventually. You always do," Ah Veng said over his shoulder.

"I still haven't met this chick. When are you going to let me?"

"Sometime soon."

"That's what you always say," Zhen yelled. Ah Veng simply shrugged and disappeared around the other side of the neighboring house before he let out a snicker.

He loved any opportunity to annoy Zhen, but he really did need to figure out what he was going to do with his life. The feelings that he had for the girl were real, but something was off. It worried him and made him even more confused.

He sighed, and realized that Zhen was now in front of him, leaning against the wall and glaring at him.

"Ahh, goodness! You just can't leave me alone, can you?" Ah Veng exclaimed, jumping back a bit.

"You were zoning out again. Now, when do we get to meet the girl?"

"Can you stop calling her the girl, please? She has a name, you know. It's Rose."

"Okay, fine, when do we get to meet the mysterious Rose?" Zhen said, wiggling his fingers in the air.

"You're being quirky. Stop it. And I already told you, I don't know."

"Nope, not going to leave you alone until you give me an answer."

"I just don't think she'll feel very comfortable being around a whole bunch of guys."

"It's one time, Ah Veng. Then we'll stop bugging you. But you have to let us meet her just once. Plus, I've been dying of curiosity about which girl caught your eye that night at the party. I don't recall a Rose being there, but maybe she was one of the quieter ones. I'll probably recognize her face once I see her."

"That's the thing . . ." Ah Veng trailed off.

"What?" Zhen asked.

"Never mind, it doesn't make any sense," Ah Veng said, shaking his head.

"What doesn't?"

"I swear Rose is the same girl I saw at the party, but a lot of things just don't line up."

"Like what?"

"It's just . . . she hasn't ever mentioned the party or the note or any of that."

"Maybe she just assumes that you both don't need to talk about it. I mean, you have been seeing each other for a long time now," Zhen replied.

"Well, it's not just that. It also doesn't really make sense as to why she was wearing rich people's clothes at the party when I've seen her closet and she doesn't have anything even relatively close to being that nice."

Zhen shrugged. "Maybe she borrowed it."

"Possibly, but she also never wants to talk about her past or about herself in general. I want to get to know her better, but it's like she's not letting me."

"Okay, I will admit, that's a little weird."

"I don't know. It just bothers me," Ah Veng sighed.

"You know, what you could do is bring her over for lunch tomorrow on our day off and I could totally help you figure out why this is so bothersome to you." Zhen grinned.

"Aw, you're just using that as an excuse. Nope, I don't think so."

"Come on, Ah Veng. I could tell you if I saw her at the party or not. And we could probably try to get her to talk about herself a bit more. With you, maybe she's scared that you'll judge her or something. If she's meeting new people, though, she wouldn't want to seem rude."

"I guess that makes sense. I'll talk to her tonight and see if she'll want to come."

"Yes!" Zhen shouted, pumping his fist in the air.

"Will you stop being weird for once? I have work to get back to and you do too."

Zhen stood there, grinning stupidly.

"Go on." Ah Veng shooed him away, and his friend finally ran off to tell the other guys.

The rest of the work day moved quite quickly, and before he knew it, he was bouncing on the balls of his feet impatiently as he waited for Rose. They were short of workers at the movie theater and she had to stay a bit longer for the first time. He was worried for her because she always seemed miserable after work these past few weeks.

"Sorry for the wait," she said, pushing open the door.

"It's alright. I was just a bit worried is all," he replied, giving her a hug before they started walking.

"I don't know if I can keep working there," she said suddenly, grimacing, "but I need the money."

Ah Veng didn't know what to say. Finally, he lamely responded, "I wish they didn't treat you so badly."

"Well, that makes two of us."

Silence took over again as they walked through the streets, lost in their own thoughts but content with each other's company. It wasn't until they had almost reached Rose's house that Ah Veng blurted out, "Can you come over for lunch tomorrow? You're off work, right?"

"Yeah, but don't you live with a bunch of your coworkers?"

"That's the thing. They want to meet you," Ah Veng said, rubbing his neck.

"Oh, um . . . sure, I guess."

"It would just be this once; they're the only important people to me besides Jian-min, but you've met him several times already. My coworkers have been complaining that they don't even know who you are."

"Well, okay, yeah. I'd love to go over for lunch tomorrow," she replied, forcing a smile since she was reluctant but wanted to do something for Ah Veng's sake for once.

"Great! I'll be here at eleven to pick you up—or rather, walk you over," he said, laughing a bit.

"Alright, I'll be waiting."

They said their goodnights before Ah Veng turned and made his way back. The walk had become a lot shorter once he found the hidden shortcuts and learned to pick up his pace.

He was still nervous and wasn't sure why. Rose mixed up all kinds of feelings in him, and yet their relationship was still more of a friendship. He wanted it to be more; however, something was holding her back, and he couldn't put his finger on what it was. Perhaps he would find out tomorrow.

Ah Veng opened the front door of the workhouse and glanced around. The house was silent, which was weird. He shrugged and headed upstairs, thinking that the guys had either gone out or went to bed, but when he opened his bedroom door, he screamed.

Crossing his arms to glare at all the guys laughing on the floor, he demanded, "Don't you ever scare me like that again!"

"You should have seen the look on your face," Zhen howled.

"It was priceless," Cheng chipped in, doubling over in laughter.

Ah Veng couldn't help himself; he cracked a smile and started laughing as well before getting himself together.

"Seriously, guys. Why are you all in my room?!" he exclaimed.

"We just wanted to know if your girl was coming over tomorrow," Cheng said.

"Yeah!" the other guys added excitedly.

"Oh, goodness. Yes, she's coming. I'm picking her up at eleven."

The guys started whooping and hollering obnoxiously.

"Alright, I told you. Now get out of my room! Out, out!" he shouted, swatting at them.

"We're going, we're going," they yelled, running past him and out the door.

Only Zhen hung back. "See, that wasn't so hard," he said with a smug grin.

"Stop, yes it was," Ah Veng said. "Now leave me alone. I'm going to have to deal with all of you tomorrow."

Zhen rolled his eyes.

"We're not that bad, but alright," he said as he walked out.

"Goodnight," Ah Veng called. He didn't bother showering or changing because he was too exhausted and wound up about the next day, and the bed looked too enticing. He curled up underneath the blankets and in a matter of minutes slipped into the dream world that had followed him every step of the way.

* * *

Trees were changing colors. Leaves drifted and fluttered to the ground in assortments of colors. Shades of brown, orange, yellow, and red. Falling. Descending. Plunging into streams of water. Diving into fragments of puddles. Autumn was making itself known. Stealing the show from summer's soft glow. The seasons shifted, one after another. Summer, fall, winter, spring, a continuous cycle that some parts of the world had never touched or experienced before. They shifted faster and faster, whipping the air into a whirlwind. Ah Veng tried to escape its hold, his head spinning, his mind racing, the dizziness overwhelming. It was uncontrollable. He was finally flung out, falling, descending, like the leaves of a tree. The tornado loomed over him, but he was snatched away by some unknown force, saved from hitting the ground and plunging to his death. Gently, and sweetly, he felt himself laid in a pile of discarded leaves, left to stare at the bare tree above.

* * *

Ah Veng's eyes opened to find his bare ceiling staring back at him. He glanced down and noticed that he was lying on top of the mess of covers. *Did I not curl up underneath the blankets?* he wondered, sitting up to stretch before grabbing some clothes and heading to the bathroom to shower. This day was not one he was looking forward to, but on a good note, he didn't have to work.

It was about ten thirty when he started walking briskly to Rose's house, wringing his hands nervously the whole way. He silently prayed to the nature gods that his coworkers would not mess things up for him. They could be such nuisances at times. His heart stopped when he saw her. Her hair was combed for once, and he could tell that she tried to look decent in the one dress that she owned.

"Hi," she said, smiling.

"Hi," he breathed. It was almost like he was seeing her for the first time, like that night at the party, her gaze holding steady, unwavering.

"Well, what are we waiting for?" she asked, holding out her arm to be escorted.

Ah Veng smiled back and took her arm. The two of them chattered happily the whole way back to Ah Veng's place.

"I have to warn you that these guys can get pretty nosy or annoying at times."

"That's alright. When are guys not?"

"Hey," he said, playfully.

"What? It's true," she retorted.

Ah Veng laughed. "Okay, sometimes."

They stopped outside the house. As he reached to open the door, it was thrown open by Zhen.

"She's here," he yelled behind him before taking a close look at the girl.

He froze. He knew her. He knew who she was. He knew who she was not. He knew that she would never step foot at one of those important parties. In fact, everyone in the town knew who she was. *How could Ah Veng not?* He glanced at his friend's glowing face, unsure if he should say something.

"Well, are you going to let us in?" Ah Veng asked.

"Um . . . yeah," Zhen said, stepping back.

The other men ran to the door to greet them, but they all halted when they saw the girl.

"Guys, this is Rose," Ah Veng announced, smiling down at her.

Zhen stood behind them with a finger to his lips, shaking his head and hoping that the other men would not say anything. He knew that he had to tell his friend the truth eventually, but he suspected that the girl was in on the deception, and he wanted her to be the one to let it slip out.

"Nice to meet you," Cheng finally said, stepping forward to shake her hand.

The other men followed suit, introducing themselves one by one before slowly filing out to head to the living room or kitchen.

"Lunch is in the kitchen, and you're welcome to sit anywhere you like," Zhen said, motioning towards the kitchen.

"Thank you," she replied as Ah Veng led her to the food.

"Wow, did you seriously cook all this?" Ah Veng asked, shocked at the amount of food on the countertops and amazed that his coworkers actually cared that much.

"We woke up super early to do it," Cheng said, nodding.

"Well, let's eat," Zhen announced, grabbing plates and handing two to Ah Veng and Rose before taking one for himself.

The other men piled in, waiting for their turn to dig into the food.

Rose wanted to stay at the kitchen dining table, so Ah Veng sat next to her and Zhen. Cheng and a few other guys gathered around as well. The rest of them went to sit in the living room to talk amongst themselves. Most of the conversations were about the girl, so they kept their voices low, not wanting her to know that they were talking about who she was.

"So, you work at the movie theater, right?" Zhen asked, determined to make the girl talk about herself so that Ah Veng could figure out that she was not who he thought she was.

"Um . . . yeah," she replied.

"How long have you worked there?"

"I can't really remember. It's been a few years, though."

"Wow, that's a long time."

"Yeah." She laughed nervously.

"So, how'd you meet Ah Veng?" Cheng asked, catching Zhen's eye and trying to figure out what was going on.

"Oh, that's kind of an embarrassing story," she replied, blushing.

"Enlighten us. We've probably heard worse stories," Zhen said.

"You don't have to answer their questions, you know?" Ah Veng cut in.

"But, Ah Veng, we want to know the story."

"I just don't—"

"It's fine, they're just curious," Rose said, laying a hand on Ah Veng's arm.

"Yeah, Ah Veng. You're ruining our fun."

He shifted, uncomfortable because they were pushing to get Rose to talk. *If she doesn't talk to me about her personal life, what makes them think they can get her to talk about it?* He realized that Rose was telling the story.

". . . was the first time I saw him. I asked him if he wanted to buy a movie ticket and, honestly, I thought that he was a really rude guy for not wanting to buy one. Then a few days later, I realized that he was following me home every single day and it honestly scared me," she said, laughing.

"Like, here was this creepy guy stalking me. I was scared that he was going to kidnap me or something, so I practically ran home each day until I decided to confront him about it. Then he asked to walk me home and all, and then everything just kind of went from there."

Ah Veng sat up straighter in his chair. She didn't mention the party. There was no mention of the note he passed her and then her reply, telling him where to meet. *Is she embarrassed about that part of the story?* Zhen watched him steadily, paying close attention to his response and wondering whether Ah Veng would say anything. He didn't.

"That's not a bad love story," Cheng said, snickering. "Nice move, Ah Veng. Follow the girl around to creep her out in order to win her over. Works every time, doesn't it?" he laughed, winking.

"Erm, yeah," Ah Veng said, clearing his throat.

Zhen was still staring at him, and it made Ah Veng restless. He couldn't directly look at his friend and he didn't know why.

"So, how long have you all worked with Ah Veng?" Rose asked.

"Oh, it's been a couple of years, I'd guarantee. Believe it or not, he's the oldest one here," Cheng replied.

"Ah Veng, can I talk to you for a moment?" Zhen asked, motioning for him to step out into the hall.

"I'll be right back," Ah Veng told Rose.

When he got into the hall, Zhen pulled him further down towards the front door.

"I know you heard her," he said, looking Ah Veng directly in the eyes.

Ah Veng tried to look away, but couldn't. "I know," he finally said, tearing his gaze away.

"And? Why didn't she mention it?"

"I don't know! I really don't," Ah Veng cried, infuriated and frustrated. His mind was a muddled mess as he tried to sort everything out.

"Did it ever occur to you that maybe she wasn't there? Because I'm certain that I did not see her at the party that night."

"No! I know that it was her," Ah Veng insisted.

"Come on, think. It only makes sense."

"No, nothing's making sense."

Zhen sighed, uncertain if he should tell or not. He finally let the words tumble out.

"Everyone knows who she is," he said.

"What?" Ah Veng said, snapping his gaze back to Zhen's face. "What do you mean by everyone?"

"Literally. Mostly everyone in the entire town knows who she is."

"Then she would have been at the party that night," Ah Veng said, feeling slightly relieved.

"No, Ah Veng. They know her because . . . I can't be the one to tell you this," Zhen said, starting to walk away, but Ah Veng grabbed his friend's arm.

"Wait, I need to know. Even if it might break my heart, I need to know," he stated a little more firmly.

"She . . . has a sister," Zhen replied hesitantly.

"What does that have to do with anything?" Ah Veng asked. "I know she has a sister."

"I don't think you get what I'm saying. She has a biological sister, Ah Veng."

"Yeah, I've seen her sister at her house."

"No, listen to me. Everyone in the town knows her because her biological father is Yuen Kaew. Now, I know that you know that name because everyone knows his name. He's one of the richest people, and that movie theater that Rose works at is owned by him."

"That still doesn't make any sense, though. She lives in a poor . . ." Ah Veng trailed off. His eyebrows furrowed together as he tried to think.

"Yeah, she lives in a poor area because her father gave her away as an infant for business purposes. He gave her to a poor family, to acquire more workers, and they had their own kids, so that's the sister that you were thinking of."

"What?" Ah Veng whispered. "Why would anyone do that?"

"That girl that you saw at the party is none other than Rose's real sister. She played you, Ah Veng. I had my doubts, but I wasn't sure."

Ah Veng slid down the wall with his head in his hands.

"I'm so sorry, my friend, but Rose is not the girl you met at the party. I can guarantee that she wanted to set you up with her sister on purpose. I bet she's even been tormenting Rose at work about the fact that you think that she's her. About the fact that you won't want Rose when you learn the truth because she's not the wealthy girl you saw in the very beginning. She's tricked and messed with your hearts."

Ah Veng hit the ground in frustration. He was crying. He didn't know what to think. He liked Rose, but the fact that he thought she was her sister messed with his head. She probably knew he thought she was someone else, which was probably the thing holding her back and probably why she was always upset after work.

"Ah Veng?" Rose called worriedly from the end of the hallway.

"Why didn't you tell me?" he shouted.

"Tell you what?" she asked, shocked at his outburst and slightly afraid.

"You know what I'm talking about," he said, rubbing his eyes.

Rose burst into tears once she realized what he meant. "She made me. She said that if I didn't go along with it that she would tell her father to fire me, and you know I need the money, Ah Veng."

"Please leave," he said.

"Ah Veng, I promise, I didn't want to," she said, rushing over.

He pushed her away. "Leave."

"Please believe me," she pleaded. "I do care about you. It wasn't just an act."

"I said leave," he yelled.

"Come on, I'll walk you home," Cheng said, gently dragging her towards the front door. "He just needs some time, but I promise you that he'll cool down. He'll be knocking on your door again in no time."

"I'm sorry," Rose called, sobbing as Cheng led her out the front door.

Ah Veng curled up even tighter. He felt someone tap him on the shoulder and heard voices in the distance. He didn't want to move. His heart felt crushed. His mind was a mess. He didn't want to think about anything. Someone lifted him off the floor, and he complied. Everything was blurry through his tears. Somehow, he ended up in his room and then on his bed. He was out cold before the door even snapped shut.

* * *

Gunfire. Explosions. Screaming. Shrieking. Smoke was so prominent that nothing else could be seen. People were falling left and right. What was going on? He flew higher, trying to see, but choked on the gas that was spreading ever so quickly. Everything blacked out. He expected to wake up in bed, but instead, he woke up in the middle of a cotton field. Someone was crying out in pain. The sound of a whip echoed. A slave was being beaten. That scene faded. He ended up in a hospital. People were dying. So much death. It went dark. Then there was a street. A child was getting kidnapped. A bank was being robbed. A building was crumbling. A bomb had gone off. Time ticked. At every second, something went wrong.

Each little tick marked a diabolical sentence of doom, doomed to be repeated throughout history.

* * *

Ah Veng jolted awake covered in sweat. His watch was ticking in his ear. He pulled his hands out from under his head and rolled onto his back to look out the window. It was still dark. His heart hurt. He couldn't believe that he was stupid enough to fall for that trap. He also couldn't believe that he fell for Rose when she had been forced to act like she liked him. *Is it weird that it feels like my heart is bleeding?*

He thought about the red roses he'd seen that day when he first walked Rose home. Roses as red as blood. Crying, broken-hearted, bleeding red roses.

CHAPTER 11

BE A MAN

August 1960

"AH VENG. AH VENG!" ZHEN SAID a little more insistently, shaking his friend awake.

"Go away," he mumbled, pushing at the hands disturbing his slumber.

"No. I will not go away. You need to stop this nonsense. They're going to fire you soon if you don't get yourself together. It's been over a month! I will not tolerate this any longer."

"I know," Ah Veng replied sleepily, rubbing at his bloodshot eyes.

"Then why aren't you doing something about it?! That girl has been worse off than you. She's been crying all the time and she even comes by to check on you."

"She has?"

"Yes, we just never let her see you because you've been so out of it lately. We're afraid of what you'll do, and I'm serious about that. You need to figure out your life and let go of things. It wasn't even Rose's fault to begin with, and you know that. You're just not accepting it."

Ah Veng sat up slowly before he started crying again.

"Just look at me. How manly is it for a guy to cry as much as I do? She deserves better. Not some stupid guy that fell for her sister's games."

"You don't get it, do you?" Zhen sighed, shaking his head. "She doesn't care, Ah Veng! And she does like you. I saw it on her face. She's in love with you as much as you are with her. You just need to stop acting like a baby and be a man. At least go see her. Apologize or something. Because when you told her to leave, she wilted, just like the petals of a flower. It was like she didn't know what else to do. Please, Ah Veng. Let it go. You both deserve better, and you have the chance to fix this and create a better life for the both of you. So don't miss out on your one chance. And make your decision before it's too late," Zhen said, pausing by the door and glancing back at his lost and depressed friend once more before going downstairs to grab breakfast and head to work.

Ah Veng sat there. He didn't want to feel anything. He didn't want to think about anything. But Zhen's words resonated in his mind. Perhaps it was time that he got his life together. Jian-min had been by to see him a few times, and yet Ah Veng had not been in the mood to talk even to him. He felt bad about that. He should do this for the man that saved him from worse paths in life, to make him proud.

Ah Veng stood and went to the top of the stairs. Zhen was heading out the front door.

"I'll do it," Ah Veng said.

"What?" Zhen asked, turning in shock to finally see Ah Veng out of his room.

"You're right. I need to get myself together and fix this before it's too late. I'm sorry. I just needed—"

"Time," Zhen finished for him with a small smile.

"Yeah," Ah Veng sighed, running a hand through his hair.

"We get it. Honestly, it just worried us how long you were taking, and I should have talked to you a while ago, but I was scared you would get more upset." Zhen laughed nervously.

"Sorry about that. I guess I was kind of a mess."

"It's alright. So, you're going to go see her today, right?"

"Yeah, I'll do that."

"Great. I'm proud of you, my friend," Zhen said. "I'll be sure to tell the bosses that you're talking to her today and that you just need one more day. Hopefully they'll be okay with that."

"Thanks, I really appreciate it."

"No problem. Anytime," Zhen replied.

Ah Veng went back to his room to grab a change of clothes before going to the bathroom to shower for the first time in at least a week. Over the last month, his coworkers had to drag him out of bed to eat, shower or go to work. He was extremely grateful for them and felt somewhat guilty that he could not find a way to express his thanks. He shook his head and grabbed his towel. *Now isn't the time to be thinking of those things. There is always later to show gratitude.* His first priority should have been Rose, but his mind was reeling. *What do you say to someone after breaking their heart? I'm sorry? How are you doing? Are you okay? Do you forgive me? There aren't that many options.* He hadn't seen her in so long. And then it dawned on him. He missed her. A lot. It wasn't her sister that he had fallen in love with. It was Rose.

* * *

He shifted from one foot to another across the street in order to keep himself from running away. He hated having to wait to see if she was even working that day. It was so nerve-wracking. It worried him that she was not in her usual spot, but then again, he hadn't been there in a while, and they could have changed her position. He tried going over what he was going to say to her. He couldn't remember if he was going to apologize first or give his speech and then apologize. *Which one would be better?* he wondered.

His head snapped up and he narrowed his gaze on the front door of the theater. She stepped out and said something to someone inside before bowing her head and hurrying down the street. Ah Veng took off after her, wondering what was wrong and why she ran off so quickly. He followed but made sure to stay a safe distance away. It reminded him of the first time he trailed after her. The thought crossed his mind that he should probably approach her or at least call out before he freaked her out again; however, it was too late because by the time he got the nerve to call out to her, she disappeared around a corner and was gone.

He stood there, baffled. *Where did she go?* They were in the middle of the forest. *Is she hiding or something?* He glanced over and noticed that they were near the cemetery. Chills went up his spine. The silence was eerie. He contemplated saying her name, but was too scared to open his mouth. *Seriously, where could she have gone?*

"Hello?" he stuttered. It came out as a soft whisper. "Rose?"

No answer. Complete silence.

"Rose?" he tried calling a bit louder. His voice wavered.

Still no answer. Ah Veng shivered. Not a breeze rustled the leaves, and it was already getting dark even though it was barely afternoon. Perhaps a storm was brewing and would arrive soon. *Why aren't there any noises at all? Where is all the wildlife?*

"If you're hiding, you can come out," he said. His voice rose higher, ending in a squeak. He took a tiny step forward and jumped when a branch snapped. Suddenly, he heard someone sniffle. His focus shifted to somewhere behind a row of larger tombstones.

"Rose, if that's you, please come out. I just want to talk," Ah Veng said a little more confidently. He took a step closer.

Something poked him in the back, and he screamed.

"Ah Veng! Calm down, it's just me!" Rose reassured him after he had spun around.

"You scared me," he said, trying to catch his breath.

"I didn't mean to, but you scared me too, following me again. I thought I already explained to you how creepy it is when you do that," she scolded.

"I'm sorry. I couldn't think of what to say to you," he admitted sheepishly.

"It's alright. I'm just glad to see that you've finally stepped foot outside of the house," she replied, smiling softly.

"I've missed you, and I'm sorry about everything that happened and if I said anything hurtful and that I didn't put enough trust in you and that—"

"Ah Veng, stop," she said, laughing slightly. "It's okay. I'm serious. I forgave you a long time ago, and I was just waiting for you to accept what happened and move on."

"Really?" Ah Veng asked. "So does this mean that we're okay?"

"Of course we're okay," she said, smiling and holding out her hand to him.

* * *

September 1960

Soft music played in the background as Ah Veng waited anxiously under the shade of a tree. He looked out across the little field, slightly nervous but excited. He was one step further towards building a life. His mind went to Rose. He wondered how she felt at the moment. It was crazy to think that this would have never happened if he hadn't talked to her that day.

A lopsided grin played on Ah Veng's mouth as he leaned against the tree waiting for his signal.

Zhen smirked, joining him under the shade to escape some of the heat. "Well, somebody's really happy."

"What do you mean?" Ah Veng asked, quickly wiping the smile off of his face, but he couldn't help laughing. "You know, I didn't think that she would say yes."

"Why wouldn't she? I told you, she waited outside the house almost every day to see if you were ready to see her. It was like you passed on the lovesick-puppy disease to her or something; even I can attest to the fact that you're pretty infectious at times."

Ah Veng grinned. "Hey! I did not pass it to her. She caught it on her own, so I'm not the only weird one."

"Oh, shut up," Zhen said. "You stalking a girl is way creepier than her hanging around outside the house just because she wanted to talk to you."

"Alright, alright. Fair enough," Ah Veng admitted.

"Hey, look, there's Jian-min! He made it!" Zhen exclaimed, pointing. Jian-min had taken a seat towards the back.

"Oh, good. I was afraid that he wouldn't be able to come."

"Aw, you know that he wouldn't miss it for the world. He's literally the reason why you're even standing here."

"I know, and I still feel as though I haven't thanked him enough."

"There's only so much you can thank a person, you know. It's not like you can go about following them around to thank them every single second. Which . . . I can actually see you doing, with your stalker instincts and all."

Ah Veng threw his friend a glare.

"Write him a note or something. That way he'll have it forever and can look back on it whenever he wants to." Zhen shrugged.

"That's a good idea," Ah Veng said, smiling at his friend.

He remembered how immature Zhen used to be, and it made him proud that his friend had matured so much, especially during the times Ah Veng had been down. He couldn't help but think about what would have happened to him if so many caring people hadn't come into his life. Zhen snapped him out of his thoughts.

"Hey, that's your cue," he said, nudging Ah Veng.

"Oh, right. Wish me luck."

"Yeah, you're going to need it," Zhen snickered, pushing Ah Veng playfully.

He threw his friend another glare over his shoulder and walked out front where he faced the crowd, impatiently waiting for Rose to show up and walk down the aisle. His hands were getting sweaty, and he briefly rubbed them together before looking at all of his coworkers, bosses, and friends in the crowd. He glanced around until he found Jian-min. Their eyes met, and he was given a huge grin and a thumbs-up before the music started; the bride had arrived.

He sucked in a breath. She was gorgeous. They may not have had very much money, but her adoptive mother had done a very good job at sewing her a dress. It flowed behind her and swirled through the rose petals of red, white, and pink littering the ground. His smile grew even wider as he realized that she was holding a single red rose in her hands. Her veil hid her face, but he knew that it was just as lovely as the rest of her. He didn't stop staring, even after she was standing in front of him and even as they exchanged vows and exchanged rings. What he desired most of all was to see her face—for her to lift up that veil. He barely heard the words spoken throughout the ceremony. His mind drifted to that wedding he had seen in his dreams; he'd seen what it was going to be like, but he never thought that it would feel this way. The emotions were overwhelming.

Finally, he heard the words that he had been waiting for.

"You may now kiss the bride."

She slowly lifted the veil, and the fluttering wings of a blue butterfly clip holding her stray hairs caught his attention. It was beautiful, but she was even prettier. Her eyes were mesmerizing. The kiss didn't last as long as he wanted it to before the people were cheering and clapping. He held his wife's hand and smiled at her before they turned to face their loved ones in the audience, eager to embark on a new journey and path in life, yet slightly fearful for what was to come.

* * *

1961

"AH VENG, YOU NEED A HOUSE," Jian-min said. "Your wife is pregnant, and you can't keep living in that workhouse. It's not fair to her or the baby, and that one room is too small for the three of you."

"We could make it work."

"I don't doubt that, but I want to do this for you."

"That's what you always say, but you've already done way too much," Ah Veng insisted.

"There's never too much that can be done. You're technically my adopted son, and I treat you like my own. You know that. So please, let me do this."

Ah Veng sighed.

"Alright, but I don't want you spending extra money on workers. I'll build it when I'm not at work, and I'm sure that my friends and coworkers wouldn't mind helping as well."

"Are you sure? It would drag out the process," Jian-min said hesitantly, wishing that Ah Veng didn't always argue with him on things like this.

"Yes, we have time. It was just recently that we found out she's pregnant, so we have a few months until the baby will get here anyway, and there will most likely still be a few months to spare."

"I guess that'll be okay then. I'll pay the down payment for the land tomorrow and then find out where we can order materials. Hopefully after all that is settled, you and your friends can get to work. Your coworkers know how to build a house, right?"

"Um, not exactly," Ah Veng replied, laughing nervously.

"Ah Veng!"

"What? We just work with wiring. But I can teach them! It'll be a learning experience!"

"Seriously, I put way too much trust in you. Do you even remember how to build?"

"Of course. I did it for most of my childhood."

"Okay," Jian-min breathed. "I'm trusting you on this one."

"It'll be fine," Ah Veng said, waving his hand nonchalantly.

"Tell me that once everything's already said and done or when the house is finished," Jian-min said before he walked out of the room, mumbling to himself.

* * *

"You're kidding me right?" Zhen asked, gaping at the empty land. "We're starting from scratch?!"

"What did you expect?" Ah Veng replied, bending down to pick up a hammer.

"Well, I knew that we had to build it but not from completely nothing."

"Ah Veng, what is this?!" Cheng cried, running over.

"Yeah," the other guys chipped in nervously.

"Hey, you all need to calm down. I think that you have forgotten that I used to build houses, and I plan on teaching you all. It'll be a great experience, don't you think? I mean, you'll be able to say, 'Yeah, I helped build that house,' and bragging rights are always great."

The men continued muttering hesitantly.

"Guys, maybe we should have a little more faith in him. If he says that he's going to teach us, then I'm sure that he's going to do it, right?" Zhen asked the men.

"Right," some of them answered.

"So, let's get to work! Tell us what to do, Ah Veng, and we'll do it!"

* * *

"Oh my gosh, did you see that? Did you?" Zhen asked, pointing excitedly.

"See, I told you that it wasn't that hard," Ah Veng replied, grinning proudly at his friend.

"This is actually kind of fun!" he exclaimed.

"Yeah, I expected it to be gruesome work, but I'm actually enjoying myself as well," Cheng called from where he was hammering a nail into the wall.

"Now, this is some good brotherhood bonding moments. Don't you guys forget it!" Zhen yelled with a whoop.

"Okay, you're getting a little too excited," Ah Veng said, rolling his eyes before checking on the guys in the back.

He was really impressed with how quickly the guys were able to learn. Perhaps it was because they were electricians and knew the general layout of houses. He circled back around to the front. Jian-min stood there, admiring their work.

"Ah Veng, just the guy I was looking for," Jian-min said, smiling.

"Do you like what you see?" Ah Veng smirked.

"Don't be all smart with me. I believed in you and your friends."

"Not until I convinced you."

"Okay, that's somewhat true, but I've always had faith in you."

* * *

"Is that it? Is that it?" Cheng asked excitedly.

"I'm pretty sure," Ah Veng said, stepping back to take everything in.

"It's finished!" Zhen yelled.

The men all let out a cheer and laughed, slapping each other on the backs. Ah Veng couldn't help the grin that spread across his face. He let the men celebrate for a bit before making them quiet down so that he could speak.

"I just wanted to say thank you so much for helping me with this. I know that myself and Rose appreciate this so much. When my child is born we will also tell him, or her, that you all were the people that built us the house that we live in. I also want to thank Jian-min, who was the one that made all this happen by buying the land and materials and supplies. I really wouldn't be standing here today if it was not for him."

He looked towards the back where Jian-min was standing—the man who was so much like a father to him. The men all clapped and cheered before rushing forward to congratulate Ah Veng. They then talked excitedly amongst themselves and pointed out certain things that they did on the house. Zhen walked over and slapped Ah Veng on the back quite forcefully.

"Ah, why'd you hit me so hard?" Ah Veng winced.

"Because look at you. Successful in commanding your own team of builders and with a wife and a child on the way. Remember that time I had to tell you to stop being a baby and to be a man?"

"Erm, yeah," Ah Veng laughed, a little embarrassed.

Zhen smirked. "Well, you finally are one. Took you long enough."

"Hey, I don't see you with any wife or kids," Ah Veng shot back.

"Yeah, yeah, I'm working on it," Zhen replied, rolling his eyes and walking away.

* * *

June 1961

The heat was already overbearing, and it was only morning. Ah Veng paced outside their home, listening carefully and waiting patiently. He looked closely at the house to distract himself and marveled at the work that was put into it.

Ah Veng winced as his wife screamed again. *Why is it taking so long? Do births usually last for hours?* He ran a hand through his hair, which was wet with sweat. The shade under the tree looked enticing, but he wanted to be near the house so that he could hear what was going on.

Ah Veng was startled once more by a scream. It was frustrating and worrisome. *Is everything going okay in there?* He paced closer to the front door, wishing that someone would at least tell him what was going on. Rose's adopted mother had specifically told him that he wasn't allowed to go inside until he heard the baby's cry or was told that it was okay to go back in. That was at least two hours ago. He sighed, and busied himself with his own thoughts as the memories of building the house came back to him.

He heard it. The baby cried—he was absolutely sure of it. His hand hovered at the door. *Should I go in? Should I wait?* He wasn't really sure. Just as he reached for the handle, he had to jump back because the door flew open.

"It's a boy!" Rose's adopted sister exclaimed, beaming with pride in being the one to tell him the news.

"Can I see him?" Ah Veng asked, hardly able to contain his excitement.

He'd wanted his firstborn to be a son but hadn't thought that it would actually come true.

"Yeah, come in, come in," she said, waving him in.

Ah Veng hurried after her into the bedroom where his wife was holding the little bundle of joy. Her face was pale, and she was drenched in sweat, but she still managed to smile at him when he entered. He slowly walked over to stare in amazement at his child, captivated. The soft blue blanket wrapped around him had butterflies stitched along the edges, and Ah Veng gently ran his fingers along them.

"Do you want to hold him?" Rose asked.

Her voice was weak, but she still managed to get the words out.

"Can I?"

"Of course you can," she said, laughing softly before handing the baby over to his father.

Ah Veng cradled the tiny child in his arms. It was such a beautiful moment of warmth and love. At that point in time, it seemed as though nothing could possibly go wrong—that life was abundant, that blessings filled it to the brim, overflowing and spilling out to be shared with the rest of the world.

"Ah Tap," Ah Veng said.

"What?" Rose asked.

"That's his name. Ah Tap."

"Oh," she smiled, "I like that. Is it his nickname?"

"Yes," Ah Veng said and smiled back before asking, "Who made the blanket?"

He fingered the trail of butterflies along the edges.

"My mother," she replied, enjoying the look on Ah Veng's face. She had never seen him so fascinated with anything before, and it was adorable to watch, especially when his significantly larger hand stroked the top of their child's. He examined the tiny fingers.

"How are they so small?"

"I don't know," Rose laughed weakly. "We were all that small at one point in time."

"That's crazy to think, though. It doesn't seem realistic."

"What do you mean? We had to come from somewhere."

"I know, it's just . . . I don't even know what to say."

Ah Veng handed the baby back to the mother, watching lovingly as she held the child close to her chest. He couldn't believe how much he loved their little family, and he knew that he was going to have a hard time leaving for work every morning.

"Alright, everything's cleaned up already," Rose's adopted mother said, entering the room. "Ah Veng, let the mother and the child rest. Rose really needs time to recover. Come on, out, out." She shooed him out of the room.

He glanced back longingly at the love of his life and their small child before he stepped out, wondering who that child would become in the future. Ah Veng was going to work hard to provide for his family and to let his children have the opportunity to experience things that he never had the chance to experience. *Is this what being a man means? Working hard to provide for my family? Isn't that what Father always told me, all those years ago as we stood next to the river? Am I to be both provider and protector?*

He didn't want his childhood to be experienced by his own children, so he sure hoped so.

CHAPTER 12

SHELLS FROM THE SEA

September 1963
Seria, Brunei

THE CHILD WAS CRYING TO THE point of a shrill shrieking. They did not know how to ease her suffering. She was only a year old, and yet her pain was immense as the virus took hold. Her name was Ah Hiang, and the crying was good; it was the silence that scared her parents the most. The extremely high fevers made them tremble in fear. Ah Veng looked helplessly at their pale little girl fighting for her life. Rose would take her to the Brunei hospital today. They could not wait any longer; Ah Hiang needed the treatment even if they had to scrounge up all the money they had. It was a risk that they had to take.

Unfortunately, Ah Veng had to stay behind and work while his wife and their eldest son, Ah Tap, stayed with Ah Hiang. He wished he could stay with his family, but he needed to keep working to pay the hospital bills that were about to pile up, sky high. Rose was packing a few of their things into a bag, throwing them in quickly and not paying attention to how they were arranged. The screams started to give Ah Veng a headache, but that was the least of his worries. Rose was stressed almost to breaking.

"How far is it again?" she asked as she tried to decide what else she would need to bring.

"About an hour or two. The bus stop at the edge of town should take you straight there. You won't have to switch buses if you tell the driver ahead of time that the hospital is where you're headed."

"Okay, and when I get there, I just have to say that she has polio and needs treatment, right? Ah Veng, I don't know what I'm doing," she said, breaking down into tears.

"Shh, it'll be alright," he said, sitting down next to her on the bed to simply hold her. "It will all work out. I don't know what will happen for sure, but I know for a fact that it will all work out in the end."

"Ah Veng! Look at her. It scares me . . ."

He started crying, pushing aside the fact that men were not supposed to let their emotions show. Hundreds of people were dying from the polio virus every day, and here they were with barely any money, trying to do everything they could to save their daughter. It was so discouraging, so heart-breaking that they could not provide her with the best care. But they were trying to make do.

"You should get going. The quicker she gets care, the better."

"You're right," Rose said, wiping her face.

Ah Veng helped her finish packing before giving his wife a kiss and his son a hug. He stood in the doorway, watching them walk off with bags and a screaming baby in hand. Tears streamed down his face as he shut the door. He sat down at the kitchen table with his head in his hands. Some decisions in life were just so difficult to make. He'd had to leave Jian-min, his coworkers and all his friends behind to get his daughter closer to the treatment she needed. His mind went back to the day that he had to tell all the important people in his life that he was leaving.

* * *

"Hey, did you hear that Malaya is now named Malaysia?" Zhen asked as they walked back from work one day.

"What? Why?" Ah Veng questioned, scrunching up his face, not sure if he liked the new name.

"I don't know, but I'm pretty sure it's because we united with Malaya, Singapore and North Borneo, I believe."

"We, as in . . . ?"

"Sarawak."

"What? When did that happen?"

"Sometime recent. I heard the other men talking about it, and everyone in town is too. Isn't it crazy to think that we're literally a new country now? It's like they piled us all together and handed us a new name. The fact that Singapore is a part of it makes me laugh, though. I doubt they'll even last a few years before they either get expelled or claim independence for themselves."

"Malaysia, huh?" Ah Veng laughed before he veered off the path.

"Where are you going?" Zhen called.

"I have to talk to the bosses," Ah Veng replied.

"Is everything okay?" Zhen asked, concerned.

"You know that it's not," Ah Veng sighed.

It was then that Zhen knew Ah Veng's intentions.

"Please tell me you're not leaving."

"You've been over and seen Rose, Ah Tap and especially Ah Hiang. I have to do what is best for them. You know that."

"But, Ah Veng—"

"They're offering treatment in Brunei," he said, cutting his friend off. "I applied to work with the Shell Oil and Gas Company a while back, and I just got a reply. They want me to start next week."

"What!? That's in a few days!" Zhen exclaimed, not prepared to lose his best friend.

Long-distant friendships were too hard to maintain, which meant that they would most likely not stay in touch unless Ah Veng came back to visit.

"I'm sorry. I just couldn't bring myself to tell any of you. I mean, Jian-min knew, but that was because he was the one that told me I needed to be closer to where my daughter can receive care. He's also the one that found me the job through some of his connections."

"Ah Veng," Zhen whined before sighing. "I'm going to miss you, a lot."

"I know, and I'll miss you too. But don't worry. I'm sure that I'll be back one day. This is just a step that we have to take right now."

"It's understandable, though. Too many people are dying from the virus."

A chill ran up Ah Veng's spine. He didn't want to even think about the possibility of losing his child. "I should get going," he said.

"Are you coming over to the workhouse later?"

"Yeah, I'll tell everyone else then."

"Okay, see you."

Ah Veng waved as he walked off to the company's offices.

He hesitated when he reached the door, unprepared for the changes that were about to happen. The door opened and he moved away. A worker walked out briskly as if he was angry. Ah Veng frowned, hoping that the bosses were in a good mood. Everyone knew that they hated losing workers since it meant that they would have to find a replacement. He walked in.

"*Tunggu sebentar*,"[36] the receptionist said to someone on the phone before greeting Ah Veng. "Ah Veng! What are you doing here?"

"I need to talk to the bosses, but I'm not sure which one."

"Well, what do you need to talk to them about?"

"I'm leaving. My daughter needs treatment in Brunei and I got a job over there."

"Oh, I'm really sorry to hear that. One sec. Let me go check."

---

36 Wait one moment please.

She headed towards the back offices and poked her head in one of the doorways before motioning to Ah Veng.

"You can talk to Tong-mu as soon as he gets off the phone," she said.

"Okay, thank you," Ah Veng replied before walking in to take a seat.

He looked at the man in front of him, taking in the big frame of someone who held an abundance of power. The top of Tong-mu's head glimmered underneath the ceiling lights, complementing the clean suit he wore. His tie was a bright red, the only splash of color present in the room besides the golden watch that hugged his wrist tightly. Tong-mu was one of the most important bosses in the company since he handled all the financial aspects and made sure that there were enough employees. Ah Veng glanced away. The man was intimidating, leaning back in his chair and stroking his chin as if deep in thought about what the person was saying on the other end of the line.

"*Tidak, saya minta maaf, tetapi saya tidak bersetuju. Selemat tinggal,*"[37] he said, slamming the phone down and making Ah Veng jump at his suddenness.

"Sorry about that, Ah Veng. People can be so annoying at times. Now, what is it that you wanted to talk about?"

Ah Veng hesitated. He wasn't sure if he could get the words out.

"This is bad news, isn't it?" Tong-mu sighed. "Alright, let's get this over with. Come on, just tell me."

"I'm taking my family to Brunei because Ah Hiang needs treatment for the virus and I had to get a job over there," Ah Veng finally blurted out.

"I see. That seems to be happening quite often now."

Ah Veng couldn't look his boss in the eyes. Instead, he stared at a drawing on the wall that the man's child had created. It was a field covered with flowers, rabbits, and their native butterflies.

"However, I do understand. You need to do what's best for your family. Was today your last day, then?"

---

37   No, I'm sorry, but I do not agree. Goodbye.

"Yes," Ah Veng said, snapping his attention back to the conversation.

"Alright, I'll put it down and make sure to let the other bosses know. Thank you for telling us and not simply leaving. Some guys just take off and disappear one day."

"No problem," Ah Veng answered, standing to make his way out the door, eager to leave the man's presence.

"I noticed that you were admiring the drawing on my wall," Tong-mu said.

Ah Veng stopped and turned back around.

"My daughter made it, and if you ask me, it's pretty impressive for a five-year-old."

"It's pretty," Ah Veng said, smiling. Tong-mu was silent for a while, and Ah Veng started to wonder if he should leave, but Tong-mu started talking again. "Ah Veng, I understand how it feels wanting to do what's best for your daughter. Just take care of yourself and your family, alright? Don't worry about what other people think."

"Thank you so much," Ah Veng replied with tears threatening to fall from his eyes.

He blinked them back and walked out. The receptionist wasn't at her desk, so he left without saying a proper goodbye. Stepping out the door, he wasn't sure if he was ready to tell his coworkers, but he forced himself to walk towards the workhouse anyway. They had to know eventually, and he might as well get it over with. *Why do goodbyes have to be so difficult?* he thought, looking up at the clouds in the sky. For once, it was not raining, and the sun beamed down as if it were trying to lighten the mood of the day.

A cloud blew past, casting a shadow on the earth below. Ah Veng stopped at the front door of the workhouse, hesitating once more before shaking his head and forcing himself to knock. Zhen opened it and gave Ah Veng a sad smile before opening it wider so that his dear friend could step inside.

"They're all in the living room," he said.

"Thanks," Ah Veng replied, taking a deep breath. "I might as well get this over with, right?"

"That would probably be best, and you'll be much more relieved after it's all said and done."

"Yeah, you're right," he said, slowly walking through the front hallway of the house that he spent so many years living in with such caring and supportive men.

It would be his last time stepping foot in that house, and somehow, he knew it.

"Hey, guys, Ah Veng's here!" Cheng yelled when he saw Ah Veng standing at the doorway.

"Ah Veng!" some of the men exclaimed. "What are you doing here?"

"I need to talk to you all," Ah Veng replied.

"Alright, hey, settle down," Zhen shouted. "Okay, that's better. He's here because of a serious matter, so just hear him out, okay? And don't give him any trouble about it."

"Thanks," Ah Veng said, glancing at Zhen before speaking to the rest of the men. "As some of you know, my daughter, Ah Hiang, has polio, and she needs treatment in Brunei." He stopped to take a deep breath before continuing. "Therefore, we're moving there. My last day working was today because I start my new job next week."

The men started murmuring.

"Where are you working?" one of them asked.

"On the coast of Seria in Brunei. I will be working for Shell, an oil and gas company there."

"Are you getting paid well?" another called out.

"Well, I think the pay is okay. I'll get paid 120 a month, but that's hardly enough to live off of and pay for the treatment, so I don't know. I'll figure it out, I guess."

"We're going to miss you," Cheng said, standing and giving Ah Veng a hug.

Usually it would have been weird to receive hugs from his coworkers, but he actually felt as though he needed the hugs, and slowly, one by one, each of the men he worked with over the years stood up to say their goodbyes. They laughed a bit, cried a bit, and shared their memories from over the years before Ah Veng walked out for the last time, never to return to that home.

* * *

November 1970

Clouds started to gather in the far east, but the sun was still shining brightly from above. The waters glistened and gleamed. Ah Veng frowned. He didn't want to participate in the competition. His wife really wanted him to, and he knew that it would greatly benefit his family; however, the pool seemed too restrictive for him. He preferred to swim in rivers or lakes where nature was not impeded from living to the best of its ability. He sighed before walking back to his car.

The small, milky Volkswagen Beetle sat just where he had left it. He took pride in having a car in good condition. It meant that he could transport his family, especially since they drove back to Miri sometimes to visit friends and relatives, although they did not go back often since the drive was long. It took about two or three hours traveling on a sandy road, and the car would get stuck in the mud sometimes if they got a lot of rain. He had also gotten back in touch with his sisters and stepsiblings, and while they didn't have the best relationship, they at least visited each other occasionally, so they weren't complete strangers.

Ah Veng started the car and headed back home. His stepsister was getting quite annoying these days. She insisted on moving in with them, which made no sense. The only explanation he could muster up was that she wanted something. So the answer was always no. Their little home was too small anyways, and there were already too many people squeezed into it.

The house came into view, and he smiled when he noticed that the children were playing outside. Ah Hiang stood at the top of the steps, clearly bossing her younger siblings around while her older brother stood to the side, not looking amused. Ah Veng felt his heart squeeze with joy. Ah Hiang had crawled for so many years that they were afraid she would never have a normal life. But she had survived and was now able to walk.

"Papá is home," Ah Lay, his second son, shouted and pointed at the car pulling into the driveway.

He always felt happy when he could go home. He was thankful the company provided housing; otherwise, his family would be on the streets. His kids waved, and he waved back through the window as he shut off the engine. There was Ah Tap, his eldest son, then Ah Hiang, the eldest daughter, followed by Ah Lay, Ah Den, Mimi, and then King King, who was not outside because he was only a little over a year old, and Rose usually liked to keep an eye on him. There was also one more child on the way. He was hoping for another girl but would be content with either a boy or a girl. It was funny to think that the names given to his children were not the actual names that they went by. The midwife that delivered his children liked to keep a common surname across all the boys and girls in one family; it eventually got too confusing, and so their kids went by nicknames.

"Papá, Papá," his youngest daughter, Mimi, giggled as she hobbled over to fling her arms around him. Ah Den and Ah Lay ran over as well.

"What have you all been up to today?" he asked, smiling down at them.

"Chores," Ah Lay replied, rolling his eyes and pouting.

"Well, you must have finished early if you all have time to play right now," Ah Veng laughed.

"We weren't playing," Ah Hiang called.

"No? Then what was going on?" Ah Veng asked, walking to his two older children.

"Ayi is mad," Ah Tap said, jerking his thumb towards the front door. "Those three made a mess," he then grumbled as he narrowed his eyes at his three younger siblings.

"Hey, it wasn't all their fault. They don't know better," Ah Hiang argued, glaring at her older brother.

"If there is no consensus on whose fault it is, then it might as well be everyone's. I'm going to go on in and talk to your mother." Ah Veng moved around his kids and went into the house to find his wife scrubbing the kitchen floor.

"You really shouldn't be on the floor doing that. Let me help. What happened?" he asked.

Rose looked up and sighed before she handed him the rag. He helped her stand up, and she sat down in a chair before talking.

"They tried to cook without supervision when Ah Tap and Ah Hiang were out. I must have been busy with King King, and, I mean, it wasn't exactly their fault, but I couldn't handle them in the house anymore, so I told them to stay outside."

"What is it that they spilled?" he asked. Whatever it was, it was obviously hard to get off.

"I have no idea. I don't even know what they were trying to cook. Did you think about what you're going to do yet?" Rose asked.

"What? Oh, you mean the competition tomorrow." He trailed off.

"Yes, please do it for the sake of all of us. We could really use the money."

"I know," he sighed and looked up at her. "I guess I'll just do it, then."

"Really?" she piped up.

"Yeah. I went to look at the pool before I came home, and I don't want to, but I will," he replied, standing up to wash the rag in the sink.

"I'm sure you'll do great."

"I hope so," he said, hanging the cloth up to dry. "Should I ask the kids to come in, or do you want them to stay out there for a bit?"

"Have them stay for a bit longer. I need a breath of air for a while," Rose answered, closing her eyes to rest a bit.

"Alright, I'm going to shower and head to bed," he said, walking out of the room.

It was not until later that night that he heard his children file back into the house. He was tired and eventually fell asleep to their indistinctive chatter.

* * *

A brilliant world of blue stretched its arms in glorious vastness. Creatures swam beneath the surface of that distant world, relishing the feelings of security within their mother's arms. She wrapped around them as they swam, caressing and stroking, sending a message of assurance that they were loved. Ah Veng sat in the sand of the shore, watching as people and kids ran in and out of the water, laughing and splashing as they enjoyed their present happiness. They failed to acknowledge the fact that they were playing in the arms of a whole 'nother world. The unreachable. The place where humans could not live. Where humans could never uncover the deepest and darkest secrets within. No matter how hard they tried, it was impossible. Their worlds were meant to be separate.

A rhyme floated through his mind:

> *That glistening body shined oh so bright.*
> *On the surface, the waters of love and light.*
> *On the inside, the waters of secrets and fright.*
> *The waters of the ocean.*

* * *

Ah Veng yelped and sat up in bed. Something wet and cold had hit his face, and his children were laughing.

"What . . ."

He rubbed his eyes and looked at them. Ah Den was holding a bucket of water, and Ah Lay stood next to him. They were both grinning mischievously.

"Why are you all up so early?" he asked, glaring at them. "That was not nice, you know. Make sure you don't ever do it again or you'll really be in trouble."

The two of them hung their heads but snickered.

"We just thought that we should prepare you for the swimming competition today," Ah Den said quietly, holding back a laugh.

"And it was a bad decision on your behalf. Now, clean up this water. It better be gone by the time I'm about to leave or you're not going."

The boys ran from the room to find a cloth.

"What was that about?" Rose asked from the doorway, saying, "They asked for a bucket of water, but I didn't know what for."

"This," Ah Veng replied, pointing at the wet sheets, table and floor.

"Oh." She trailed off. "Sorry about that." She grimaced. "I shouldn't have given it to them."

"It's fine. I told them that they have to clean it up or else they're not coming with us."

"Fair enough," she said. "You should probably get up and get ready anyway. You don't want to be late."

He rolled off the bed and stood up to stretch before following his wife to the kitchen. Breakfast was already on the table, and some of the kids were eating.

"*Selemat pagi,*"[38] he said to them before sitting down to eat his share. "Did you all sleep well?"

Mimi's head bobbed up and down.

"No," Ah Tap blurted out and scowled. "The other two woke me up really early to ask for a bucket."

"At least they didn't dump water on you."

"Is that why your hair is wet?" Ah Hiang asked.

"Yup."

"Why'd you tell them where the bucket was?" Ah Hiang demanded, glaring at her older brother.

"I didn't! I told them to go away."

"You had to have told them. Otherwise they wouldn't have known

---

38 Good morning.

where it was."

"They asked me," Rose interrupted. "Now hurry up and finish eating. We don't want to make your father late."

Ah Veng put his plate in the sink and left the room to get ready. His kids had such different personalities, and he loved each and every one of them.

"We're finished," the two mischievous boys said in unison, standing up quickly when their father entered the room.

"You're sure it's all cleaned up?" he asked, glancing around them.

"Yes," they answered.

"Alright, go eat your breakfast, then, before you mother gets upset with you as well."

They scampered out. By the time he walked out, most of the kids were already playing outside while they waited, and Rose was holding King King by the door.

"You ready?" she asked.

"Yeah, I think so,"

"Alright, let's go," she said, pushing open the door and calling to the kids.

Ah Veng unlocked the car and waited as his children figured out a way to pile in comfortably at the back.

"No, you sit at the bottom," one of them whined. "You're smaller."

"I don't want to."

"Stop pushing me," another one grumbled.

He waited patiently; this was a common occurrence. He wished that they had a larger car, but they were lucky enough to have one at all, and they had to make do with what they had. Finally, they seemed to settle, and he shut the door for them before he got in the driver's seat so that they could head off. He was not prepared for this at all and hated that people would be watching him swim. It shouldn't be that big of a deal. It wouldn't even matter what place he came in. He just had to pass, and he would get the promotion, meaning that he would be able to work offshore and get a pay raise. It seemed simple enough, but the more he thought about it, the more it freaked him out.

"Look, we're here," one of his kids yelled from the backseat, and his heart skipped a beat.

Quite a few cars were already there, and people were in the pools warming up. He pulled into a parking spot and turned off the engine. The kids scrambled to get out of the car, but he didn't move.

"You okay?" Rose asked.

"Yeah, just thinking."

"Stop worrying. You're good at swimming. You've just never swam in an actual pool before, and there's not much of a difference. Just think about it as if you were swimming in a lake or river or something. Imagine yourself somewhere else if it really freaks you out that much."

He took a deep breath and opened the car door.

Rose took care of rounding up the kids to take them to the stands while he went in search of the bosses he was supposed to check in with. He finally spotted some of his coworkers.

"Hey, it's Ah Veng!" they yelled, waving.

He waved back and joined them. His boss was standing there as well, and he marked Ah Veng off.

"Alright, you might want to warm up with a few laps, and then whenever you're ready you can let me know and we'll time you."

"How many laps is it?" he asked.

"Just one when you're actually timed."

"Okay, thanks," he said, stripping down to his swimming trunks.

He looked uneasily at the water, unsure if he wanted to go through with this.

"Hey, man, are you alright?" one of the guys asked.

"Yeah, I'm fine."

He looked up at the stands to see his wife and kids waving at him. He felt a little bit better and smiled as he waved back. He walked to one of the empty lanes and dipped his foot in. It was freezing cold. He shivered a bit and then dove in, figuring that he should just get it over with. After a few laps, he got a little bit more confident and swam a few more before hopping out to tell his boss that he was ready.

"You warmed up enough?"

"Yes sir," Ah Veng replied.

"Alright, we'll time you in this first lane here. Just get in line behind those other men and watch for when we tell you to go once it's your turn."

He nodded and then did as he was told, looking up to search for his family again. More people were in the crowd, and when he finally found them, he gave them a thumbs-up. His wife smiled at him and seemed relieved. It made him glad that he was doing this for them.

Someone nudged him from behind. "Hey, you're next."

His attention snapped back to his bosses.

"You ready?" one of them asked.

"Yes," he answered.

"Okay. Ready . . . Set . . . Go."

He dove in and swam as fast as he could, envisioning himself fighting a current in a river. The water seemed to split before him as he cruised through. He had never felt his adrenaline pump so quickly before. The sensation was thrilling. His hand hit the wall. People started cheering when his time was called out. *Did I do good?* he wondered, pulling himself out of the water and padding over to where the towels were. He wiped himself off before grabbing his clothes to pull them on. By that time, his heart rate had gone down, and he had control over his breathing again.

"You did a really good job," someone behind him said.

"Oh, thanks," Ah Veng mumbled, briefly giving the guy a smile before going up into the stands to sit with his family.

He wasn't really in the mood to talk to the other guys because he wasn't quite sure if they would be genuine or sarcastic about how he did.

"That was great! I knew you could do it," Rose exclaimed once her husband found them.

"Are you sure?" he asked.

"Yes, I'm positive."

"Should we leave now?"

"What, no! We must stay for the results. It shouldn't be too much longer."

"I'm pretty sure I passed, but I doubt I would have placed, so we really don't have to stay."

"Come on, sit," his wife demanded. "You never know."

He sighed and took a seat, turning his attention to his kids to talk with them.

"You were fast," Ah Hiang said as she stared at the water below in fascination. The eight-year-old girl felt the desire to swim but was uncertain if she would be able to do so.

"Was I?" Ah Veng asked.

"Yeah," some of his other kids chimed in.

"It was like they said go and then you just dove in and you weren't there, and then you were going so fast we couldn't see you, and it was like, whoa, you were a fish or something."

Ah Veng laughed at Ah Lay's interpretation of the swim.

"It was like whoa, huh?"

"Yeah, it was crazy," the little boy said, nodding in excitement.

"Oh, Ah Veng, they're starting to announce names!" Rose said, clenching his arm.

He turned his attention to what they were saying.

"Then in third place we have Bao Sheng."

People clapped as the man who had congratulated Ah Veng earlier stood to make his way back down to the pool in order to receive his medal.

"In second place, with a time of 30.19, Chia Ah Veng."

"What?" he gasped, looking at his wife. "I think they made a mistake."

"No, don't be silly. Now go and get on down there," she scolded, nudging him.

"There's no way."

"Go on," she said, pushing him a bit harder.

He finally stood up and went down to receive his medal. He was shocked and had a hard time comprehending it.

"Congratulations," Sheng said.

Ah Veng smiled, sticking his hand out to shake the man's hand. "Thanks. Congrats to you too."

"I guess this means that we're getting sent offshore together."

"Probably," Ah Veng laughed.

He looked down and rubbed the medal around his neck. It was heavy. He gently traced the etchings on the silver. It shone brightly whenever he held it a certain way. His face glowed just as brilliantly when he held up the medal towards his family. His kids were bouncing up and down and his wife was beaming.

This was a moment he would never forget. They celebrated that night by simply sitting in their living room together to eat snacks and tell stories or sing songs while he played the guitar. The home was filled with such warmth and love, as if the whole family were being held in the arms of a greater being up above.

* * *

December 1970

"I don't want you to go," Mimi whined at the door.

"I have to, though. I'll only be gone for two weeks, and then I'll be home for a whole two weeks after that," Ah Veng replied, hugging the little girl.

His other children stood behind him, and he hugged each one before kissing his wife goodbye.

"Yeah, but then you'll just leave for two more," Ah Hiang said.

"I know." He didn't know what else to say. Then an idea came to mind. "What if I brought something back for you all?"

His wife looked at him sharply and raised her eyebrows.

"I promise that I won't spend money on it. It might be something that I find or something that is given to me," he reassured her.

"Yeah!" the kids piped up.

"Alright, I really should get going now, but just remember, I'll bring something back."

"Like what?" Mimi asked.

"It'll be a surprise," he said, grinning down at her before he walked out the door and got into the car.

His family waved to him as he drove off towards the harbor. The drive went by quicker than he anticipated. When he got there, everyone was already gathered at the shore, but they weren't on the docks yet.

"Hey, you made it," Sheng said.

The two of them had become friends after the swimming competition and occasionally hung out after work. Now, they were getting shipped offshore together.

"Yeah, it was difficult to tell my family bye."

"Goodbyes are always difficult. Well, I'm sure that these two weeks will go by quick."

"Hopefully," he sighed and shifted slightly to look at the boats waiting to be boarded.

He felt something hard under his feet and moved away. It was a shell. He bent to pick it up.

"What is it?" Sheng asked.

"A shell," Ah Veng said, holding it up.

"Hey, that's funny. We work for Shell and you found a shell," Sheng laughed.

Ah Veng put the shell down to glare at his friend.

"Nope, you need to try harder with the jokes. They're still not cutting it."

"What? That was funny!"

"Keep thinking that," Ah Veng said, shaking his head and looking down at the shell in his hands. It was the perfect thing to give his children. He looked around for more.

"What are you doing?"

"I promised my kids that I would bring them something, so I'm looking for more."

"Ah, well, here's one," his friend said, bending to pick it up and handing it to Ah Veng.

"Thanks."

"No problem."

Soon enough, he had seven shells. He would hang onto the seventh one until the baby was born. He put them in his pocket and ran his hand along the rough edges as they walked up the dock.

"You ready for this?" Sheng asked.

"Not really. How about you?"

"I'm not really sure. But it's going to be an adventure for sure. Think about it. We're working in the sea!" he exclaimed.

"I wish I had your enthusiasm," Ah Veng said as they boarded the boat. The bosses were at the entrances checking off names and assigning people.

"Chia Ah Veng. Okay, let me see. You're our electrician."

Ah Veng nodded and moved on board. He waited for Sheng and they headed towards the back.

"This is crazy. I've never been on a boat before," Sheng said.

"Really? I don't think that I have either."

"See, isn't this exciting?"

"Sure," Ah Veng said slowly and bent over the railing to look down at the waters below.

He reached into his pocket to feel the shells again, tracing their intricate, woven designs. He briefly remembered having a dream about the ocean, but he couldn't remember what it was about exactly. There was a whole other world down below.

He took a deep breath of the ocean air, lifting his head slightly when a breeze blew by. The ocean stretched so far out, its vastness and beauty hard to comprehend. He gently wrapped his hand around the shells in his pocket as if they were prized possessions. *Well, they are*, he thought. *Shells from the sea. Each shell is created so uniquely, much like each person is created to be unique.*

CHAPTER 13

SALVATION

March 1975

"Ah Veng, when you're finished over there, please come check the wiring for the thermostat. It is way too hot in the rooms on the second floor," Sheng called down to him.

Ah Veng put the cover back on the box he was working with before collecting his tools and making his way to the stairs.

"Hey, that's our boat!" someone yelled.

Ah Veng stepped out of the way as everyone rushed to the edge of the platform. He looked where they were pointing and frowned. Their boat never came early, and they still had a week before their shifts rotated. He shrugged and continued up the stairs. The men chattered excitedly.

"What's that all about?" Sheng asked.

"I don't know. Something about our boat."

"Our boat? But it's not our turn to rotate yet."

"Exactly," Ah Veng said.

"Well, that's weird."

Ah Veng took the covering off the thermostat and checked to make sure the wirings were all connected correctly. Meanwhile, Sheng loitered nearby and made conversation.

"There are still problems going on between Malaysia and Singapore."

"When is there not?" Ah Veng asked.

"Well, it's a little more serious now."

"I thought it was worse when Singapore got expelled."

"No, I think that was just the starting point," Sheng replied.

"How long ago was that again?"

"It was, like, August of 1965, so it's been about ten years."

"Then why are we still talking about it? You would think they would have got themselves together by now," Ah Veng said.

"Well, that's the government for you. They always have their ups and downs, but I just hope they can iron out their problems. I do not like the thought of larger disputes or possibly even war."

"I doubt they would ever go to war. Large disputes are a possibility, but definitely not war," Ah Veng said, shaking his head and bending to get a better reading on the temperature before saying, "I don't see anything wrong with the wiring, but I set the temperature a bit lower, so that might help a bit. If it doesn't, let me know."

He put the covering back and stood up.

"Alright, I—" Sheng started to say, when someone came running up the stairs, yelling, "Ah Veng, Ah Veng! The boss wants to see you!"

Sheng looked at his friend sharply. "That can't be good."

Ah Veng rushed down the stairs after the messenger to find the other workers crowded around the dock where the boats came in.

"Coming through, coming through," the guy yelled, dragging Ah Veng along with him.

They finally stumbled through the crowd and made it onto the boat. He was so confused about what was going on. One of their bosses was writing something on a clipboard, and the other was watching over his shoulder.

"Ah, there you are," the one with the clipboard said, looking up.

"Sir, you wanted to see me," Ah Veng said, standing a little taller.

"Yes, we have heard news of your mother-in-law."

Ah Veng shifted uncomfortably, not sure what they meant or if they were referring to Rose's real mother or adoptive mother.

"Um, which one?" he asked.

"Your wife's adoptive mother, I believe. She's fallen quite ill, and your wife is already in Miri tending to her. Before she left, she told us to inform you and asked if you could take time off to go be with her or your children. So, we've come to take you back. You'll have three weeks instead of the normal two."

Ah Veng felt relieved for the extra time but worried for his family. *Did she leave the children by themselves?*

"Thank you," he said.

"Is there anything you need to get before we head out?"

"I have his stuff!" Sheng said, pushing past a few people and onto the boat to hand it to his friend.

"Wow, perfect timing," Ah Veng laughed. "How'd you know?"

"One of the other guys told me. I send my love to your family. Best wishes to you, and I'll see you in a few weeks."

"Thanks!" Ah Veng called after him.

"Are you ready?" his boss asked him.

He nodded and watched the dock pull away as they slowly departed. His coworkers were waving to him like crazy from the dock and he waved back. His grin widened when he noticed Sheng waving enthusiastically from the top floor.

That friend of his was something—always thinking that he was better than anyone else, but he was still a great guy. Ah Veng leaned against the railing of the boat the entire trip, looking down into the waters below and out into the horizon. His wife must be having a hard time. She was quite close to her adoptive mother, and it would be hard for her to lose her.

The shore was getting closer. He squinted to see it better.

"I'm quite sorry about the suddenness of all this. But we realized that you would probably need to know and be with your family right now," his boss said, snapping him out of his thoughts.

"Oh, thank you, I really appreciate it."

"We were looking at your file earlier today and you've done good work. You're probably one of the most loyal and one of the best workers that we have."

Ah Veng looked at them, a little surprised at the compliment. It was rare for the bosses to interact with the workers, much less give them a compliment.

"Do you find that surprising?" the other boss asked, noticing his expression.

"Just a bit," Ah Veng replied, slightly embarrassed.

"We're serious, though, and we wanted you to know that before you have to deal with everything that you and your family are about to go through."

"Most people think that we're scary and avoid us just because we're in charge, but honestly, we would get to know you guys more if we could, and we do care about your lives," the other one chimed in.

Ah Veng gave them a small smile as the boat came to a stop. They were at the docks.

"We send our condolences to you and your family."

"Thank you," Ah Veng called behind him as he disembarked, completely confused about the interaction that had just occurred. *That boat ride felt like the shortest one of them all*, he thought as he tried to remember where he parked the car. He spotted it under the shade of a tree.

As he drove back to his house, he worried that he would find it in complete chaos. He trusted his two eldest children to take care of the younger kids but was still worried that the responsibility might be overwhelming. They had not been left alone like this before. He parked in the driveway and cautiously went to the front door, wondering why it was so quiet. *Perhaps Rose took them with her?* He opened the door.

"Hello?"

"Papá!" his youngest daughter yelled and came running.

He smiled when he saw her and gave her a big hug, remembering how happy he was when she was born. Her name was the most difficult to decide, but they had finally settled on the nickname Philly.

"Hi," he laughed, hugging the other children who came running. "Have they been good?" he asked Ah Tap and Ah Hiang.

"Yes, we were just telling them stories," Ah Hiang replied, smiling.

"So, they let you off work?" Ah Tap asked.

"Yes, I'm getting three weeks instead of the normal two."

"Are you going to Miri for the funeral though?" Ah Hiang asked.

"The funeral?"

"Oh, did they not tell you?"

"They said that Ayi[39] was sick, but they didn't say that she passed."

"It was recent. They probably didn't know yet."

"When is it?" Ah Veng asked.

"Tomorrow," Ah Tap said.

Philly and King King were tugging on his arm. He looked down at them.

"Wait, Rose didn't take these two with her?"

"No, she wants you to take them."

"Aright, well I guess we're leaving in a little while, then. Go play, okay?" he told the youngest two, shaking himself free and heading towards his bedroom.

"Can we come too?" Ah Lay and Ah Den asked, chasing after their father. He shook his head.

"I'm sorry, but you all have school."

"What? That's not fair. Why did Ah Tap and Ah Hiang get to miss school these last few days?"

"Because they had to take care of your two younger siblings, who are not in school yet. But they aren't going either. They'll be going back

---

39 Formal and respectful way of referring an elder or one that is of higher authority in a family, in Mandarin Chinese, literally meaning "aunt."

to school tomorrow."

The two boys pouted and ran off. Ah Veng simply shook his head and grabbed a bag to start packing. He then packed his kids' bag before setting everything down at the front door. He checked to make sure that he had packed everything his wife would need for the younger kids before walking into the kitchen to make sure that his older ones would have enough to eat.

"Are you about to leave?" Ah Hiang asked.

"Yes, just about. Do you think that you all will be okay for a week?"

"Yeah, we're good," she said, smiling to reassure her father.

"Okay then. I'll be heading out. King King, Philly," he called.

The two kids came running.

"King King, can you take this bag and your sister to the car?" he asked.

His son obediently did as he was told. Ah Veng picked up his own bag and said goodbye to his other children before getting into the car and starting the engine. As they pulled out of the driveway, the two in the back pressed their faces against the window and waved goodbye to their siblings.

"Where are we going?" Philly asked, moving to sit closer to the other window.

"To see Ayi."

"What's a funeral?" King King asked.

Ah Veng sighed, realizing that it was going to be a long drive.

"It's like a service that is held in memory of someone that has died."

"Someone died?" Philly gasped.

"Oh no," King King said, looking at his sister wide-eyed.

Ah Veng stayed silent. He did not want to be the one to tell them that their grandma had died. Although they did not know her well, they still knew who she was. He zoned out, letting them talk and laugh with one another. The area had not gotten much rain, so the roads were not that bad, which was a relief since he was not in the mood to push the car out of the mud.

They got to Miri in about two hours. When he pulled up to his adoptive mother's house, he turned and noticed that his children were asleep. He couldn't carry them both, but he didn't want to wake them up either, so he quietly got out of the car and knocked on the front door. Rose answered. Her eyes were red and swollen as if she had been crying, and her hair was sticking up in places.

"I wasn't sure if they were going to let you come, but I tried," she said, sniffling.

Ah Veng hugged her and held her for a bit before saying, "King King and Philly are asleep in the car; do you think we should bring them in?"

"Yeah, let me move some things off the bed."

Ah Veng walked back to the car and got his daughter out first before going back for his son. He and his wife watched the two children sleeping peacefully, oblivious to what was going on in the world. It would be nice to have such innocence and not have to worry about anything. He turned to Rose.

"I know this probably isn't the best time, but there's something that I need to talk to you about."

"We can do it now. I don't mind."

"Are you sure?" he asked.

"Yeah, we can sit in the kitchen," she replied, turning to leave the bedroom. Ah Veng followed her, silently hoping that she would be okay with what he was about to tell her.

"Alright, what is it?" she asked once they sat down.

He took a deep breath before starting. "Money is tight," he said quickly.

"It always has been. What do you mean?"

"At the start of my job, I was told that they only pay for four children to go to school."

"We know that, and we've been paying for Mimi."

"Well, that's the thing. King King is going to start soon, and then a year later, Philly will start. We just don't have the money to pay for all three of them, and we already struggle to pay for Mimi right now."

Rose sighed and rubbed her temples, not wanting to think about the struggles they were facing at the moment.

"I was thinking . . . perhaps we should move back here since they were either born here or are citizens. That would mean that their education would be free, and we wouldn't have to pay for any of them."

"Do you think Ah Tap and Ah Hiang will be able to come back or will want to, though? They're almost done with school."

"Well, they could stay if they wanted to. Shell will still pay for up to four children, so we could just have the youngest three come back over here to study."

"Ah Veng, where are we going to live? In this house? You know that my sister is ill as well and wants us to adopt her kids when she passes, right? This house is not big enough for fifteen children."

"What? When did that happen?"

"Recently. I found out almost as soon as I got back."

"Why is it our responsibility? Where'd her husband go?"

"He left. And seriously, where are the children going to go? They'll be left to the streets. I can't allow that to happen even if you don't like them," Rose insisted.

"So, that means that we'll have to move back anyway. I mean, we can make this work. Every time I am back for two weeks, I could work on building an extension to this house and repairing it since it needs some work. If some of the older kids want to stay in Brunei to study, then we'll let them continue living in the house provided by my company, and the rest of them will come back over here for school. I guess you and I could just drive back and forth to check on them when I'm not offshore."

"That sounds kind of absurd—a family living in two places at once."

"Well, what else are we supposed to do?"

"I don't know. I guess it could work."

"We'll be okay," he said with a reassuring smile. "I'm sure of it."

* * *

February 1987

THE RAIN CAME DOWN IN SHEETS like tears pouring down a face. Ah Veng banged his fist against the steering wheel in anger and leaned his head against the window of the car door. *How could life go so wrong? It just isn't fair.* He was being forced to retire at age fifty-four, but the actual retirement age was fifty-five. He was so close and yet so far. They said that they would pay him a lump sum for retiring early, but all his coworkers told him that it wasn't true.

He needed the money and he needed a job. His kids were all emigrating overseas, and there was no way he could pay for all of them to go to universities or to start new lives. *They just couldn't hold on to me for a few more months, could they?* he thought bitterly. *No, they just had to have young workers because it would be more productive and help the business.* He hit the steering wheel again and winced in pain. Something fell on the windshield. He looked closely. It was a dead butterfly, pelted down by the rain. It's blue wing hung crookedly, and Ah Veng cringed when he used the windshield wiper to wipe it away.

He settled against the window again. Life had started to go downhill once his family adopted the children of Rose's sister and moved back to Miri. Actually, life had turned absolutely chaotic after that. He reflected on those times and remembered when the conflict between the two sets of children just got to be too unacceptable.

* * *

"Why are you touching our stuff?!" one of the cousins yelled.

Mimi glanced up in shock and stuttered, "This is for everyone to use—"

"Who says?"

"Well . . . it's—"

"No! Nobody said that. So, get out! You're not even supposed to be on this side of the house anyway! Get out, get out!"

She scampered back to her siblings.

"I don't understand why they have to be so mean," Ah Den said, crossing his arms across his chest and glaring at the doorway.

"I don't either," Ah Lay agreed.

"They just want their way all the time, and I'm afraid that they're going to kick us out sometime soon," Ah Hiang said from the back of the room.

"They can't do that!" King King cried.

"Umm, yeah, they actually could. But I don't think I would mind. I'd rather live somewhere else than be bossed around by those seven. I feel bad for David; how did he even deal with them growing up?" Ah Den asked, shaking his head and sitting on his pile of blankets on the floor.

"Well, he got lucky. I can't believe Ayi and Papá actually saved up money to help send him to university in England. I wish I was the one over there," Mimi sighed, thinking of their cousin—the only one of their aunt's kids that Ah Veng and Rose officially adopted.

Ah Veng stepped into the doorway. He felt bad that he had been listening in on their conversation, but he didn't want to interrupt.

"Oh, Papá!" Mimi said, shocked and embarrassed that her father had been listening.

"They were rude and stole again, didn't they?" he asked.

None of them wanted to answer.

"It's okay. They approached me when I got home and told me that they wanted us out. So, you know what? We're going to get out of here. I'm tired of them, and I know that your ayi is tired of them, and I know that you all are tired of them. So, we're leaving. Pack up your stuff because once we leave, we're not coming back."

His children immediately began to gather up their stuff. Only his eldest was slow to start packing. "Where are we going to go?" Ah Tap asked.

"There is a distant relative that we knew quite well before Ayi passed away. She said that she is willing to take us in until we find ourselves a house. I have already found a place, but it will take a while to contact the owners and get the rent set in place and everything. So, we should only be staying with her for a few weeks."

Ah Tap's eyebrows scrunched up with concern.

"It doesn't cost that much, does it?" he questioned, not wanting his father to have to add another bill to his plate.

"No, it's just about thirty dollars a month."

Ah Tap frowned but stopped asking questions. Instead, he bent to gather up his blankets from the floor. Ah Veng sighed and left the room, knowing that his son was upset that they were going to have to pay for a place to live when they shouldn't have to.

* * *

The rain lightened up a bit, but it was still not light enough to start driving. Ah Veng was probably going to have to push his car out of the mud once he started traveling down that dirt road.

He dreaded the news that he would be bringing home. They struggled hard enough to put food on the table, and his kids did not even have proper beds growing up. They slept on the floor. At times they were starving because they did not have food at all, and he hated that they had to grow up like that. He blamed himself, and now he was jobless, unable to help each child get where they wanted to get in life.

He glanced out the front windshield and figured that he might as well start driving. It would be better to just get it over with.

Time seemed to pass so slowly, as if it were draining him completely—as if he himself were stuck in the mud. He was not motivated anymore. He wasn't even sure if he wanted to think. All he wanted to do was retreat into a dark corner of his mind and sit there, staring out into nothing.

He had no memory of getting home or what happened when he did. He just knew that somehow his family heard the news, and he ended up in bed. Every day after that, all he wanted to do was sleep, but sometimes someone would disturb his slumber and force him to eat or shower.

"You have got to stop acting all depressed like this," his wife demanded one day.

"Go away," he mumbled.

"No, I'm serious. I can't stand this and seeing you like this. I shouldn't be the only one working to provide for this family. This is supposed to be your job, and yet I had to go out and find a job. You know where I'm working? The hotel. A hotel! And I'm just like a maid, washing and drying their bedsheets. You need to get out! Find a job or at least socialize with people!" she huffed.

Ah Veng merely groaned and put the pillow over his head. Rose turned on her heel and walked out the door, almost running into Ah Hiang. "You!" she exclaimed, pointing at her daughter. "Talk to your father. He's useless," she grumbled.

"Umm, okay?" Ah Hiang said, shocked at her mother's suddenness. She walked into her parents' room.

"Papá?"

"What? Not you too," he groaned, removing the pillow from his head and looking at his daughter. "What do you want?"

"Nothing. I just wanted to tell you that I'm going to try and talk to your company about getting the money that they never gave you."

"Why would you want to do that? There's no point."

"Yes, there is. That money belongs to you, and therefore they should have given you what they promised. You can't just let people step all over you and take what belongs to you. That's not right," she insisted.

"Well, fine. If you can do it, then do it. Oh, and when you go back, could you get my radio for me?"

"Your radio?" she asked.

"Yes, it would be in the office. Please. It's really important to me."

"Okay, sure. I'll try to get it, but I can't promise anything."

"Great. Now let me sleep," he mumbled, closing his eyes.

He slipped off into the dream world before his eldest daughter even left the room.

* * *

Something drifted through the air, intangible. A line of swirling sounds, pushing and pulling to make music that was pleasing to the ears. He dropped down to see where the extravagant melodies were coming from. People danced and twirled and swirled up a storm. It was such a lively event, with lights strung all about. Cheers and laughs and barks added to the atmosphere. Musicians stood upon a stage and played till their hearts were content. They whistled a tune to which everyone clapped or tapped and danced. A lively event indeed.

* * *

Ah Veng woke to music in his ears. He sat up and listened carefully, wondering if it was playing from his radio. The sudden excitement quickly died down when he recognized that the music was coming from Ah Hiang's piano. Somehow and someway, she had saved up enough money by working different jobs to buy herself a piano. He couldn't remember how many years it had been.

"Ah Hiang," he called.

The music stopped.

"Yes?" she said, quickly walking into the room.

"Did you get my radio?" he asked.

"I got the money," she said.

"I asked about the radio."

"Um, no, there was some love-crazy guy in there, and he was weird and scary and I just couldn't do it. I'm sorry, Papá. Please don't be angry."

"Humph, well, you said you got the money? How did you manage to do that?"

"I just talked to the company and they apologized, saying that they had the money ready, but it never got sent out."

"Sure they did. I bet that's a lie," he grumbled.

"I don't think so. They handed it right to me, and when I got home, I gave it to Ayi."

"You can leave now," he said, pointing to the door. "I don't feel like talking anymore."

Ah Hiang lowered her head and left, upset that her father didn't seem to care about anything anymore. Her mother was heartbroken that the man she married had changed so much. It wasn't until Ah Hiang was gone from view that Ah Veng broke down in tears. He cried for days until his eldest daughter couldn't stand it anymore.

"Ayi, you have to quit your job," she said to her mother one day.

"What?!" her mother exclaimed. "I think you've lost your mind."

"No, I'm serious. You need to take Papá to live with Ah Lay in KL."[40]

"How is that going to help him?"

"It's going to get him out of the house at least! He needs to get out of bed," Ah Hiang said desperately.

"Do you think he'll even want to go?"

"It doesn't matter if he wants to or not because he's going. I already contacted Ah Lay and told him that you all will be going over there soon."

"Soon!" Rose exclaimed.

"Yes, like next week. Please, Ayi. I can't go on seeing you both like this."

Her mother sighed. "Okay. I will tell them tomorrow that I am resigning."

Ah Hiang was about to say something else, but sobbing came from the bedroom, and the amount of sorrow she heard was too much for her to bear. She walked outside, wondering where she could go to escape the sounds of suffering.

* * *

---

40   Kuala Lumpur.

March 1988
Miri, Sarawak, Malaysia

"I thought he was better," Ah Hiang said in frustration.

"Well, he is, but he's still depressed," her mother replied.

"I mean, it's good that he's no longer in bed, but didn't the year in KL help him at all?"

"I told you. He was the same over there. All he wanted to do was stay in the room. Sometimes we could convince him to go out with us, but it took a lot of effort."

Ah Hiang sighed. Everything was accumulating and getting even more frustrating. Rose looked at her daughter and saw the pity she had for her father.

"Why don't you go talk to him again? He seems to listen to you sometimes," she said.

"I'll try." Ah Hiang walked towards the bedroom. "Papá," she called.

Her father was sitting in a chair, looking out the window. He didn't answer. She walked in front of him to block his view.

"Papá," she said a little more firmly.

"What," he stated, slowly lifting his gaze.

"Stop this. It's been over a year since you lost your job. You need to find a life. And if it's not a job, at least go out and find friends. You're causing everyone to worry, and it would be helpful if you could at least try to help yourself instead of dragging this family down."

Ah Veng winced. It was the first time in a long while that he paid attention to the words that were spoken to him, and it made him angry.

"Fine! You all keep wanting to kick me out, then I'll get out! But don't complain when I don't come home that often! You all were the ones that started this in the first place!" he yelled, grabbing his wallet and storming out of the bedroom and then out the front door.

"Well, that went well," Ah Hiang said, walking to her mother, who stood gaping at the door.

"You got him to get out, though," she said in shock. "We haven't been able to do that."

"But, Ayi, where exactly is he going to go? What if he finds the wrong people?"

Her mother nonchalantly waved her hand. "He's a grown man. He can take care of himself. He has enough sense to at least know right from wrong."

Ah Hiang furrowed her eyebrows. Her father wasn't in the best state of mind right now.

"Are you sure?" she asked.

"Yes, now stop worrying. We have things to do," her mother said, turning to finish the dishes in the kitchen. Ah Hiang lingered for a bit before following suit and going back to what she had been cooking.

Out on the streets, Ah Veng fumed that his family didn't care or want him at home. *After everything I've done for them, and this is how they repay me.* It was getting dark. He turned another corner and heard music in the background. People were laughing and cheering. He followed the noise until he came to a sign that said, *SYURGA MANUSIA LAMA.*[41]

The place was packed with people, and he wondered why he had never stumbled upon this open-spaced hangout before.

"Hey, you!" someone yelled, noticing Ah Veng was just standing there watching.

He searched for the source of the voice and found that it came from a serious-looking set of guys in a far-off corner. He frowned and made his way over to them.

"Well, someone doesn't look happy," one of the guys said, breaking the serious atmosphere by laughing.

"Sit," another told him, pointing to an empty chair.

Ah Veng sat and noticed that there were lottery cards on the table.

"What's your name?" the guy that looked to be in charge asked

---

41   Old Man's Heaven.

him.

"Ah Veng," he replied.

"You new here?"

"Not to Miri, but I've never been to this place before."

"What do you mean? Everyone knows about this hangout. Where've you been, locked up in your house or something?" the guy asked, smirking and looking at the other guys.

Ah Veng shifted uncomfortably, unsure of where the conversation was going.

"Hey, I'm Ying by the way," the guy said, turning to meet his gaze again. "You ever played?" He motioned to the cards in front of him.

Ah Veng shook his head.

"Well, you should," Ying said, grinning and picking up one of the cards. "It only costs a ringgit,[42] and think about all the possibilities that could befall you if you just happen to win the big jackpot."

Ah Veng hesitated, knowing that he shouldn't. *A few cards couldn't hurt, though,* he thought, and he couldn't possibly disappoint the men he just met.

"Alright, I'll take three," he said, pulling out his wallet.

The men cheered when Ying smacked three cards down in front of him.

"That's my man," one of them shouted, clapping him on the back.

* * *

August 1989

It was about three in the afternoon when Ah Veng started to prepare for the ceremony. His life was about to change completely. He had worked so hard to recover after falling into a deep hole of darkness and gambling. It wasn't until he hit the bottom that he realized he needed to climb back up. His debt was piled high, and he was taking out loans

---

42   Malaysia's currency.

left and right. The guys that he called his friends were nothing but deceitful brokers who constantly lied and tricked people for money. Now he had to pay back all the money he owed.

"I can't believe I fell into all that," Ah Veng said, feeling incredibly guilty.

"It's okay, Papá. You know that you're forgiven now, and look! You're even getting baptized!" his eldest daughter, Ah Hiang, exclaimed.

He smiled at her, thankful that she had forgiven him, but there was still sorrow in his heart that his relationship with his wife would never be the same. There was so much to regret, especially since he had forced each of his children to send him money so that he could give it to Ying, who promised him land. But that was a lie. There was no land.

He walked out into the living room and picked up his Bible, thinking back to the day his life had changed for the better. If it wasn't for Ah Hiang's friend showing up that day, he'd still be stuck at the bottom.

* * *

"Ah Hiang? Are you coming?" her friend Shu called from the doorway.

"Yeah, give me a few minutes. You can come in and wait," Ah Hiang yelled from the back of the house. Shu tentatively stepped in and saw her friend's father sitting in a chair, staring at the wall.

"Uncle?" she asked, trying to get his attention.

"Hmm?"

"Are you okay?"

"Oh, umm . . . yeah," he said, snapping his attention to the person that had entered their home.

"You know, there's a dinner at the church tonight. You should come!" she said excitedly.

"I . . . think I'm alright," he replied, shaking his head, not wanting to go to anything that had to do with a church. Church had changed his daughter completely, and he wasn't sure he wanted to partake in something like that.

"Please," the girl begged. "You don't even have to stay for the part after if you don't want to. You could just stay for the dinner. Ah Hiang and I would love for you to join us."

"What?" Ah Hiang asked, rushing into the living room.

"I'm trying to get your father to join us for dinner."

"Oh, Papá, you really should come," Ah Hiang said, but she doubted her father would agree to go.

"I'm thinking," he said.

"Come on, Uncle, it'll be fun!" Shu said, walking over to him and holding out her hand to help him out of the chair.

He eyed the hand and reluctantly accepted it.

"Alright, let me change and I'll be right back."

Ah Veng walked out of the room and Ah Hiang turned to her friend. "You did not just do that. No way."

"What?" Shu asked.

"He's actually coming? I haven't got him to do anything in years!"

Shu shrugged. "Maybe he just wasn't ready yet? Or maybe it's just because I'm not a member of the family?" she proposed.

Ah Veng walked back out, decently dressed.

"Okay, let's go and get this over with," he said. "Lead the way."

* * *

He thumbed through his Bible, loving the feel of the pages running along his fingers.

"Are you ready?" Ah Hiang asked.

"Yeah," he said, walking out the front door to start the car.

The two of them drove in almost complete silence. He didn't know what to say. For some reason, he was both nervous and excited.

"You're really quiet," Ah Hiang observed.

"Just thinking," he said.

"You know, God worked miracles in our life. We're one lucky

family."

Ah Veng didn't respond. He didn't know how to. They pulled into the parking lot, and he smiled when he saw the sign that read, *CALVARY CHARISMATIC CHURCH.*

It was the one place he loved to be, and he also loved the people.

"You ready for this?" Ah Hiang asked.

"Yes," he said, his smile growing even wider.

They got out of the car and walked inside where he was immediately greeted by several of the church members and the pastor.

"Ah Veng! How good to see you! This is an exciting day!"

"Papá, I'll be sitting in the front after the baptism, okay?" Ah Hiang said, walking off with some of her friends.

People were already filing into the sanctuary, and he heard the music playing. The service was about to start.

"Here, let's go on into the back," the pastor said, motioning to Ah Veng.

He followed and went to a room where he changed into baptism clothes while the pastor made an announcement for friends and family to go out the side door if they wanted to see the baptism. Once Ah Veng was changed, he went outside to the baptism pool. Everything was moving so quickly, and it was hard for his mind to process.

"Are you ready?" the pastor asked.

He nodded and stepped into the water.

"Thank you all for gathering here today to see the baptism of Chia Ah Veng. Is it true that you have accepted Jesus Christ as your Lord and Savior?"

"Yes," Ah Veng replied, smiling up at his daughter, who stood in the very front.

"I now baptize you, my brother, in the name of the Father, Son, and Holy Spirit."

He was dunked under to be submerged, and as soon as he came up, he felt completely new. It was like a revelation. The feelings were glorious, like his old self was being stripped away to make him into a new person. He thought about his daughter's words in the car as the people cheered. A small movement caught his eye, and his attention focused on the very creature that had followed him throughout his life—a small being with such a pure heart. The butterfly flitted down and landed on the side of the pool. *Perhaps a spirit has been with me all along—a true heavenly father.*

His family had been saved. All along, God had been guiding his family. The number of miracles that had blessed them was incredible. If anything, he should not even be alive at this point. God had truly saved him.

CHAPTER 14

BLESSINGS

August 2001
Kuala Lumpur, Malaysia

"AH VENG," HIS FRIEND SHENG SAID, trying to get his attention.

Sheng was visiting family in KL and had made the time to visit his dear friend as well.

"How many times do I have to tell you? It's Henry now," Henry replied, rolling his eyes.

"But I like calling you by your old name."

"It's been over ten years since I've changed it. You should be used to it by now."

"Well, I'm not. I don't visit you that often since you moved."

"Yeah, yeah," Henry said, waving his hand.

"Ugh, you have got to be kidding me!" Sheng exclaimed, throwing his newspaper down on the table.

"What?" Henry asked, picking the paper up.

"Read it! I don't understand why there is so much fighting going on. Like, seriously!"

Henry looked closely at the article. "Dozens arrested? Ethnic clashes? Is this about those ethnic disputes again? Why are people getting arrested for it?"

"Why else? It's getting out of hand," Sheng retorted.

"It says it's between Malays and ethnic Indians."

"Yeah, it always has been, but this is like the worst it's been."

"Why do you always like looking at the bad news? There's good news too," Henry said, flipping through the paper to find something.

"You know that the bad is just as important as the good. It's important to know about everything that is going on in the world."

"Oh, hey, that's interesting," Henry said, quickly scanning something that he found.

"What is it?"

"Malaysia and Singapore are finally fixing their long-standing disputes, and they want to build a new tunnel and bridge."

"No way," Sheng said, standing to read the article over Henry's shoulder. "It took them long enough," he laughed.

"Yeah, that's for sure. Do you—"

He was cut off by the sharp ring of the home phone.

"Ah Lay," he called.

His son walked out of the bedroom and sleepily rubbed his eyes as he answered the phone. The two men watched the exchange over the telephone. It looked serious.

"Are they okay? Yes, yeah, I can do that. Do we need to go today? I understand. So, they will issue a visa?"

"Visa?" Sheng said, looking sharply at his friend.

Henry was concerned. *Why would a visa need to be issued?* His son hung up and rubbed his face. Tears were in his eyes.

"What's wrong?" Henry asked.

"There's been a car accident in America. Mimi and Ah Hiang and her family were all affected. That was the hospital and they said that they couldn't tell me everything but that Ah Hiang broke her arm and Mimi . . ." Ah Lay trailed off, tears running down his face.

"What?!" Henry exclaimed, standing up, pleading to God that his daughter was not gone.

"They don't know if she'll make it. She's unresponsive and in a coma. She wasn't wearing a seat belt and it was a head-on collision. She was thrown forward. They are calling the US embassy here to see if a visa can be issued immediately for you and mother to go over there."

Henry paced the room as his friend watched with concern.

"Who else was in the car?" he asked.

"Mimi's boyfriend, Ah Hiang's husband and their eighteen-month-old daughter."

Henry stopped pacing. "My granddaughter. Is she okay?"

"Yes, they said that she was the only one not injured, physically."

"Physically? What's that supposed to mean?"

"I don't know. She wasn't hurt, though, so that's what's important."

"Thank God," he said with relief.

His friend walked towards the door. "I should get going," Sheng said, "but my thoughts go out to you and your family." He nodded at them before walking out.

"So, what do we do now?" Henry asked.

"There's not much we can do. I guess we just have to wait," Ah Lay replied.

And wait they did. The visas came within a couple of weeks, and Rose and Henry were on the first flight they could book. Henry entered the United States for the first time through San Antonio, Texas, where the two of them split ways. Rose flew on a connecting flight to Georgia in order to care for Mimi, who was recuperating after waking up from a two-week coma. Henry was picked up by Ah Hiang's best friend and her husband. They drove him to Snyder, Texas, where his eldest daughter, her husband and child were back home.

He couldn't imagine what they had gone through, especially since they had to fly back to Texas from Georgia. The visit excited him, though, because he would see his granddaughter for the first time. Rose got to see her when she was born, but he hadn't had the chance. The entire drive, he looked out the window, examining the beauty of the vast landscape. He saw incredible things that he had never seen before. The plains were dry, and sandy wind blew tumbleweeds across the road. Odd green plants with spiky points were scattered alongside the road for miles and miles. More vegetation started to show up closer to urban life.

His heart beat faster when they pulled up to the apartment complex, and he nervously knocked on the door. Rustling came from inside before the door opened.

"Papá!" Ah Hiang exclaimed and rushed to hug him.

He noticed the cast on her arm, and inside, he saw that her husband also had a cast on his arm, as well as his leg. A sharp-pitched sound drew his attention towards a keyboard in the corner of the living room. A little girl was playing with the keys and the buttons on the board.

"Is that . . ."

"Yes," Ah Hiang said, smiling, and he immediately felt love for his grandchild.

Over the next few months, he spent his time taking the little girl to the park or playing with her at home since she never let him take care of her. She always wanted her mom for things like food or baths. So, instead, he became her playmate.

The time spent with that little family was precious. However, he was soon on a flight to Georgia, to check on his daughter and meet with his wife before they flew back to KL. He was sad that they had to leave, but the US had opened a door to endless opportunities, and he knew that he would be back one day.

* * *

September 2005
Stone Mountain, Georgia, United States

"Is this really happening?" he asked.

Mimi laughed. "What do you mean?"

"That we're actually here to stay permanently," he said.

"Of course," she replied, grinning at her parents and her brother Ah Lay, who were walking around the house, getting acquainted with their new home.

They each had their own bedroom, and the house was three stories, so she was sure that they would be able to find their favorite places eventually. She went into her office, leaving them to explore.

Rose and Ah Lay had already gone to check out the basement, so Henry ventured upstairs, taking his bag to the bedroom that he knew was his. It was perfect for him, and he started unpacking all his things, starting with his Bible, which he placed on the table right next to the bed. While he unpacked, he thought about his new life and how it was going to be from now on. It was hard to comprehend that he was finally in the US. He had the opportunity to work in America when he had just started working for Shell. However, he had turned it down, and he couldn't really remember why he did. It was disappointing to think about it now; he could have provided his family with a better life. But things didn't turn out that way.

Everything seemed to be turning out okay, though. Mimi was a project accountant; Ah Hiang was busy taking care of her daughter while her husband worked; Ah Den was an engineer in Australia, and he and his wife were raising two kids; Ah Tap was an architect back in Miri; David was an engineer in England with a wife, and they were raising two kids; Philly was in KL with her son; King King was in Singapore working offshore as an engineer; and Ah Lay was about to start studying there in the States. Henry's love for his family ran deep. He sat on the bed and grabbed his Bible to reflect on some of the things he had written in it.

* * *

Life from then on was filled with happy times. Weeks flew by and then months, and then years. He got to watch his granddaughter grow up, and then his grandson, Philly's son. The boy lived with Ah Hiang and her family for a year when he was about eight and then went to live with them permanently when he was twelve so that he could go to school in the US.

Henry loved thinking about all the good memories. He often went to Texas to visit Ah Hiang, and he would build things for her family. One of the things his grandkids liked the most was the four-wheeled scooter he would pull and roll them around on. He also built them a swing since his granddaughter always begged for one. She was an adventurous little one and enjoyed climbing on top of her parents' cars to just sit up there, looking down.

He helped build her a bed, and he built a compartment for their footrest. The memories were endless, but the holidays were his favorite, especially Christmas since they got to celebrate the birth of Jesus. He loved to remember one Christmas in particular since it was filled with such excitement, despite starting out with much disappointment.

* * *

"Are they not coming this year?" Ah Lay asked.

"I don't know," Mimi replied, upset that she had not heard anything from her sister Ah Hiang or her family.

"They will probably call in a few days," Henry said.

"But Christmas is a few days away. If they were coming, they would have already said so. Do you think we should just drive there and surprise them?"

"That's a really long drive," Ah Lay said.

"Yeah, but—" Mimi was cut off by faint singing at the front door.

"Away in manger, no crib for a bed . . ."

Someone knocked, accompanied by the sound of a stringed instrument.

"Umm, it's almost midnight. Carolers don't come out at this hour. You get it," Mimi said, nodding to Ah Lay.

"No, I think you should be the one to open it," he insisted. Henry watched the two of them argue. However, Rose had somehow made it upstairs and already pulled the door open. They heard familiar voices.

"Surprise!"

"What? We were just talking about how we thought that you all were not going to show up," Mimi said, rushing to greet her sister's family.

Henry grinned happily, and his granddaughter went up to give him a hug. She was holding her viola but also something else—a leash.

"Merry Christmas!" she exclaimed as a dog ran inside. It was cute, big and black with touches of light brown.

"What is that?" Mimi exclaimed.

"He's for you!" the granddaughter said. "His name is Buddy, and his little tag around his collar says that he wants to be your buddy and he's wondering if you'll take him in."

"You shouldn't have," Mimi said, taking the leash from her and bending down to pet the dog.

"How old is he?" Ah Lay asked.

"About a year old, so he's still a puppy."

"What do we do about the cats?" Mimi asked.

"They'll get along eventually. I'm sure of it," the granddaughter answered.

"It's so great to see you all," Mimi said. "I can't believe that you all ended up surprising us because we were thinking about surprising you instead."

"Yeah, it was kind of a last-minute plan, but it worked," Ah Hiang said.

"Well, come in, come in," Rose said, motioning her family into the kitchen and shutting the front door.

* * *

"Kong-kong! Look," his granddaughter said, running up to him at another Christmas gathering.

She was holding a little grasshopper in her hands.

"Oh, you caught a bug. You know what you could do with it is make it into a delicious meal," he said, grinning.

"Ew, why would you eat it?" she asked, scrunching up her face.

"Well, people in the past didn't always have food to eat, so sometimes they had to eat anything they could find."

"But we live in America," she said. "We don't have to do that here. We have food."

"True, but it's protein."

"That's disgusting," she said, bending down to let the grasshopper go. "Can you tell me a story about the past?" she asked when she stood up.

"Umm . . . I don't remember," he replied, not keen on thinking about his life before he came to America. He liked to think that he was forever moving forwards instead of backwards. It did no one any good to dwell in the past. He enjoyed the positive memories but didn't really want to think about the negative ones.

"Come on, you have to remember at least one," she begged, but her grandpa shook his head. "Didn't you used to play the guitar and harmonica?"

He shook his head again.

"What about swimming? Didn't you do a competition or something? My mom told me about that after I started swimming competitively because she said you did and then that's why she got into swimming and now I swim."

Again, her grandfather shook his head. "Sorry, I don't really remember much."

The girl pouted and trotted off before turning and asking, "Have you seen Billy?"

"No," he replied, wondering where the cat could be, and then snickered when he realized that it must be hiding from her. "Check the basement." He went to the front of the house to look at how their Christmas decorations turned out, and she followed.

Lights were strung all around, and a huge wreath hung above their garage door. There was also one hanging on the front door. He touched the pine needles and then pushed the door open to head inside. Pudgy, their other cat, raced past him, making him step back. His granddaughter frowned.

"Why don't they like me?" she asked.

"Maybe it's because you chase them," her mother, Ah Hiang, called from the kitchen.

"I just want to play with them."

"You better not. Otherwise your allergies will act up again," Ah Hiang said.

Henry motioned to his granddaughter. "Here, come here."

She followed him as he grabbed a marker from a drawer in the living room and then pointed to the doorway with the height markings. She bounced up and down excitedly.

"Cousinkins!" she yelled, calling for her cousin, knowing that he wasn't a fan of the nickname.

"You don't have to yell. I'm right here," he said, walking in from the kitchen.

She stood up tall against the wall and waited for her grandfather to mark her.

"No cheating," the grandson said, pointing at her feet.

"I'm not," she shot back.

"Okay," her grandpa said, and she stepped away to look.

"Ah, I grew!" she exclaimed.

"Of course you did. We're always growing," the grandson said, rolling his eyes and standing against the wall.

After he was marked, the two of them wrote their names next to their markings and then put their ages as well, which were ten and thirteen. It was one of the most exciting things they did each holiday season, as well as watch Christmas movies every night. Some of them showed on TBN, Henry's favorite television channel, or Hallmark, but most of them were DVDs that their aunt Mimi had bought.

"You two," Ah Hiang said, "come help in the kitchen."

The grandson immediately went, but the granddaughter whined, "Do I have to?"

Henry tried to hide a laugh. She definitely did not like cooking and would probably rather be off exploring, reading, or practicing a piano if she had one here. He walked off before he could hear her mother scold her. His room seemed like a good place to be before dinner was ready, so he went upstairs. He noticed that the door to his grandchildren's room was open and went inside.

There was a bunk bed and a rainbow beanbag that his granddaughter loved to sit on and read. A teddy bear sat in the corner, familiar to him since she often took pictures with it when she was younger. It made him smile. Picture frames lined the dressers and tables. He bent to look closely at each one. There were so many. His favorite one was the picture of her in a poodle skirt. She was sitting at a piano.

He went to his own room and picked up his journal to write. That was one of his favorite things to do besides read his Bible or read anything else he could find. He also loved staying up to date on the news and events happening throughout the country and within their city. He thought about what he should write and finally settled on writing some notes to put in his grandkids' Christmas presents. He did it every year. He put his pen down on paper, wondering what he should say this time. He wrote: *My granddaughter, you are one with us in The Holy Home of Christ Jesus. GOD BLESS you, AND WE LOVE you. Back to School; Study Hard.*

He didn't finish before he fell asleep.

* * *

The streets were quiet, and the atmosphere was thick with humidity. It seemed to be squeezing and choking the life out of everything around. The world looked dead. The earth shifted slightly. It trembled and quaked; two tectonic plates slid past one another, ever so slowly, and yet it threw everything off balance. Henry flew a bit higher, afraid of the ground beneath. It was unstable, shifting until the road cracked. It splintered and twisted, the crack carving a path for itself, demanding that everything around it conform. Houses crumbled, one by one, crushing everything beneath. Dust showered the scene. People ran out of their homes, but some were already trapped deep in the rubble. And then the trembling stopped, but the damage had already been done. One last tremor made itself known, as if the earth were shivering at the horrific sight.

* * *

"Kong-kong."

Someone was shaking him awake. He opened an eye and saw his granddaughter.

"Dinner's ready," she said, grinning and tugging on his arm.

He got up and followed her downstairs to where everyone else was already gathered. There was so much food that it made him wonder if any recipes had been reserved for Christmas day.

"There you are," Ah Lay said, handing his father a plate.

Henry went to an empty seat and sat down before helping himself to the food. He then waited for everyone else before they said grace and dug in. After dinner, he waited patiently as the others grabbed jackets and put foldable chairs into the car. He was already ready, as usual, but it always took a while for everyone else to pile in to the car before they headed to Stone Mountain. There was a laser show that night, like there was almost every night. He wasn't complaining. It was always fun to watch, even though it became repetitive at times.

He stared out the window and occasionally listened in on the conversation, laughing or commenting when it seemed necessary. It wasn't long before they pulled up to the front gate. They were waved through since they had a pass for living within the park's limits. His grandchildren talked excitedly in the back about the mountain. They always loved trips to see the show or to simply take a hike or a bike ride, and they were the first ones scrambling to get out of the car once it stopped.

"Come on, we're almost late," the granddaughter called, trying to open the trunk to get her little chair out.

"Don't worry. There's still time," Mimi said, coming around to help.

Everyone helped to carry something, and they set out down the path towards the huge lawn. It was already crowded with people, and although they had a hard time finding a good spot, they were all situated before the show started. He smiled when he heard the music start. The beginning told the story of a family and their travels, and then played a few catchy songs that he liked to listen to. The images always reflected what the songs were about, and he loved the stories they told. He eagerly waited for the best part at the end when all the fireworks went off and people clapped and cheered.

"There it is, there it is," his granddaughter said excitedly, pointing to the first firework as it exploded in the sky. It lit up the darkness, shining like a bright star, standing still for just a second before diminishing and disappearing completely. More followed until the night was almost as bright as day, but they too diminished until nothing was left but smoke, making the clear skies appear cloudy. Other people packed up to leave, but Henry's family stayed for a little while, letting traffic clear a bit before they started gathering their things to head back to the car. He listened in on his grandchildren's conversation on the way back home.

"Oh, my goodness, I just realized! Tomorrow's Christmas Eve!" the granddaughter exclaimed.

"Well, yeah, what'd you think it was?" the grandson asked, clearly annoyed.

"I don't know. I just didn't think that it was that soon," she said. "I mean, we haven't been here that long."

Henry zoned out and looked back out the window. He was the first person to notice a tiny snowflake had fallen from the sky. He didn't say anything but merely observed, and soon enough everyone in the car was chattering excitedly about the snow drifting down lazily and gradually getting stronger. They would be having a white Christmas that year.

* * *

"Cousinkins, Cousinkins," the granddaughter called Christmas morning, shaking her cousin awake. "It's Christmas morning. Come on, get up. Why is everyone still sleeping?" she grumbled.

"Because." He looked at the clock. "It's seven in the morning," he said, rolling over and throwing the covers over his head.

"Well, fine, I'll wait. At least Kong-kong is up, meaning there's someone that's excited about Christmas besides me."

"Alright, alright, I'm getting up," he mumbled.

"Great," the granddaughter said before running off to find her next victim.

Henry was trying to read his Bible and do his early morning quiet time, but all he could hear was his granddaughter running all over the house and up and down the stairs. *What is she doing?* His grandson stumbled into the living room, rubbing his eyes while a few other family members filed in as well. *Ah, that's what she's doing,* Henry thought, slightly amused.

"Remind me to lock my door next Christmas," his grandson said.

"Oh, good idea. Let's all lock our doors," Ah Lay chimed in.

Henry couldn't help but laugh. Their facial expressions were too funny; they were clearly not happy with having to wake up so early.

Finally, when everyone was gathered in the living room, the very enthusiastic little girl started reading the labels on the presents and passing them out to everyone.

"Wait, wait, wait," said Ah Lay, the cameraman of the family. "I need to get my camera." He ran downstairs before coming back up, where he immediately started taking pictures.

The granddaughter tore into her presents first, and then everyone else followed. There were exclamations and comments, and many notes of thanks were given out as well. Henry looked down at the gifts in his hands and realized how blessed they were. Growing up, he had never received a gift besides things needed to survive. Yet here they were, exchanging luxuries, all to remember the greatest gift of all—the gift of a savior. It made him recognize that sometimes things were taken for granted, but he was thankful that his grandchildren had a life oblivious to the hardships of the past, to the hardships of extreme poverty. They would hear stories, and they would learn about it, but he did not want them to ever experience it.

He then thought about all his regrets and remembered something someone important had told him. His mind turned as he struggled to think clearly. He was almost certain it had been Jian-min who told him that although life had many regrets, the blessings outweighed them all in the end.

Well, he was certainly right. It just took almost an entire lifetime before it was made known.

"Aren't you going to open your gifts?" his grandson asked.

"Oh, yes," he said, snapping out of his thoughts and turning his attention to the carefully wrapped gifts.

He was delicate as he tore open the wrappers, and he could immediately tell which grandchild gave him what. A lot of it was food, but there was also a cross.

"Thank you," he told them, smiling and enjoying this sweet family moment where everything was in unison, as if all the puzzle pieces had come together at once to create a beautiful image. *Yes, this family is blessed,* he thought. *Life must go on.* Not everything was accomplished yet, and there was still much to be done. Life had a lot more to offer, a lot more precious moments in store, and a lot more blessings to give. There was still more.

CHAPTER 15

PROUD AMERICAN

October 2011

The building sat there, tall and still as Henry entered it for the last time. He had been taking a citizenship class for about two years, and today was the last class before his test. He pulled open the doors and walked through the halls, excitedly entering the classroom to take a seat.

"Henry!" a friend greeted him. "You're taking the test soon, aren't you?"

"Yes, in the next few days."

"Oh, isn't that exciting?"

"Yes, but I will miss coming here. When do you take yours?" Henry asked.

"I don't really know. It could be soon, or not. I think it just depends on when my son decides I'm ready, and who knows if he'll ever think I'm ready."

"Why do—"

"Oh look, here comes the teacher! We better pay attention," his friend said, cutting him off and turning around to face the front.

"Good afternoon!"

"Good afternoon," everyone said.

"I think we have someone that is about to leave us, and while we're sad, we should also be happy for him because Henry Chia takes his citizenship test this Thursday!"

Everyone in the room clapped, and some even cheered.

"That's right. Be sure to wish him luck when you leave today. But I'm sure he's going to do great! Now, for the lesson. We'll be talking about the different states, and for those of you that already know these things, it will be review."

The teacher pulled down a map of the US on the wall.

"Can anyone tell me what this state is?"

"Texas!" someone shouted out.

"Yes, now tell me one interesting fact."

"Umm, it's the biggest state."

"Well, not quite. It's actually the second biggest state. Alaska is the largest."

"It has different environments, right? Oh, and it's primarily Republican, I think," someone else answered.

Henry thought about his family in Texas and wondered what his granddaughter and grandson were up to. He hoped that they were studying hard and doing their best in school and in everything they did. His granddaughter was swimming in an upcoming state competition.

The teacher had moved on to other questions.

". . . so, they might ask you something along the lines of . . . let's see." The teacher paused, looking at the questions packet. "Oh, here's a good one. Which state has the largest population?"

Someone in the front raised their hand.

"Yes?"

"Is it Texas?"

"Wow, you all must love Texas today. No, again, Texas is second in this case. California actually has the largest population of 37.68 million, and even though Texas is second, they only have 25.65 million."

"How does that state fit so many people in it, and why doesn't Texas have the most if they're so big?" someone asked.

"Well, because Texas has different environments, remember? They have deserts and forests, some of which a lot of people don't want to live in. Also, California has a lot of big opportunities that people look for. For example, there is a beach, and a lot of famous people live there."

"Yeah, that's where Hollywood is!" someone shouted excitedly.

"Exactly," the teacher said before pointing at another state.

Henry tried not to zone out, but sometimes he couldn't help himself. He started thinking about the vastness of America. *Do other countries ever get jealous of us?* There were literally all types of environments and climates in this one country, from snow, to mountains, to hills, to deserts, to rivers, beaches, lakes, and so much more. It was difficult to comprehend. *How did they gain all that land?* He tried to remember the history lesson about that, but it was kind of fuzzy. He moved on to thinking about the faces on Stone Mountain. Now, those were important people. They were extremely vital in shaping America into what it was today.

Henry hoped that one day his entire family would end up in this country, or at least in a country that had great opportunities. He noticed people shuffling to gather their stuff and realized that class was coming to a close.

"Don't forget to practice writing. I'll see you all next week, and, Henry, good luck on Thursday!"

He smiled at his teacher and stood to leave. Some of his classmates stopped him on the way out and wished him well on the test. He thanked them and waved goodbye before climbing into his daughter's car. The whole ride, he smiled happily, watching the scenery pass by. Leaves littered the ground, piled in little heaps, and pine needles and cones gathered together as if attending an important meeting. When they got home, he noticed an abundance of debris covering their yard, and so he grabbed a rake from the garage and made his way to the front of the lawn, scanning the area. The yard was huge. He wondered where he should start and shrugged before raking the very spot where he was standing.

As he raked, he went over answers to questions in his head. He didn't want to admit it, but he was somewhat nervous for his test. He was prepared, but that didn't stop the nerves. The test would consist of questions about the states, history, or the government. Then there was the writing portion to see if he could write, but he didn't have a problem with that. He grew up writing, reading and speaking English along with Malay and the Chinese dialect Hakka. His wife would have trouble if she tried to take the test, though. Her English was limited, and she couldn't really write. Mandarin Chinese was her primary language, but she also spoke Malay, and their whole family spoke Hakka, which was what they all preferred to converse in.

He thought about Rose and wondered if she would ever forgive him. Their relationship was still strained, after all these years. She only talked to him if she had to or about a meal she had put on the table. She avoided him, but he was guilty of doing the same thing. When one of them walked into the room, the other walked out. That's just how things were, and when he tried to talk to her, she would wave him off, saying that she was busy and didn't have time to talk.

It didn't stop him from trying, though, and he would keep trying. He would be persistent unto his last days. Sometimes he even tried to give her gifts. With each refusal, his heart was wounded further, ripping farther apart, creating a rift that would never be sealed; but no matter what, he would not give up. Henry stopped to wipe the sweat from his brow and saw that Rose was gardening in front of the house. He sighed and continued to rake.

It wasn't until the sun started to set that he finished cleaning up the yard and went inside to shower before heading to the kitchen to find something to eat. There was already food on the counter, and no one was around, so he ate it. When he finished, there wasn't much of anything else to do, and so he went upstairs to his room to open his Bible, reading until he fell asleep.

* * *

Birds called to one another. Wolves howled. Bears growled. Henry wondered what was going on. A high-pitched squeal pierced the air and gradually grew louder. He shook his head, trying to get rid of the sound, but it persisted. Other animals whimpered and whined. A loud thud cut off the ear-splitting noise. The ground shook. He flew a little higher to try and see above the trees. Animals were running frantically. He moved towards the sound and saw all kinds of machines. They were cutting and sawing away. Men were shouting to one another and pointing and directing. The natural environment was no longer safe. Mankind was distorting and shifting and changing the land. Time evolved. The forest gradually disappeared, tree by tree, animal by animal. The last tree hit the ground. It reverberated for miles and miles. Gone. Never to return.

* * *

The sound of something hitting the ground and shaking the house woke Henry. He looked at the clock. It was already ten in the morning. He got up and looked out the window. There were workers in their next-door neighbor's yard, and a tree lay on the ground. He remembered them saying that they would be cutting down some of their trees that morning. He got dressed and went downstairs to find something to eat before curling up in his favorite chair.

At first, he didn't know what he should do that day. There was always the TV or more yard work or finding something to read. Instead, he stayed lost in his thoughts and started thinking about his granddaughter. She always asked him for stories about his past, and yet he never told her anything. He felt like he should let her know, but he wasn't sure how. *Perhaps I could write it?* he thought. That gave him an idea. He had an extra journal in his room. He went back upstairs and got it before grabbing a pen.

That's what he would do. He was going to write his life story for her, and he would give it to her as her high school graduation gift. He started to write.

* * *

August 31, 1933. That was the birthday they gave me. I couldn't remember the day I was born as I was homeless on the streets. A poisonous fish killed my father, and my sister took me away to escape an abusive stepfather. But through it all, God was good to me. He sent a good Samaritan. People came, and people went, and not a single person ever stopped to help. But there was one guy. He stopped and he talked with me. I didn't know it at the time as I was not yet a believer, but God was guiding my life each step of the way. In life, we always reach a point where we believe that no one cares. But that's a lie that tricks us. It leads us astray. It leads us down dark paths until we think that there is no light left to see. Don't fall victim. There is so much more to life.

People do care.

I walked the streets aimlessly through the nights, and yet there was always light. No matter what we believe, where there is darkness, there is also light. I used to think that I could hide. I used to think that if I could hide, all my pain and suffering could slip away, melting like butter in a hot pan on the stove. I also used to think that nothing could get worse. However, I soon saw the truth—that life could throw so many unexpected curves, even when someone thinks that they have control. God knew what he was doing because he promises to never give more than what someone can handle. Seeing this firsthand and all the good that came out of my suffering-filled life, I know it to be true.

Believe.

Have faith.

Miracles are real.

Life is not easy, but where there is sadness, there is also joy.

Even if you can't see it, search deep down because I'll tell you a secret— it's there.

* * *

He spent the rest of the day writing. There were so many stories to write and so many more tales to tell. He wanted to share not only the story of his life, but the wisdom that he held. He wanted the younger generation to know and understand that there was so much more out there, that there was so much more beyond the walls of one's home. Adventures and different experiences awaited. Both the good and bad needed to be revealed. Truth must be told. Life was a book, and yet it went beyond the words on a page. Each person needed to find its meaning and purpose for themselves. Then and only then would the revelation of a lifetime of memories be found.

These were the reasons for his writings. He desired for his voice to be heard by the younger generations because he cared so much for them.

Time flew by, and before he knew it, it was Thursday and he was on his way to his test.

"Do you remember everything you learned?" Mimi asked her father.

"I think so."

"That's good. Hmm . . . let's see, what is the supreme law of the land?"

"The Constitution," Henry replied, thrilled that he knew the answer.

"Good. How about, how many years do we elect a president for?"

"Four."

"Alright, just one more since we're here. What is the highest court in the US?"

"Umm . . . that's the Supreme Court!" Henry exclaimed.

His daughter laughed.

"See, you're going to do great!"

They got out of the car and walked into the building where they were greeted by a receptionist.

"Good morning. Are you all here to speak to a representative or take a citizenship test or—"

"Citizenship test," Mimi said.

"Alright, if you'll take this clipboard here and fill out these forms in the waiting room right over there. Once you're finished with them, just bring them back here. We'll be sure to put you down on the list. What's the name?"

"Henry Ah Veng Chia."

"Okay, thank you. Oh, and I see that he had an appointment scheduled. We'll be right with you once all the forms are finished."

Henry sat in one of the chairs in the waiting room, and Mimi joined him a little while later. He noticed that there were a lot of people in the room and wondered if they were all there to take the test as well.

"Henry Chia," someone called from a doorway. He stood and followed the person into a room.

Mimi watched as he disappeared from sight and prayed to God that he would do well and pass. She was not completely relieved until he came out with a big smile on his face. He handed her a piece of paper.

"That was easy," he said.

"You passed!" she exclaimed, hardly able to contain her excitement.

Henry was really excited as well. He couldn't believe that he was going to be an actual US citizen.

He could hardly sleep during the following nights because he was anticipating the ceremony that would make it official. At times when he couldn't sleep, he would crawl out of bed and go downstairs for a cup of water. Billy would be lounging on the couch, and Henry sometimes sat beside him, stroking the animal. That cat was something special. He had never met an animal with such a gentle and loving spirit. Something about the cat pulled on his heartstrings. He remembered when his granddaughter was younger. She would often pull the cat's tail or pinch its nose, and yet not once did Billy scratch or bite. He would howl in pain, but he never did harm to anyone, even if they were harming him.

Perhaps Henry liked the cat so much because it reminded him of Jesus. Their personalities were sort of parallel. Both were tortured in some way, and yet they never wanted to harm anyone or take revenge for what those people did to them. Now, that was an amazing quality, such humility. He got up and grabbed his journal, writing while he had the words in mind.

* * *

Humble.

I ran across the meaning of this word several times throughout my life, although I did not necessarily know it at the time. The first includes all the moments my sisters were abused. I watched as they refused to fight back, continuing to show respect even when they had every right to stand up for themselves. I watched as they obeyed every command without a word, without a complaint, and without question. If only I had known better, maybe things would have turned out differently. There were moments where I looked back and replayed memories in my mind and wondered what would have happened if the scene played out in another manner.

Now, I choose to forget.

Regret rips and ruins people on the inside, and I went through that corruption at one point, and tears rained down in waves.

Sad tears.

My wife and children trusted me to lead them by example. They trusted me to provide and protect, and I did so well until regret and doubt in myself swallowed me whole. I sat in the house for months, refusing to move or go out with my tear-stained face. My job had let me go and I saw no point in trying anymore. I kept thinking to myself that if only I worked harder, maybe there was a small chance that they would have kept me, despite my age. I fell apart, and it took so much effort from others around me to bring me back to life again. They pulled me away from the depression and gambling that I fell into. I did not think that it was possible, but there is always hope.

Another chance.

Soon after that, I had an encounter with God. My eldest daughter had a friend over who convinced me to step foot in the church. Although I was reluctant, I thought that a simple dinner could do no harm. However, as soon as I walked through the doors of that church, I was treated with unexplainable kindness. I cannot really describe in words how I felt. The atmosphere was just something completely different, and I finally felt accepted again after such a long time of feeling like an outcast. I found my place, and not long after, I found faith in God. The miracles were in front of me the entire time, and he had been trying to make his present known, but I pushed him away. I cried happy tears after my baptism because I finally realized that everything in my life had happened for a reason. It had brought me to that special moment in time.

Happy tears are a real thing.

Even when change seems impossible, if tears can transform from sad to happy, anything is possible.

* * *

About a week later, Henry noticed that Billy was getting weaker. The cat was as thin as a rail since he wasn't eating as much, and he hardly ran or jumped around anymore. The cat was getting quite old. Mimi had gotten him around the time his granddaughter was born.

"Do you think something's wrong with Billy?" he asked his daughter one day as she worked in her office.

"I don't know," she said.

Henry went downstairs and asked his son the same question.

"He's just getting old," Ah Lay said. "He's probably just losing energy."

A few days later, they found Billy lying on the bathroom floor. He had peacefully passed away sometime in the night. Henry cried out and couldn't help the sobs. That cat was so dear to him and had touched him in such a unique way. It was the first time Mimi had heard him cry like that. It was the first time she had witnessed him losing something so sentimental. Henry let himself cry until he felt as though he could pull himself together. *At least he passed peacefully,* he thought as they buried their dear pet.

That night, he wrote about the precious cat so that his grandchildren would be able to remember and hold on to those memories. The cat was dear to them too, and when his granddaughter heard of Billy's passing, she regretted the way she had treated him when she was younger. However, it was not her fault. She was so young at that point and didn't know that it was wrong. He set the tip of his pen down on the paper and wrote, *God gives and takes away. Enjoy the blessings and remember the happy moments. Don't rely upon the past. BEHOLD and BE BOLD. He LIVES so that we may have life.*

There were some days that he wrote in order to think about everything he was grateful for. After being in the United States for so long, he had fallen in love with the country. It had so much to offer, and he was thankful that many of his children and grandchildren would be able to receive its blessings.

He thought about the same things when he finally stood at the naturalization oath ceremony to recite and pledge his allegiance to America. His smile was contagious because he was so happy and proud. He and Mimi went out to celebrate afterwards.

"Can we go to Dollar General?" he asked when they were on the way home.

"Dollar General? Umm, sure. Is there something you want to buy there?"

"Yeah."

"Okay," she said, turning into a Dollar General that was close to their house. "What are you wanting to buy?" Mimi asked once they were inside.

"Hold on." Henry went down an aisle. "This!" he said, holding up an American flag. "I want one for my room and one for the living room, and then we can take one to Stone Mountain tonight too."

Mimi laughed. Her father was too cute sometimes. They paid for the flags and went outside, but Henry didn't get in the car. Instead, he grabbed his passport and stood at the front of the store.

"Take my picture."

"What?"

"I want a picture," he insisted.

His daughter took out her camera and shook her head at his excitement. It was a really proud and special moment in his life, and he wanted it documented. She snapped a few shots and then got in the car.

"Okay, let's go home and get ready for tonight. We'll see if Ah Lay and mother will want to go as well."

As it turned out, all four of them went that night, which was surprising since Ah Lay and Rose usually stayed at home. They arrived at the mountain early for once and got a pretty good spot right in the center. Henry held his flag and snacked on some of the things they brought before the show started. He expected it to be the same, but it was different. He sat up a bit and paid attention.

This time, the laser show told the story of a girl at school who was learning about history. Henry got excited when he realized that he knew some of the facts being taught. The next song was all about the fifty states. The tune was catchy, and he smiled when he realized that he knew a lot about the states as well. It was as if he finally fit in and could understand. He wondered why the show was different this time.

The next song and story was about soldiers during war. They were serving their country to help make it a safer place for all citizens. He watched the projection and felt immense gratitude for those men and women who served with such honor. The depiction of their bravery was very moving. The whole show illustrated the story of America, showing the history, the families, the wars, the battles. It went through the good, the bad, the happy, the sad. He had never seen anything like it. It made him all the more thankful to be a citizen of a country that held so much. The beauty of it all almost brought him to tears.

The Star-Spangled Banner played next, and everyone stood. He noticed that other people were holding flags as well, and he held his a little higher as he put his hand over his heart. *Is there a special occasion?* he wondered. It was then that he realized it was Veterans Day. *Well, that explains it,* he thought. Fireworks went off and people cheered. However, it wasn't completely over yet; the last song that played was "I'm Proud to Be an American." Henry was awestruck at the perfect timing.

"Papá, look at that. This song is for you!" Mimi exclaimed.

"How does it feel to be an American?" Ah Lay asked, smiling at his father.

Henry grinned.

"Proud. I'm proud to be an American," he replied.

The fireworks lit up the sky just like they did every night. However, this time was different. It was a special night as the US welcomed a new citizen. Henry was not surprised to see the silhouette of a butterfly projected on the screen, fluttering past fields of green. A great symbol of red, white and blue waved in the background. The symbol of freedom and beauty. The symbol of a glorious country. The symbol that encompassed all of America—from sea to shining sea.

CHAPTER 16

BUILDING A FOUNDATION

July 2016
Miri, Sarawak, Malaysia

SWELTERING HEAT POURED FROM THE SKY. Everything seemed as though it were melting. Henry wiped the sweat from his brow. It was dripping into his eyes and blurring his vision.

"Papá, can you bring me that wood?" Ah Lay asked, pointing to a wheelbarrow.

Henry stood and wheeled the cart full of wood to his son, who was hammering a nail into the doorframe. They were building a house on his property because the government was going to take it away if they didn't do something with it. Other workers were working on it, but he wanted to help finish since it was his land and his house.

He was already eighty-one years old, and he had to think about who he was going to sign the property over to. What he really wanted to do was give it to all his children, but he wasn't sure if he could do that.

"Do you think we'll finish it in time?" Henry questioned as he picked up an extra hammer.

"We're pretty close to being finished, so I'm going to say yes. We'll definitely finish in time."

The two of them continued working in silence, and Henry thought about how blessed he was to be able to take this last trip back to Malaysia. He needed to finish up some things, starting with his property and the fact that he desperately wanted the family of his eldest son to be saved. *Is that going to be accomplished?* he wondered. *Possibly.*

"Henry!" someone called.

He turned to see who it was.

"I thought that I might find you here," his friend Sheng said, walking through the front of the house. It had been forever since Henry had seen him.

"How'd you know I came back?" Henry asked, grinning widely and walking over to shake his hand.

"Eh, people talk," Sheng replied, shrugging before going on to ask, "How have you been? How's America? Like, wow, how many years has it been?"

Henry laughed. "Good and good, and it's been too many."

"Yes, it has! And while you've been off adventuring, nothing's really changed here except expansion, but that's not new. We're always expanding and building new restaurants, shops, or stores. The construction is never-ending. And look at you, building a house again. Never fails."

"How's your family?" Henry asked as he put his tools away; it was about time to head back to the house for the day.

"Oh, they're alright. My kids all have families of their own now, but they stay close by, except for one of my sons who decided to study in KL. They're definitely not like yours that spread out across the world. How do you even visit all of them?"

"Well, I usually don't because they visit us, but I've made a trip or two."

"Ahh, I bet it gives them the opportunity to see America. A lot of people have been talking about how hard it is to get a visa."

"Papá, we should get back so that we don't miss dinner," Ah Lay called from the front doorway.

Henry looked at his friend. "I wish that we could visit a bit more, but there will be other times that we can. I'll be here for a few months," he said as they walked out of the house.

"It's alright. And make sure that you do come visit! You know where to find me," Sheng said and got into his car on the side of the road.

Henry waved before watching his friend drive off. He and Ah Lay got into their own car and drove back to the house of his eldest son. Ah Tap was the only one that had stayed in Miri, while Henry's other children emigrated to other countries. Henry glanced out the window and admired all that he saw, not realizing how much he had missed the country of his birth. Deep down, he had needed to see it one last time. They pulled into the driveway of the small home.

"Kong-kong, Kong-kong!" his youngest granddaughter yelled, running out of the house. "*Lihat*,"[43] she said, holding up a cage.

He bent down to see what was inside and cringed when he saw a tiny mouse.

"Did you catch it?" he asked. The little girl nodded enthusiastically before running back inside. Her older brother stood at the window and greeted his grandpa once he walked in.

"Hi, Kong-kong."

"Hi, how was school?" Henry asked as he slipped on his house shoes.

"Okay," the boy said before flopping down on the couch to change the channel on the TV.

Ah Tap walked in from the bedroom.

"Hello, Father. Dinner is almost ready, and don't forget to pack for tomorrow."

---

43 Look

"Tomorrow?"

"Yes, we're going to Bintulu, remember?"

"Oh, right. Yes, I will pack tonight."

He walked into the kitchen to find Ah Tap's wife setting the table.

"Hi, Papá," she said.

"*Saya mahu makan*,"[44] his granddaughter said, bouncing in her chair.

"Please be patient," her mother scolded as she went to grab more chopsticks from the drawer and placed them on the table. "Okay, *makan malam*,"[45] she called once she carried the last dish over.

Henry sat down at his spot as his two sons and grandson came in. They immediately started to grab food and eat.

"Wait, the blessing," Henry said.

His grandkids stared at him.

"We have to bless the food. Father, thank you for this day and for this food that you have given us. We thank you. Amen."

He looked up and smiled before digging into the food himself. Everyone else picked up where they had left off. The two kids didn't finish their food before running off to play again, and Henry helped to clean up the kitchen before heading to the living room to see what they were up to.

"What's that?" he asked his grandson.

"An iPad. It has games and stuff on it."

"What are you playing?"

"It's just a game." He briefly showed the screen to his grandfather. "You're trying to get this over there, but you have to go through this maze."

"Kong-kong, this! Look, this," his granddaughter said, trying to get his attention.

She was blowing bubbles and popping them. It made her giggle. He laughed at her reaction, and she handed him the bottle.

---

44   I want to eat

45   dinner

"You," she said.

"I blow?"

The little girl nodded, so he dipped the small stick in the solution and blew. Bubbles of all shapes and sizes formed and floated through the air. Some of them disappeared. The girl twirled through them, swinging around a doll she had grabbed off the couch. He looked at Ah Tap's two kids, thankful that he was getting to spend time with them. This trip was his first time seeing them since he hadn't been back to Malaysia in so long. They weren't even born until long after he left for America.

"Again," his granddaughter said.

He blew out some more and watched her twirl around once again. That went on for a while until he got up to head to his bedroom.

"More," the little girl whined.

He shook his head. "I have to pack."

"Pack?"

"*Saya perlu bungkus untuk esok.*"[46]

"Oh, *saya juga!*"[47] she said, running into her room to find her mom.

Henry grabbed the backpack that sat beside his suitcase and emptied it out. Ah Lay must have already packed; a bag sat beside the door, and he was already in bed, probably exhausted from all the work they did that day. Henry tried to be quiet as he packed what he thought they might need. They would only be gone for a few nights. He put a couple changes of clothes in the bag, as well as his Bible and other sundries, before getting ready for bed. Once he closed the door and lay down, he was out, and the dream world came to life.

* * *

It was dark and gloomy. A light mist filled the air and shifted at the slightest twitch. Somewhere, a light flickered. It cast a glow and a shadow that trailed behind one's feet. Someone moaned as if in pain.

---

46   I have to pack for tomorrow

47   me too

Henry flinched. A man was slumped against the wall of an abandoned building. Several cans lay next to him, and he held a bottle in his hands. A drunk. Shouts came from another alleyway. Someone was screaming for help, but the sound of beating drowned it out. A gang. Voices filled the air, coming from all directions this time. He wished he could drown it all out, but they persisted, growing louder and louder. A liar. A thief. A killer. A prostitute. A drug dealer. A cheat. The shadow was getting closer and closer. Such brokenness littered the streets. The drunk tossed the bottle in anger. It shattered into a million pieces.

* * *

Henry jerked awake, breathing heavily.

"You broke it, you clean it!" his grandson yelled accusatorily.

"I didn't mean to," his granddaughter whined.

Henry got out of bed and opened the bedroom door to find the two kids standing over a broken plate.

"Why did you take a plate into the living room anyway?" Ah Lay asked.

Henry turned to see his son standing behind him, and he moved out of the way, careful to avoid pieces of glass.

"Because she wanted to feed the mouse, and I told her to just grab the food, not the plate, but no, she just had to bring the plate in here," the brother said, glaring at his younger sister.

"No, you said feed it," she shot back.

"I did not."

"What happened?" Ah Tap asked, walking in from his bedroom and rubbing his eyes. His wife saw the mess and shook her head, walking away and coming back with a broom. She began sweeping it up and shooed her kids away.

"*Pergi berpakaian,*"[48] she said as the two ran into their parents' bedroom.

---

48   Go get dressed

Henry turned and went to do so himself; they were going to leave soon.

Their breakfast was a quick one so that they could pack things into the car, and soon they were on their way. The kids chattered happily in the backseat but would occasionally fuss when one of them got too annoying. Other than that, it was a decent car ride that wasn't too long. Bintulu was only about three hours from Miri, and throughout the drive, Henry thought about who all he knew that lived there. He knew that one of his sisters did, but he couldn't recall which one. He didn't stay in touch with most of them and only heard what his friends told him about how they were faring. He wasn't sure if he wanted to visit the one in Bintulu. The only sister he did like to see was the one that lived in KL, and he had seen her a few weeks ago. Ah Lay had something to do that day, so he had taken a *teksi*[49] to his sister's house.

They pulled into the parking lot of an office.

"I have to run in and get something," Ah Tap said. "I'll be right back."

Henry had almost forgotten that his son worked in Bintulu. Their visit here made a lot more sense.

They would be traveling to other places as well. Ah Tap wanted his father to have the chance to visit relatives and see more of his hometown and country for the last time. Henry's children had decided that this was his final trip. They didn't want him traveling so far again because his age made the exertion dangerous. He wished that it weren't true but knew that they were probably right to be concerned.

Ah Tap came back to the car with a stack of papers, and he put them in the trunk before climbing back into the driver's seat. They drove off again towards the center of the town to find somewhere to eat.

"Can we get *ais kacang*?"[50] the little girl called from the back.

---

49   taxi

50   A Malaysian dessert that literally means "bean ice," also commonly known as ABC

"Maybe after lunch," her dad said, turning to park in front of a friend's restaurant.

They walked in and were instantly greeted by the owner.

"Ah Tap! How good to see you, and you brought your family along this time! Is that— Ah, Uncle!" The man rushed forward to shake Henry's hand. "It has been a very long time."

"Yes, many years," Henry said, laughing.

"So, how have things been?" the owner asked once the family was seated.

"Good, good. We're working on finishing the house," Ah Tap replied.

"Oh yeah, how's that going?"

"It's coming along and is close to being done. The workers should be working on it right now, and my father and brother have been extra helping hands as well."

"Oh wow, Uncle. You still remember how to build houses?"

"Of course," Henry replied, grinning. People always seemed surprised that he still remembered how to build. Now, that was something that he could never forget. It was one of his purposes in life—he was sure of it.

"That's great. I can't wait to see the house once it's finished. Now, what can I get you all to drink?" the man asked.

"100PLUS,"[51] the little girl blurted out excitedly, blocking out her brother's reply.

"Okay, and what was that you said?"

"Milo,"[52] the boy answered, clearly annoyed that his sister was being so rambunctious.

The adults all ordered hot tea and water.

"Alright, I'll be right back with your drinks and ready to take your order."

---

51   Isotopic sports drink that originated in Malaysia
52   A type of hot chocolate

"Should I get *nasi lemak*[53] or *char kway teow*?"[54] Ah Tap's wife asked him.

He shrugged. "I'm getting nasi lemak because I don't really want noodles."

The man came back with their drinks.

"I thought that you usually don't wait tables," Ah Tap observed.

"Oh, yes. I usually don't, but I'm low on staff right now, so I kind of have to. A lot of people have been moving away lately, but I don't think that's completely the reason since many people have moved here recently as well. Anyway, are you ready to order?" the man asked.

Henry looked at the menu again after the others had ordered. He wasn't quite sure what he wanted, and everyone else was waiting on him. *Maybe something spicy,* he thought.

"I'll just have *mie goreng*,"[55] he said, pointing to the picture of the dish on the menu.

"Alright. We'll have those right out for you."

Henry tried to think of the last time he ate that particular dish. It had been a while. He realized that he had missed Malaysian food in America. Although at times his wife would cook food that resembled their native dishes, it still wasn't the same.

They didn't have to wait long before their food came out, and once the kids finished most of their food, their parents ordered ais kacang for them. Shortly after that, they were on their way to find a place to stay for the night.

Over the next few days, they traveled and visited friends and relatives or simply went sight-seeing. Henry enjoyed catching up with people he hadn't seen in years. He was also reunited with some of his sisters and found it in him to forgive all of them. He used to think that would be impossible, but he felt so much better when he did. He also forgave his stepsiblings and all his family members that had hurt

---

53 Malaysian fragrant rice dish

54 Malaysian noodle dish that literally means "stir-fried rice-cake strips"

55 Malaysian spicy fried noodle dish

or wronged him.

After forgiving all those people, he did not understand how he could have held a grudge for so long. In fact, he didn't understand why people held grudges or sought revenge. Life was so much more enjoyable when one reflected on the cheerful times instead of dwelling in misery on the dark moments of the past. He thought about all the people he encountered and realized that so many people were lost to the darkness and in desperate need of salvation.

The night they returned to Miri, he wrote in his journal:

> *Be the light in a dark world.*
> *Save the people.*

He took advantage of every opportunity to write things down in his journal, even if it was a simple phrase or word that came to mind. Progress on the house they were building was also something that he recorded daily, and looking back through the notes he had made, he realized they were closer to finishing the house than he'd thought.

* * *

Some weeks later, Henry hammered in the last nail just as the last screw was tightened.

"Is that it?" Ah Lay asked.

"Yes! It's finished!" one of the workers shouted.

The others cheered and stepped back to take a look. The house that loomed over them was immense, holding over ten bedrooms in addition to several other rooms.

"Uncle, what are you going to do with this house? This is huge!" one of the guys exclaimed.

"I'm not sure," Henry said.

Ah Lay was on the phone with Ah Tap, urging him to bring his family over to see it. Henry stared up at it. *It would have been nice if my kids had a house like that when they were growing up instead of a home that hardly gave them enough room to even sleep on the floor,* he thought. But his kids would have a great house now—if he could sign it over to all of them.

"Ah Tap is coming over now, and then we can go over to the Land and Survey government office afterwards to see if you can sign the papers. Do you still want to do that?" Ah Lay asked.

"Yes, I do. I want you all to have this," Henry said, smiling up at the house.

"Well, I don't know what we are going to do with it. People are going to think we're rich or something."

"We are."

"Umm, no, Papá, I don't think that we are," Ah Lay argued, unsure of why his father thought that they were.

"Yes, because we are rich in blessings. We are rich in the eyes of God."

"Right, that's true," the son said, nodding and walking away to greet Ah Tap, who was pulling into the driveway.

"*Itu besar!*"[56] Henry's granddaughter exclaimed excitedly as she jumped out of the car and ran up to the house.

"Woah," his grandson said, standing there in shock.

Their reactions amused Henry.

"Papá, it looks good!" Ah Tap said, coming over to pat him on the back.

"Go look inside," called one of the workers stacking the extra materials to the side.

The kids pushed open the front door and started running from room to room and up and down the stairs.

"I like this one!"

"No, this one's better!"

"Wow, it has two kitchens," Ah Tap's wife said.

---

56   It's big

"Should we wait to do the papers tomorrow?" Ah Tap asked Ah Lay, but Henry overheard them.

"No, today," he said.

"I mean, if we go now, we'll probably have time," Ah Lay stated, looking down at his watch.

"Okay. *Mari pergi!*"[57] Ah Tap yelled as his kids ran down the stairs.

"We're going already?" the boy asked.

"Yes, come on."

They piled in to the car and waved goodbye to the workers who were cleaning up outside. The office wasn't too far, and Henry was excited. He remembered when his children had first informed him that he had to build a house or he was going to lose his land. At first, the news troubled him; he didn't think that there was enough money to build one, until all his children decided to chip in. They were the real reason why this was happening.

The car stopped. Ah Tap turned off the engine and handed the keys to his wife.

"You and the kids can go somewhere for a bit or wait inside."

She simply nodded as the three guys got out of the car and headed inside where they were greeted by a lady at the front desk.

"*Selemat petang,*[58] can I help you?"

"Yes, we are here to see if our father can sign over his property to his children," Ah Tap said.

"Ah, yes, I'll see if my boss is available to help you with that." After a brief call she said, "He says that you can go ahead back to his office. If you'll go through this door to your right and walk all the way down, his office is the last door at the very end."

"Thank you."

They followed her directions and knocked on the door, pushing it open when they heard someone say, "Come in." The man seated behind

<hr>

57 Let's go

58 Good afternoon

the desk rose to shake their hands before they all took a seat. "Hi, welcome, welcome, my name is Guotin. What can I do for you today?"

"Well, we just finished building a house on my father's property today, and he was wondering if he could sign it over to his children. Right, Papá?" Ah Tap said.

"Yes, I want my kids to have the house and land."

"How many kids do you have?" the man asked Henry.

"Seven of my own, plus one of their cousins that's officially adopted."

"Oh, yikes, that's quite a number of kids. Let me see what I can do here. What's your name?"

"Henry Chia."

"Alright, I'm pulling up the information on your property now. Yeah, I can see that everything is under your name, and you're saying that you want it signed over to all your children. Are your other kids nearby?"

"No, most of them are overseas."

"Oh wow, okay. I'm not completely sure that will work. We would need them to be here in person in order to sign the form." The man grabbed some papers from his printer and placed them in front of Henry. "See, and here, it only has a place for up to three people to sign. So, you could sign it to your two sons right here, and then possibly, in the future, they could add their other siblings on if they ever come back to Miri."

"Are you sure there isn't a way that we could all be owners of it?" Ah Tap asked.

"It's alright. I'm texting in the group chat now, and most of them have said that they are okay if they don't own the land, and I am as well. I don't think I want to be on it," Ah Lay said.

"Can I sign it over to you?" Henry asked his eldest son.

"If you want to, Papá, but it's entirely up to you. I'll take care of it no matter what."

"So, are we signing it over to him?" Guotin asked.

"Yes," Henry replied, nodding.

"And you're sure."

Henry nodded.

"Alright, then if you could just sign here and here, and then have your son sign on this line on the following page," Guotin said, pushing the papers forward and handing Henry a pen. "I'm sorry that there isn't really a way to get all of your children on there. It's just difficult to handle when there's too many people that have ownership."

"We understand," Ah Lay said. "It probably will get too messy when you try to sell it or make renovations or repairs."

"Yes, that was exactly one of my worries. If there's more than one owner, it's harder to agree on what must be done, and it's even harder if most of your siblings live overseas."

Ah Tap handed the papers back to Guotin.

"Is there anything else that we need to do?" Henry asked.

"Yes, one more thing. I need the new owner to fill in his information on this sheet," he said, passing another paper to Ah Tap. "We'll be getting in contact with you soon; we have to follow protocol by telling you what it means to be the owner of this property. Also, if you choose to rent it out, we'll need to be informed."

Ah Tap handed the form and pen back to the man.

"Thank you for your help," Ah Lay said, standing to leave. "We appreciate it."

"Yes, thank you very much," Henry said, standing to shake the man's hand once more.

"Thank you," Ah Tap said.

"It was my pleasure, but I really am sorry that we weren't able to do what you wanted."

"That's okay." Henry smiled reassuringly.

"Well, best wishes to each of you, and I'll be in touch with you soon," Guotin said, pointing at Ah Tap.

They walked out and went back to the car.

"Can we go to the store?" Henry asked. "I want to get some things to bless the house with."

"Bless the house?"

"Yes, I want to go back there after dinner."

"Won't it be dark?" Ah Tap asked.

"Yes, but I want to bless it."

"Okay," Ah Tap said, looking at his brother, who shrugged and got in the car.

"*Saya lapar,*"[59] the little girl whined from the back. "Why'd you take so long?"

"Shh," her brother said, "that's not our business."

"We're going to stop by the store first and then we'll go home for dinner," Ah Tap said. "Ah Lay, we can take Papá once we finish eating."

They drove back towards their house and stopped at a store close by.

"Do you have money?" Ah Lay asked.

"Yes," Henry said, nodding and getting out of the car.

A few minutes later he returned to the car with a small bag.

"*Apa yang awak beli?*"[60] his granddaughter asked.

"Candles."

"Candles? What's that?"

"*Lilin.*"[61]

"Oh, why you buy that?"

"Stop asking," her brother snapped at her.

Their dinner that evening was a quick one since they were just eating leftovers, and soon enough, Ah Tap, Ah Lay and Henry were on their way to the house. The sun had not started to set yet, but it would within the next hour. When they got to the house, Ah Tap and Ah Lay lingered outside because they wanted to give their father his privacy, not exactly sure what he wanted to do. All they knew was that he had a stool, a hammer, a picture frame, nails, candles, and matches.

---

59   I'm hungry

60   What'd you buy?

61   Candles

"We'll wait out here, okay?" Ah Lay said when they got to the front door.

Henry nodded and entered the house by himself. He set all his things down and went to work. Using the remaining daylight, he set the stool by the front door and picked up his hammer and a nail. He stood on the stool, eyed the center of the doorframe, and hammered the nail in partway. He then retrieved the picture frame he had brought and got back up on the stool to hang it before stepping down to admire it. The words were in his handwriting above a cross that he drew. It read **GOD BLESS THIS HOUSEHOLD.**

He bowed his head to say a prayer and then picked up the candles and matches. Walking up the stairs to the second and third floor, he placed a candle in the middle of each hallway and lit them, then went back downstairs to do the same. He also put one in each of the living rooms before he made his way back to the front door. Starting there, he placed his hand on the wall and moved along, tracing every inch of the house from one point to the next until it led him up the stairs and back down again. He kept doing that, saying silent prayers and whispering. His mind focused on one thing and one thing only. He wanted that household to be blessed. He wanted the foundation to remain strong, to be grounded, to stand firm. He had built it with his own hands, and it would not be taken for granted. His family had to know. They had to understand. His writings, his teachings, his reasons for everything he did revolved around that one thing. *Blessings.*

He couldn't remember how many times he made his rounds, but it was already dark outside. He blew out the candles one by one when he passed them until he finally returned to his spot at the front door. One candle remained lit. The blessings had been given, and a foundation had been built. It would stay rooted for generation after generation, never to be broken. It was as strong as it ever could be. It was as strong as a tree. That one candle illuminated the entrance to the house with a soft glow that allowed Henry to read his words hanging above the door. *God bless this household.* The candle went out.

CHAPTER 17

FLAMES
OF GLORY

March 2017
Stone Mountain, Georgia, United States

THE MOON WAS FULL, AND THE clear sky glowed with twinkling stars—a radiant, starry wonder. Henry went to bed early that night, lulled into a deep slumber by the hooting of an owl.

* * *

Disorientation. Confusion. Turmoil. Chaos. The smell of something burning. The taste, the feel, the sound of something burning. The sight of nothing but smoke and flames, choking and suffocating. The land screamed as flames licked it clean of all living things. Destroyed it completely. Scarred for eternity. The fire raged in relentless anger. It festered and burned and spread some more, running faster and faster to steal everything. It wanted life and dreams, a home, a family. The vengeful force ran rampant, destroying so much of what it would never own. It destroyed all hope, replacing it with furious, fiery light.

* * *

For once, Henry did not awake to something related to his dream. They were often confusing, but he believed that they allowed him to see the world the way it truly was, which meant exposing both the good and the bad. He didn't mind. They had become a part of who he was. Dreams were important in their family. He believed that they might even be messages from God. *We can learn so much by merely seeing the world through the eyes of someone or something else*, he marveled.

Henry got out of bed and looked at the clock. It was already nine. He put on work clothes and went downstairs to make himself a cup of Milo and a piece of toast before sitting in his chair to read his Bible. Around ten thirty he decided to go outside to do some yard work since he was tired of sitting in the house. He usually spent his days inside; he didn't have much to do. Occasionally he would take a walk or go out with his daughter Mimi, but most of the time he stayed in his room.

As he wandered outside, he thought about what he should do. There were a lot of weeds around the mailbox. He went to the garage to grab a pair of gloves, thinking that he could pull weeds by the mailbox until the mailman arrived since Henry took it upon himself to get the mail every day.

The weather was perfect as he squatted down to start his task. He hummed to himself as he worked, enjoying the nice day and his time outside. Meanwhile, his daughter was in her office working when she noticed smoke. She couldn't tell where it was coming from.

"Ah Lay!" she called down into the basement.

He was working on his computer and noticed that something was wrong when the screen blacked out for a moment before coming back on. He ran upstairs to the main level.

"What was that?"

"There's smoke. I don't know where it's coming from. I already checked the stoves up here and none of them are on. Is mother cooking downstairs?"

"I don't think so."

"Well, go check. I'll check upstairs."

Ah Lay ran back down the stairs to find his mom feeding the dogs. Her sewing machine was on.

"Ayi, are you cooking?"

"No," she said, looking up.

Ah Lay ran back up to the main level just in time to hear his sister scream, "Fire!" She ran down from the second floor. "There's a fire in Papá's room and too much smoke. I can't get the door open."

He panicked and ran up the stairs.

"No, don't go up there," Mimi said frantically, but he was already halfway.

"Papá!" Ah Lay shouted, coughing.

Smoke seeped out from under the door. He grabbed the handle even though it was hot and tried to force the door open. It wouldn't budge. He pushed even harder, and it cracked just a bit, but he was hit with a wall of smoke and saw only a glimpse of the flames before he fell backwards, coughing violently. His vision spun. He knew he couldn't pass out, so he forced himself up and stumbled back down the stairs.

"Mimi!" he shouted before coughing again.

She ran up from the basement.

"I already told Mother to take the dogs and cat outside. Google, Buddy and Bubba will be fine, but Afu ran off."

"Don't worry about that right now. Where's Papá? I need a hose."

"Will it reach?"

"Doesn't matter. We're going to try."

Mimi ran out the front door and grabbed the hose that they used to water the plants. She passed it to her brother, who took it as far as it could go. The smoke had filled up the entire second floor, a black mass devouring everything in its reach. Water came from the hose in a trickle. Ah Lay coughed and heard sirens in the distance. A fire and rescue truck pulled into the driveway, and the men yelled at Mimi, who was running back into the house.

"Ma'am, get out of the house!"

"But my father's in there!" she yelled back and went in anyway.

"It's no use," Ah Lay said.

"Out! Come on, we'll take care of it," one of the rescue men shouted just as a fire truck arrived.

The firemen swarmed, and the two siblings trailed out after the first man. Just as they walked out the front door, Henry noticed the firetrucks pulling into their driveway and stood up to see what was going on. Smoke was rising from their roof. He hurried back towards the house.

"Papá!" Mimi shouted with relief. "He's okay," she said, grabbing Ah Lay. "He's okay."

"What's wrong?" Henry asked.

"Thank God you're okay," Mimi said when he reached them.

The dogs were running around and barking like crazy.

"The house is—"

The sound of glass breaking cut her off, and they all turned to watch as the fire erupted through the windows, released from its captivity. The firemen shouted to one another.

"We need more water pressure."

"Turn it up!"

"Hold steady!"

Water and fire met in a relentless battle. It seemed to last for an eternity, but finally, fire was defeated. It shivered and died, leaving nothing but smoke and ashes. The sky above their house was black, as if marking the death of a home. Almost everything was gone. The family sat on the ground beneath the trees as the firemen ran in and out before putting up their equipment.

"How bad is it?" Mimi asked one of the men who approached them.

"Well, the attic and entire second floor is gone, burned completely. And the main level has both smoke and water damage. The basement just has water damage. I'm sorry to say that the house is probably going to need to be completely rebuilt."

"Do you know what caused the fire?" she asked.

"We think it was electrical. Wires could have potentially sparked and started burning. Or it could have been from the outlet, or an electrical appliance; it could have been anything, really. However, the room where it started has wires across the floor and remnants of what seems like many books and paper judging by the amount of ashes. That might very well be the reason."

"Yes, that's my dad's room. He has a lot of books and journals. I knew that he had wires across the floor of his room because he has a TV and fan in there, but I didn't think that it was dangerous."

"I'm really sorry, ma'am."

Henry stopped paying attention to what they were saying. *My room is gone? My stuff is gone?* He started to panic. *What am I supposed to wear if I don't have clothes?*

He then realized that all his writings were gone as well. The hundreds of pages of his life story were gone. The things he created for his family members. The pictures that he held most dear. *Gone, gone, gone. It is all gone.* He put his head in his hands. He had worked on that story for so many years, for his granddaughter to have, and now . . . it was wiped away in a matter of seconds, as if it never existed

There was no way that he could rewrite it. He was supposed to be traveling to Texas in two weeks. Perhaps he could tell her then and hope that she would understand.

"Are you all okay?" someone asked.

He looked up and saw that their neighbors had walked over to check on them.

"Yes, we are. Just a bit shocked is all," Mimi answered.

"Yeah, I bet. That must have been quite a scare. We were about to head to the store when we saw the smoke and dialed 911."

Henry zoned out again. *The fire started in my room. Is it my fault that we are now homeless?* The guilt overwhelmed him. *What if I'd stayed in my room for just a while longer? What if I'd never stacked those books in that one corner? What if I'd taped the wires to the wall instead of letting them run along the ground? What if? What if? What if?* That's all he could think about.

Forgive me, God, he thought. *If only I paid more attention.* He watched as the smoke continued to rise from the house and dissipate.

"Where are we going to live?" he asked Ah Lay.

"I don't know. I'm sure we'll find a place."

"What about the dogs and the cat?"

Ah Lay sighed.

"I really don't know, but I'm sure that we'll figure it out. Mimi is on the phone with the insurance company right now," he said, nodding towards his sister.

They sat there in silence. Henry looked to where his wife was sitting. She seemed to be lost in thought as well, simply staring up at the house.

The next few days were a blur. The insurance company had them stay in a hotel while they further investigated how the fire started and how much they were going to pay for repairs. The two big dogs were staying at a kennel while the smaller dog and cat stayed with the family at the hotel. Henry wondered if the two dogs at the kennel were doing okay.

His granddaughter in Texas had somehow convinced her parents to let her get two puppies that were brothers, not knowing that they were going to be huge. They were too big, and their house was too small for the pets. So, one of them had become Mimi's Christmas present. That was Buddy. About a year later, Mimi learned that Buddy's brother was constantly at the animal shelter since it kept running away from its new home. She took Bubba in, and the brothers were reunited. The two were inseparable from that moment on.

Although Henry missed the dogs, he wasn't terribly upset about their absence. What still bothered him was that he had to get clothes from charities and organizations. However, one thing was saved from the fire; his Bible had been left by his chair in the living room, so not everything had been lost. God's word prevailed. Henry spent the days curled up, reading his Bible, writing new notes, and watching TV. With nothing much to do, he thought about his past and where he came from. He didn't have anything to start with, and now here he was, back in the same exact state. *Is this how life works? Is it a cycle?* He grabbed a piece of paper and started to write:

> *The things of the earth shall pass away as they cannot follow us into the afterlife. There's so much more to life than material things.*
> *Treasure awaits.*
> *Souls can be saved.*
> *Pictures and notes and keepsakes should not be relied upon.*
> *There's so much more to life.*
> *There's more to everything.*
> *Stories, memories, recollections, remembrances. Never forget these things. They hold the key. They hold the answers, the truth, the lies, the songs, the melodies.*
> *Everything.*

* * *

May 2017
Denton, Texas, United States

Henry tried to stop the cough rising in the back of his throat, but he couldn't and covered his mouth with a tissue. There was blood again. His eldest daughter had taken him to see a doctor, and they said that he'd need to see an internal one and have a primary care physician. *Does that mean it's serious?* Henry had wondered.

"I think I have cancer," he said, turning to Ah Hiang.

He had been staying with her family for a little over a month after the house burned down.

"Papá, don't say that," Ah Hiang protested. "It could be anything, but don't talk like that."

He drank a sip of water from his cup before moving to the kitchen table to help her sort through the groceries.

"If something happens to me, I want to look nice when I'm buried."

Ah Hiang froze and wanted to change the conversation, but she reassured her father.

"I promise, if something happens, we'll dress you in a suit and tie."

Henry smiled happily. He didn't know why, but it gave him peace to hear that.

"Where does this go?" he asked, holding up a box of cereal.

"Up there," Ah Hiang replied, relieved that the conversation did not continue. "We have busy days ahead of us," she said, pausing at the refrigerator to look at the calendar.

"Busy how?" he asked.

"Well, let's see, there's something tomorrow, and then we have to go to something on Wednesday and something on Thursday and . . . let's just say that there's pretty much something to do every day."

"Wow, why so much?"

"The school year is ending, so there is a lot going on."

"Is it always this busy?"

"Usually, yes."

Henry grabbed the empty grocery sacks and put them away before picking up the clothes on the chair and heading to his room. The clothes were more donations from people who'd heard that he lost most of his belongings. He was touched that people cared enough to donate clothes to him, and he found that he really enjoyed Denton. He spent a lot of his time at the senior citizen facility in town where he got to meet new people and make new friends. He even participated in an exercise class, and oftentimes he joined the other guys to play board games afterwards. His granddaughter would sometimes wait at the library, studying. Other times his daughter would drop him off before running errands.

He sat down on his bed and pulled out the little journal his daughter had given him, to record the donation. He enjoyed making these notes, but he was also afraid that he might forget one day. Not only did he record everything given to him, he recorded the details as well, such as the clothing material and how much they cost if there was a price tag. He wrote everything he did each day, but he just couldn't find it in him to rewrite his life story. It still made him feel guilty, even though his granddaughter told him that it was okay. She had been quite touched that he was doing that for her and said that it was the thought that counted. She also said that his life and wisdom were his story, and that he touched everyone that knew him. That made him feel a little bit better.

The week passed by in a blur, and before he knew it, it was the night before he would be flying back to Georgia. He spent a small portion of his evening packing before heading to bed. However, he had a hard time sleeping. His cough was persistent, and he was restless, so he finally got up to get a drink of water. The light was still on in the study room. *What is my granddaughter doing awake? Probably still studying.* It was one thirty in the morning. He drank some water before crawling back into bed and finally falling asleep.

* * *

A bell rang down below, and children poured out of a building to run to the playground. He swooped down and flew in through the door as more kids ran out, their faces alight with smiles and cheerful giggles. Each one a unique bundle of joy with a load of potential. He glided slowly through the hallways as if he were taking light steps, his feet barely touching the ground. Lockers lined the walls, and several doors stood propped open. It was a school. He looked in each classroom until he found one that was empty. There were so many colors, so many letters, so many wonders inside.

He smelled food as he passed the cafeteria, but that wasn't where he was headed. It stood at the end of the hall: the pathway to everything. Worlds beyond one's imagination, sights yet unseen, experiences and facts that one had never known. He entered the library, zipping through rows of books and lightly touching their bindings. The center of it all. The glory of experience, of travel, of knowledge. It held the glory of learning.

* * *

When Henry awoke the next morning, he had to squint because the sun was so bright. It shined in through the window, touching everything. He got up and looked at the time. He had slept in quite late and missed saying goodbye to his granddaughter and her host-sister from Taiwan. He got ready for the day before dragging his bag out into the living room.

"Good morning," he told his daughter, who was sitting at the kitchen table.

"Good morning. Oh, before I forget, this is for you," she said, holding out a booklet.

He walked over and took it from her hands.

"Is this what she was making last night?" he asked, running his hand over the cover.

"Yes," Ah Hiang said, rolling her eyes. "She stayed up almost the whole night to do it because she felt so bad that she didn't spend that much time with you and that she didn't make it earlier. She also wants you to have something to remember this trip and your stay with us."

He sat down at the table and started flipping through the pages. They were filled with pictures. He closed it because he wanted to really take the time to look through each picture. His daughter was looking at him.

"Tell her I said thank you very, very much," he said.

He hugged the booklet to his chest and went to put it in the front of his suitcase with his journal. Before he knew it, the plane was taking off for Georgia. He held his journal and booklet in his hands, putting the tray table down to look through them. The memories were beautiful. He opened his small journal to read some of his favorite moments.

Sunday, April 2, 2017

We went to church this morning like every Sunday. My granddaughter played viola in the worship service. The sermon by the senior pastor was very good. He talked about repentance, and at the end, there was a time of response. After church, we ate lunch at home before going to my granddaughter's piano recital. It was their Sonatina Festival, and she played a really beautiful piece, but I don't know what it was called. In the evening, we went to Awana, which is a Christian club where the kids learn and memorize Bible verses. Awana stands for "Approved Workmen Are Not Ashamed," and Ah Hiang put her daughter and nephew in it ever since they were really young. I got to help out with their store that acts as a reward system when kids memorize lots of verses.

Thursday, April 6, 2017

There was an orchestra concert tonight, but I have never seen anything like it. They call it String Fling. My granddaughter played in the top orchestra, so they were the last group to play. Many, many groups played before them, from little kids all the way up to her group. The songs were very fun, and there was even one where people stomped and clapped and cheered. I got to take pictures around the school afterwards.

Friday, April 7, 2017

Today was one of my favorites because my grandson took me to a city called Fort Worth. He showed me many places and we ate at a really good restaurant, although I don't remember the name. We took a lot of pictures and I loved the sight-seeing. It is a very big city and reminds me of Atlanta in Georgia. My grandson told me that a lot of big cities are similar, but they all have something that is specifically unique to them. That evening, my daughter took me to see a musical at someplace on the Denton Square called the Campus Theater because my granddaughter was watching it with some of her friends. The musical was titled Oliver *and it was about a boy that was an orphan who then became a pickpocket on the streets, which reminded me of my past life when I lived on the streets. However, it ended bittersweet because someone died, but the boy ended up with a family.*

Saturday, April 15, 2017

In the morning, my daughter and I took her godchildren to an Easter egg hunt where they ran around and grabbed eggs that were filled with candy. There was then a big party with food and an Easter bunny that you could take pictures with. There were also bounce houses and games for the kids to play. Then, in the afternoon, we threw a surprise birthday party for Kaiwen, who is Ah Hiang's host-daughter from Taiwan. She is staying with them to study in the States for a year, and since the school year is almost over, she will be going back to her country soon. The surprise party was fun as well because there was a lot of food and they also had an Easter egg hunt for her and her friends who were also exchange students and had never done an egg hunt before.

Tuesday, May 11, 2017

My daughter had free Dairy Queen coupons and so we had free ice cream. I chose mint chocolate chip. Then that evening we had to take her godchildren to karate lessons, and it was interesting to watch. They were teaching them self-defense and morals. I even got to take pictures with the two boys after they were done with their lessons because I really liked their uniform, or what they had to wear for karate.

* * *

"Ladies and gentlemen, as we start our descent, please make sure your seat and tray tables are in their full upright position. Make sure your seat belt is securely fastened and all carry-on luggage is stowed underneath the seat in front of you or in the overhead bins. Thank you."

Henry closed his journal and put his tray table up. He looked out the window to watch the passing scenery down below. They hadn't quite entered the city yet. Fields and trees were scattered in all different directions. He looked further out towards the horizon. A thick cloud of smoke was rising from a ball of flames. He wondered what the source of the fire was and shuddered, thinking of their burning home. The flames were enthralling, though. He continued to watch them, that fiery orange glow.

The fire fought for what it wanted with determination, refusing to let go. The same way so many people fought to carve a path, or a life. The same way that they went through school, struggling and failing over and over again until they prevailed. The same way that they fought to survive—and even, finally, to achieve glory. *Flames of glory.*

CHAPTER 18

PEACE AT LAST

August 2017
Stone Mountain, Georgia, United States

HENRY WAS GETTING WEAKER. THE COUGH wracking his body was sometimes unbearable. It was cancer, they said, but he had known that from the start. That was not new. There was not much that they could do besides tests and scans to tell him what was wrong. He did not fear what was to come. The days passed by with him lying in bed or sitting up a bit, occasionally eating small portions, fearful that he might throw it back up. Ah Lay and Mimi took care of him, and he was thankful that they were there, but he wanted all his children to come. Most of all, he wanted his wife by his side, but of that he had almost given up hope.

Every day, his daughter Ah Hiang called him to talk, and he would sometimes hear the voice of his granddaughter as well. His grandson had recently visited, and Henry enjoyed those precious moments. One by one, his children overseas called to speak to him. He felt his voice getting weaker, but he fought it, not ready to give in quite yet. His purpose was not finished. He had one person left to forgive, and he desperately craved her forgiveness as well.

"Papá, we can video you and then you can tell Mother all that you want to tell her. We will show the video to her and then video her response. Is that okay?" Ah Hiang asked over the phone one day.

"What do I say?" he asked.

"Whatever is on your heart. You will know the right words."

"Okay," he replied, wanting to ask more but not having the energy to do so.

* * *

Later that day, Henry's friend, a cancer survivor, came to visit him.

"Henry! How are you doing today?"

He forced himself to lift his head and tried to form a smile. He winced. His head hurt.

"Have you been trying natural foods?" the friend asked Mimi.

"Well, yes. I mean, we've been blending carrots like you said, and then we're also trying that strict diet, but he can hardly hold any food down," she said.

"It's not working, is it?" he asked.

Mimi shook her head.

"What have the doctors said?" he questioned, fearful for his dear friend.

"After the biopsy, they haven't done much except say that surgery is out of the question. They're still considering other options. We haven't heard anything yet."

"Alright, keep me updated. Henry, do you know what I did to fight?"

Henry slowly shook his head.

"I wrote down all the reasons why I still wanted to live and then read through it each day, or I had someone read it to me. You might try the same. I'm sure your kids here would help you write it out."

"Okay," Henry said.

"Yeah, we'll do that tonight," Ah Lay said.

"Thank you so much," Mimi chimed in. "It means a lot that you came to check up on him."

"Oh, no problem, no problem. I love coming by to visit. Take care of yourselves now," the friend said as he walked out the door.

Shortly after he left, with the help of his two children, Henry wrote down the reasons why he wanted to live. He wrote:

Reasons why I want to live:

1. *I want to look down on my children and grandchildren everywhere.*
2. *I want to enjoy my life and praise God. (Jesus, Hallelujah!)*
3. *I want fellowship with God and my family and church members.*
4. *I want to pray to God day and night of every day of my life.*
5. *I want to get better in my life and receive more healing on the inside and out from God and Jesus.*
6. *I don't want the illnesses or sicknesses to attack my body. (God is the healer in my life!)*

Thank you, Father God. In Jesus' name, Amen. AMEN!
Love, Henry A. Chia and family

As he read the list to Ah Hiang, her face grew graver with each passing second. The things she heard did not sound like reasons for wanting to live. It sounded as though all his reasons for living could be carried out in heaven. He sounded like he was ready to go. She tried not to panic and did not let herself think about it.

* * *

A few days later, Henry was unconscious, and the two siblings were not able to wake their father. They panicked.

"We have to take him to the hospital. Now," Ah Lay said, searching for the car keys.

The two of them carried Henry to the car and drove off, hoping they wouldn't get pulled over for speeding.

"Why won't he wake up?" Mimi asked.

"I don't know. He hasn't had anything to eat or drink in like the past twenty-four hours. He's probably dehydrated," Ah Lay said, stepping on the gas to make it through the traffic light just before it turned red.

"And that's why he's unconscious?"

"I don't know."

He pulled into the emergency parking lot of the hospital, and once they got inside, their father was immediately taken back for a scan while the siblings waited anxiously in the waiting room.

A little while later, a doctor came out to tell them that Henry would be admitted and that the rest of their siblings and family members should be contacted. Mimi and Ah Lay were already making phone calls. Ah Hiang and her daughter booked an emergency flight for the next day. They were bringing Rose as well. The siblings overseas made arrangements and would gradually arrive over the course of a week. The cancer in Henry's lungs had spread to his brain, and things were not looking good.

Mimi hardly left her father's side. She was there every day and every night. Ah Lay drove to the airport almost every day to pick up his siblings arriving from different parts of the world. Rose, Ah Hiang, and her daughter were the first to arrive. They were all nervous, uncertain of how Rose would react to seeing Henry. She had seen the video of him and heard the words he had spoken, pleading and begging for her forgiveness, but she merely waved it off. Henry, however, had felt better knowing that he had finally released the one thing holding him back. He finally felt peace, and yet he wanted to hang on just a little bit longer. He longed for his children to all be gathered together. They had not been together in years, and he was certain that this would bring them back together again.

Ah Lay did not take his mother, sister, and niece straight to the hospital. Instead, he took them to eat first. They could all use a proper meal since they would be in and out of the hospital over the next few days. They also used that time to prepare Rose for what she was about to see.

"Mother, you know that Papá is in the hospital, right?"

"Ah, he's fine, he's fine," she said, waving her hand and avoiding the pictures that her son and daughter were trying to show her.

Her granddaughter winced as she stared at her grandmother.

"No, he's very sick," Ah Lay said.

"Things like this always happen, but people always make it worse than it actually is. I can't be around him when he's sick anyway. He was always in a bad temper when he wasn't feeling well."

"Mother, it's different this time," Ah Hiang insisted.

"No, it's always the same. He never changes," Rose said.

The granddaughter looked sharply at her mother, knowing that what her grandmother had just said was not true. Her mom shook her head at her, so she kept her mouth shut, but she couldn't believe that her grandma never saw the changes.

Because he did change. He had changed a whole lot, and he kept trying to win her heart back. He kept trying to show her that he was sorry and that he still loved her. It was heartbreaking to watch over the years when she grew up. Sometimes he would even hand gifts to his granddaughter to give to her grandmother. That's how much he loved her. He desperately wanted her forgiveness.

"We're going to see him after we eat," Ah Lay warned.

"Hmm," Rose said, looking down at the menu.

The conversation was obviously over.

It wasn't until she saw him that the scene became heart-wrenching. Visitors left the room to give the family their privacy. She seemed to be in shock at the sight of him lying like that on the hospital bed. Her first response was to grab his hand. She cried and told him that she should have been the one going first, not him. Everyone started crying; it was too much. Henry tried to open his eyes. He could hear, but he was just so weak. He knew she was there. After so many years, she was finally holding his hand again. He tried squeezing it a bit and knew that he could move if he tried hard enough.

"Mama, he can hear you. He knows," Mimi said through tears.

Rose kept asking if he could hear her, and Henry forced himself to nod. He needed her to know. She told him that she had heard all he said and told him not to think too much, not to worry too much. She kept repeating that and telling him that it was okay.

One by one, each person had their chance to speak to him. He could still acknowledge that they were there; if they asked him to squeeze their hand, he would. It was a light squeeze, but it was better than nothing.

The granddaughter was often speechless. It was hard to speak and not cry. She was losing the only grandfather she had ever known. There was so much that she missed out on because she was too caught up in her own life. There was so much to regret about the time that she had lost. She wished she had known. She wished she had taken the time to simply sit and talk with him; instead, she was always studying or doing her own things. Time was the one thing that could not be gained back. It wasn't possible to go back into the past. She often thought about the story that he had wanted to write for her, and now she wished that she had it.

"Kong-kong," she said one day, "you don't have to be upset anymore about losing the story you wrote me. Don't worry, because instead, I'm going to write it for you, okay? I'll find stories and contact family members, but you don't have to worry about it because I'll write it, for you."

Henry squeezed her hand. He heard the guilt lacing her voice even though he wasn't really sure why. She needed reassurance, and so he tried squeezing her hand once more. He was touched, realizing that he was blessed beyond belief. The family he had was precious.

They were talking to him now; they were making it look like he was wearing a suit and tie, and they moved the bed up a bit to make it look like he was sitting. His granddaughter desperately wished that her grandfather could make it until her graduation, but it was just the beginning of her senior year. Her cousin let them borrow his graduation gown so that she could get a picture in it with her grandpa and then both of her grandparents. They were the only grandparents she had known. She wasn't ready to lose one of them.

* * *

The next day, the hospital pressed to put Henry on hospice care, but the family insisted on waiting until more family arrived. They just needed more time. Their brother King King had already arrived from Dubai, but they were still waiting on several others. Two days later, they picked up Ah Den and his son, who were coming from Australia. It was on that day that the hospital was overwhelmingly insistent that Henry go onto hospice care.

"He'll be more comfortable there," the doctor said.

Mimi shook her head. "Please, just wait until our other siblings arrive," she said. "They're trying to get their visa."

"Ma'am, I can assure you that the hospice center will hold all your family members much better than that small hospital room."

After a moment of silence, she sighed and finally nodded.

The rest of the family agreed, and he was transported the following day. Their brother David, who was coming from Scotland, was picked up from the airport that night, and they all gathered at the hospice care facility. Prayers were said, and some of the siblings had their moments to speak to their father privately. Rose was glad that Henry had been moved to a more comfortable place, where the room could fit the entire family. She thought that he was going to get better and prayed that this would be the case.

By the end of that week, most of the family was together again. They were only missing the eldest and youngest siblings, Ah Tap and Philly, who were in Malaysia, frantically trying to apply for a visa. Ah Tap had never been to the States before and so it was a difficult process, but Philly had stayed behind to help him. They weren't sure if they would make it in time to see their father, but they were trying their best.

The small mission home that Mimi and Ah Lay stayed in was overcrowded, but they made it work. Their house was still in the process of being rebuilt. Mimi, Rose, and her granddaughter slept at the hospice center each night, and after a couple of nights, Ah Den's son did as well. Every evening, the granddaughter curled up in the recliner chair, and that was where she slept. She had brought her school work with her and would do it there, occasionally looking up to make sure her grandfather was still breathing. She was scared. But she kept her mind busy, thankful that she had short stories to read and annotate for English. They kept her mind elsewhere. She wasn't ready to think about anything else, and she prayed that her grandfather would at least make it until his eighty-fourth birthday. It was only days away . . . and when she woke up that morning, she gave a sigh of relief, extremely thankful that he did.

"Henry! Do you know what today is?" the nurse asked that morning.

It was the last day of August.

"It's your birthday, and we decorated your room! You have a lovely family, and I'm sure that they'll be singing to you soon," she said.

Henry tried to smile but simply didn't have the energy. *I do have a lovely family,* he thought. *I don't deserve them. I don't deserve to have such good children and such a good family. God, you're too good to me.*

* * *

Before everyone else went home each night, they sang hymns. The devoted grandson would play the guitar as everyone sang. He had spoken privately to Henry as well, thanking him for everything that he had done and how he been such a good father figure and role model for him.

As they sang each night, their door stood open because they wanted the songs of praise to reach people in the other rooms. The nurses also enjoyed it. They said that it uplifted the depressing mood. Every time he heard his family members sing, Henry wished he could still smile, and although he couldn't physically do it, he was smiling brightly in his mind. *If only they could see it.* He couldn't squeeze their hands anymore, but he could slowly move his head. His eyes wouldn't open either. He kept them shut and just listened.

Their songs were all beautiful. His favorites were the Malaysian songs; there was one in particular that his granddaughter sang each night. She was singing it again now.

> *Oh Tuhan pimpinlah langkahku*
> *Ku tak b'rani jalan sendiri*
> *SertaMu itulah doaku*
> *Ajarku merendahkan diri*
> *Menurut FirmanMu s'tiap hari*
> *Jadikan pelita dalam g'lap*
> *Mecari domba yang sesat*
> *Itulah kerinduan jiwaku*

Henry was so content that his family was together again, though he wished that he could hear the voices of his eldest and youngest child just once more. *Will they make it in time?* he wondered. He thought of his wife. She had finally forgiven him, and they had reconciled. Sometimes throughout the night, and every morning, he heard her talking to him. At times he even felt her dabbing a wet washcloth on his face when he had a fever. It made him feel the love that he felt when he had first met her, even though he physically couldn't see her anymore. That love had been missing for many years after they grew apart, but now, it was finally rekindled. He didn't mind that it had taken her so long. What mattered was that they were back together in the end. *Will she be okay when I'm not here anymore?* he thought. *The children and grandchildren will take good care of her.*

He enjoyed hearing his grandson from Australia and his granddaughter talking and laughing with each other. They hadn't seen one another in a very long time, and he was happy to hear them getting along so well. When they watched movies or played card games, he felt peace in knowing that they would be alright. He wondered who they would grow up to be and what kind of things they would be doing in the future. His grandchildren would all be successful—that he was sure of—because his family was blessed. He blessed each and every one of them. There was nothing left for him to do on earth. Most of his possessions were gone. He had started with nothing, and now he would be leaving with nothing.

Music was playing next to his ear, and yet it sounded as though it was coming from far away. Someone was holding his hand.

He would not be there to know how his family would react once he was gone. He would never know that his granddaughter would be the first one to notice that he was not breathing anymore and would drag her younger cousin out into the hall, unsure of what she should do. He would never know that all his family members would be woken up by a phone call and would have to drive back to the facility in the middle of the night. He would not see or hear how his wife would collapse and sob, angry at her children for not telling her what moving to hospice actually meant. He would not be there to see how each of his loved ones dealt with the grief. He would not know that his eldest child got his visa and would travel with his youngest child over to the States in time for his funeral. He would never know that all his children would finally be reunited. He would not know that his granddaughter played the piano and sang in his funeral. He would never know what his gravesite looked like and the words that were engraved there.

They would be words of love that he would never get to read.

The light was bright now. Scenes flashed before him.

A life full of suffering and heartache, and yet so much beauty.

* * *

He soared high above the clouds and swooped down into glimpses of his life. The death of his father. The near-death experiences in the forest. The homelessness. The girl. The marriage. The jobs he did. The children he had. *The grandchildren he had. The fire. The sickness. All of it, and so much more. He flew further out and reached beyond his own life and stepped into the shoes of many others. It allowed him to see what others saw, to feel what others felt, to experience what they experienced. His was a soul that traveled and sought out all the knowledge he could gain.*

The world was a beautiful place.

The world was a dark place.

The world was a place of happiness.

And of brokenness.

It held it all.

He flew over different parts of the world, seeing and believing. He saw a girl's journal with blue butterflies strung across it, much like the native butterflies of Malaysia that flew so high, desperate to touch the sky. A Bible verse was written elaborately on the front:

"*HE HAS MADE EVERYTHING BEAUTIFUL IN ITS TIME.*"

Ecclesiastes 3:11

Each continent, each country, each city, each town held separate histories that all came together like the pieces of a puzzle. Each person was put on the earth for a reason, a specific purpose, but it was up to them if they wanted to find it or not. He had found his. He had seen what other eyes could not see. Heard what other ears could not hear. He felt what others could not feel. He saw the world in a completely different way.

The dreams . . .

He saw everything. The world in and of itself. All that it entailed.

The trees blurred together now as he zipped through them faster and faster. He emerged to see a pool of water and a glowing, crystal waterfall. The water cascaded in a glorious stream. It gleamed and shined enticingly. He flew closer and hovered, shocked by what he saw. His reflection . . . could it be? He flittered even closer. The water was a roar now. Music came from the other side. It was a magnificent sound—the sound of light itself.

Droplets of water splattered his wings. His wings . . . they were the color of oceans, of waters, of streams. They were the color of the skies. A brilliant, bright blue. He fluttered lightly to touch the waters. They shimmered at his touch. He was a butterfly, the symbol of transformation, of joy, of happiness. The symbol of change. A beautiful soul of light.

* * *

Time ticked past. The tired, overworked clock slowed as if it were fading away. An ancient photograph fell, drifting away like moments and memories of another life. Time sped up, aimed on one destination.

I rose from my chair in the corner and walked over to my aunt Mimi, who was holding her father's hand. It was my turn to freeze.

Everything stopped as if the scene were encased in ice.

My journal lay open in my chair. It read:

> A single tear, dropped to the ground;
> swiftly, softly, it makes no sound.
> A symbol of a trail,
> leaving loved ones behind.
> A symbol of a change,
> that shifts and dies.
> A beautiful soul, shines oh so bright,
> the picture-perfect, bright-blue butterfly.
> It flutters and flies, to touch the sky,
> soaring higher and higher until it's out of sight.
> The gates of heaven are opened wide,
> receiving another angel that night.
> That single tear hits the ground.
> Still. Motionless, for peace had been found.

The clock struck midnight just as a cry was heard. Grief was unleashed, but joy had been earned. Henry A. Chia, the man whom everyone loved, took his final breath and suffered no more.

APPENDIX

Full family portrait. Rose and Henry seated with their children standing around them.

Henry and Rose seated with all fifteen of the children they cared for.

The home in Miri, Malaysia, where the children of Henry and Rose grew up.

Henry (right) and his friend working offshore with the Shell Oil and Gas Company off the coast of Seria, Brunei.

'Oh Tuhan'

```
C           F     G
```
Oh Tuhan pimpinlah langkahku

```
G         C
```
Ku tak b'rani jalan sendiri

```
F   C
```
SertaMu itulah doaku

```
G              C
```
Ajarku merendahkan diri

```
G              C
```
Menurut FirmanMu s'tiap hari

```
D              G
```
Jadikan pelita dalam g'lap

```
C  C7       F
```
Mecari domba yang sesat

```
C  G  C
```
Itulah kerinduan jiwaku

'Oh Lord'

Oh Lord lead my steps

I do not dare to walk alone

You are my prayer

Teach me to humble myself

According to Your Word
every day

Make light in the dark

Looking for a lost soul

That is the longing for
my soul

GLOSSARY

Translation of Malaysian Words:

ahkbar = newspapers

anda = you

bantu = help

bos = boss

datang = come

dewa alam = nature gods

di sana = there

harimau = tiger

kakak = sister

kampong = village

lihat = look

lilin = candles

makan malam = dinner

menonton = watch

merdeka = independent

restoran = diner

sila = please

teksi = taxi

tidak = no

Translation of Malaysian Phrases:

Adakah awak . . . = Do you . . .

Anda seorang lelaki besar. = You're a big boy.

Apa yang awak beli? = What did you buy?

Apa yang boleh saya lakukan untuk awak? = What can I do for you?

Bersuara! = Speak up!

Hai, bagaimana saya dapat membantu anda? = Hi, how may I help you?

Hari Merdeka. = Independence Day.

Itu besar! = It's big!

Itu kerana anda. = It is because of you.

Maaf, tidak. = Sorry, no.

Mari pergi. = Let's go.

Pergi berpakaian. = Go get dressed.

Sangat sedih. = So sad.

Saya janji. = I promise.

Saya juga. = Me too.

Saya lapar. = I'm hungry.

Saya mahu makan. = I want to eat.

Saya minta maaf. = I'm sorry.

Saya penat. = I'm tired.

Saya perlu bungkus untuk esok. = I have to pack for tomorrow.

Saya sedang mencari kerja. = I'm looking for work.

Saya takut. = I'm scared.

Selamat datang ke pusat Miri. = Welcome to the center of Miri.

Selamat Hari Jadi! = Happy Birthday!

Selemat pagi. = Good morning.

Selemat petang. = Good afternoon.

Selemat tinggal. = Goodbye.

Tak mengapa. = It's okay.

Terima kasih. = Thank you.

Tetapi saya tidak bersetuju. = I do not agree.

Tiada wang. = No money.

Tunggu sebentar. = Wait one moment please.

Places/Groups:

Jabatan Imigresen Malaya = Immigration Department of Malaya

KL = Kuala Lumpur

Perjalanan Persaudaraan = The Journey of Brotherhood

Syurga Manusia Lama = Old Man's Heaven

Teater Filem Bintang = The Star Movie Theater

Definitions:

Ais kacang = A Malaysian dessert that literally means "bean ice," also commonly known as ABC.

Ayi = Formal and respectful way of calling an elder or one that is of higher authority in a family, in Mandarin Chinese, literally meaning "aunt."

Char Kway Teow = Malaysian noodle dish that literally means "stir-fried rice-cake strips."

Mie goreng = Malaysian spicy fried noodle dish.

Milo = A type of hot chocolate.

Nasi Lemak = Malaysian fragrant rice dish.

Ringgit = Malaysia's currency.

Roti canai = A Malaysian flatbread that is Indian-influenced.

100 plus = Isotopic sports drink that originated in Malaysia.

ACKNOWLEDGMENTS

THERE ARE MANY PEOPLE IN MY life that I would like to thank, starting with God, my heavenly father and supporter and encourager through it all. Secondly, I thank my family, who stuck together and supported one another after the passing of my grandfather. They were also extremely helpful in providing me with the stories I incorporated into this book after his life story was lost to the fire. I really appreciate their willingness to share and fill in some of those "missing pieces" to the story. I would also like to thank all my loving and supportive friends who were there for me when I needed them, especially my best friends. They kept me going and pushed me to start writing this book in the first place. Their comments and excitement throughout the process was one of the reasons I was able to complete the ending; I could not have done it without their support.

I am also incredibly grateful that I had so many caring teachers throughout my life. Two of my middle school teachers read stories that I had written, and my recollection of their words and encouragement also propelled me to finish writing this book. I would also like to thank my high school history teacher Mr. Matthews for reading through certain parts to make sure that it was historically correct, as well as my high school English teacher Ms. Phillips, who constantly encouraged and believed in me, especially when I did not think that I would be able to finish. There were times where she believed in me far more than I ever believed in myself. Not only did she allow me to work on the book in her room almost every day during or after school, but she also took the time to read it, and for that, I will be forever grateful. Many, many thanks also need to be given to one of my college English professors, Dr. Elliott, who took the time to talk with me, providing valuable feedback on my writing and execution of ideas within my book. She constantly encouraged me and was there for support when I needed her, and that meant so much.

Thank you to everyone else in my life that has had a positive impact on me and in helping me grow as both a person and a writer.

CPSIA information can be obtained
at www.ICGtesting.com
Printed in the USA
LVHW041111231219
641444LV00006B/892/P